THE AUTHOR

Cyril Vernon Connolly was born in Coventry in 1903. His father, a professional soldier, was often stationed abroad and he travelled widely as a child, living briefly with his grandmother in Corsica and with his mother's family in Ireland before returning to school in England. From St Wulfric's, where his schoolfriends included George Orwell and Cecil Beaton, he won a scholarship to Eton and eventually went up to Balliol College, Oxford, as the Brackenbury History Scholar. A dazzling literary career was forecast and he began to write for the *New Statesman* and other periodicals from 1927. His first ambition was to write fiction and poetry, but his novel *The Rock Pool* (1935) had only a limited success and his true *métier* proved to be in journalism and criticism, brilliantly displayed in his collections *Enemies of Promise* (1938) and *The Condemned Playground* (1944). As 'Palinarus' he published in 1945 *The Unquiet Grave*, a collection of thoughts, quotations and impressions which won great critical acclaim.

In 1939, with Stephen Spender, Connolly founded *Horizon*, 'a critical review of our times', which was a prime force in the cultural world of the Forties and a focus for a wide variety of new writers until it closed in 1950. He had been Literary Editor of the *Observer* from 1942-3 and from 1951 contributed a weekly column to *The Sunday Times*. An *enfant terrible* in his youth, he was awarded the CBE in 1972 and was also a Chevalier of the Legion d'Honneur. Cyril Connolly was married three times and died in 1974.

THE CONDEMNED PLAYGROUND

Essays: 1927-1944

Cyril Connolly

Claudite jam rivos, pueri:
sat prata biberunt'

New Introduction by
Philip Larkin

THE HOGARTH PRESS
LONDON

To
F. J. C.

Published in 1985 by
The Hogarth Press
40 William IV Street, London WC2N 4DF

First published in Great Britain by George Routledge & Sons 1945
Hogarth edition offset from original British edition
Copyright the Estate of Cyril Connolly
New Introduction copyright © Philip Larkin 1985

British Library Cataloguing in Publication Data.

Connolly, Cyril
The condemned playground : essays : 1927-1944.
I. Title
824'.912   PR6005.0393

ISBN 0 7012 1924 6

Printed in Great Britain by
Cox & Wyman Ltd
Reading, Berkshire

NEW INTRODUCTION

It was one of Cyril Connolly's cherished beliefs that he was a failure ('so repulsive in others, in oneself of course the only dignified thing'). The reasons he advanced were various. It was something to do with having been a success at Eton, something to do with being fat and lazy, something to do with not having enough money or having been born into the wrong age. But above all it was to do with reviewing. Reviewing was what you did if you were a failure; reviewing was what made you a failure:

Reviewing is a whole-time job with a half-time salary, a job in which our best work is always submerged in the criticism of someone else's, where all triumphs are ephemeral and only the drudgery is permanent, and where no future is secure except the certainty of turning into a hack.

Certainly he spent a large part of his working life writing about books. He wrote for the *New Statesman* in the Twenties and Thirties, for his own commandingly individual magazine *Horizon* in the Forties, and for the remaining twenty years of his life for *The Sunday Times*. But he was very far from being a hack. Except for his early stint as a novel-reviewer, he chose what he wrote about, and chose it not only for the sympathy (or otherwise) he could bring to it, but for the chance it gave him to display his own talents. And these were different in kind from those of the MacCarthys and Mortimers of his day; perceptive, provocative and unpredictable, he was at his best when able to assimilate his subject into the scenario of his own temperament.

The Condemned Playground, spanning as it does his career as a literary journalist from his departure from Oxford up to the latter half of the Second World War, contains some of his most exhilarating pieces, many of them contradicting his claim to have 'gone off the boil' during the Thirties. What strikes the reader most forcibly is his commitment to literature, to the notion that being a writer is the practice of a morality as well as an art. 'There are but two ways to be a great writer (and no other kind is worth the being),' as he says in *The Unquiet Grave:*

One way is, like Homer, Shakespeare, or Goethe, to accept life completely, the other (Pascal's, Proust's, Leopardi's, Baudelaire's) is to refuse ever to lose sight of its horror. One must be Prospero or Caliban; in between lie vast dissipated areas of pleasure and weakness.

The dramatisation is forthright, and perhaps not very convincing, but is demonstrates his conviction that only the best is worth bothering about: 'the true function of a writer is to produce a masterpiece', and this is likely to mean scorned delights and laborious days. Conversely, it postulates a contempt amounting to loathing for belles-lettres, for literature as a game or a commercial entertainment, for pandering and pot-boiling as a way of life.

This led him, as a young man, to fall upon the literature of his own time with farcical ferocity – on the one hand the Walpoles, Galsworthys and Linklaters and their middlebrow reputations, and on the other the multitude of professional time-killers ('Culbertson, Torquemada, Wodehouse, Dorothy Sayers, Duke Ellington') who proclaimed England a footler's paradise. In fact his fury spilled over onto England itself; the series of diary extracts 'England Not My England' (1927-9) purports to record the closing stages of his love affair with his native land ('Really, the most deplorable country, Americanized without America's vitality or variety of race'); the virulence of his distaste ('Women all dowdy, men undersized and weedy. Pathetic voices and gestures, newspaper-fed ignorance') recalls at times D. H. Lawrence: there is a study to be made of this literary hatred of England between the Wars. Was it owing to the rise in the cost of living? The emergence of the working class? The strict sexual climate and laws against homosexuality? Whatever the reason, it meant a bunk for the boat-train and sunnier climes, with the leisure to reflect 'we have no paper for literary experiment in England, and literature is, after all, as technical a business as medicine or engineering.'

Perhaps inevitably, Connolly developed a thesis that in the last hundred years English literature had fallen away badly when compared with that of France:

English writers were not prepared to sacrifice their lives to the dictates of their artistic conscience, to be celibate like Flaubert, or to be debauched like Baudelaire and Rimbaud: they would not stand up to the matador. They represented romanticism in decay, shielded from its logical consequences by good mixing, Anglican ethics, Victorianism.

This view is developed more explicitly in the lecture 'French and English Cultural Relations' (1943):

We stood aside from the conflict [between artistic values and bourgeois materialism], with the result that in the twentieth century our art and literature became even more unreal: the fanciful pastime of well-to-do middle-aged children who had refused to grow up, and who could never hurt themselves because whenever they fell it was always on a thick green lawn.

If Connolly had extended these contentions to a full–length argument – a companion to *Enemies of Promise* – he might have found they required so many qualifications as to collapse of their own accord, but they matched the war-time enthusiasm for things Gallic that elevated writers such as Aragon, Cocteau, Malraux and Gide to an eminence they can hardly have expected. What is important is not whether what he says is true, but his passionate insistence on literary integrity: no compromise, no surrender, no children's books, no lecturing in America, no 'work for television' (and, presumably, no reviewing).

Some of Connolly's most damaging criticism, however, took the form of hilarious literary romping, for he was an extremely funny writer, as *The Rock Pool* had already shown. It is hard to read the first three paragraphs of 'More About the Modern Novel' without bursting out laughing (interestingly enough, they were written in 1935; the rest of the article dates from

1928); 'Told in Gath' transfixes middle-period Aldous Huxley with the cruelty of a one-time disciple; 'Where Engels Fears to Tread' resembles a speeded-up one-reel version of *The Condemned Playground* itself ('Barcelona' shows him grappling with the 'contemporary' issue of the Spanish war) based on the career of Brian Howard:

Some of these young poets, I realized, had even attended my university! One quatrain in particular haunted me.

> M is for Marx
> and Movement of Masses
> and Massing of Arses
> and Clashing of Classes

It was new. It was vigorous. It was real. It was chic!

So much for the pylon poets; so much, too, for A. J. A. Symons's Wine and Food Society:

'Well, now, here's a test,' said Dads. 'Here's a wine from my own modest *caves* – oh, nothing remarkable – just a well-fendered little wine – one that's honest and obliging enough to engage in a symplegma or amorous wrestling match with this charming bird we're debating . . .'

So much, finally, for the whole business of reviewing:

Never praise; praise dates you . . . Remember that the object of the critic is to revenge himself on the creator, and his method must depend on whether the book is good or bad, whether he dare condemn it himself or must lie quiet and let it blow over . . . He stands behind the ticket-queue of fame, banging his rivals on the head as they bend low before the guichet. When he has laid out enough he becomes an authority, which is more than they will.

With all its violent oscillation between defiant assertion and farcical derogation Connolly's literary method produces not so much criticism – he was never a critic in the fullest sense of the word – as self-portraiture, 'Narcissus with his pool before him,' as he ends his early and enlightening account of the later Joyce. The writers he deals with emerge exalted or damaged, the situations he analyses encourage or accuse, but always there is a faint whispering: 'I wish I were like that.' Or, conversely, 'That's why I came to nothing.' It is both his strength and his weakness.

The richness of *The Condemned Playground* resides not so much in its recognisable contentions as in its incidental satisfactions, the pleasure of meeting a well-read, widely-travelled mind in which the cushions of nostalgia alternate with the snap of deflationary epigram (the *Penguin Dictionary of Modern Quotations* has 55 entries for Connolly against 38 for Eliot). And how unexpectedly, in its last section, the book rises to its conclusion, the passages from war-time issues of *Horizon*. Here Connolly is no longer savouring the past, or savaging the present: he is looking to the future with a sober idealism that transcends the personality of the previous pages. The enemies are still there – 'poor bald old homo-puritan Pinheads', 'the Publisher, with his Cold Feet', the not-so-young poet trying to reconcile 'communism with religion, pacifism with war, property with revolution, and homosexuality with marriage', and the culture-diffusionists of CEMA, ABCA, MoI and their latterday descendants – but they will be squashed if we remember that England, 'an ancient civilisation that is not neurotic, where thought once more is correlated with action, and which fights for its beliefs . . . should, in those invisible exports like poetry and fine writing, be in a position to lead the world':

It will be a world in which the part played by the English will be of supreme importance. In fact, one might say that the whole of English history, tradition, and character will be judged in the future by how we rise to the occasion of the post-war years.

There were too many qualifications for this to be termed propaganda. In the narrow corner of the mid-war years, it was Connolly's commitment to the morality of art that surfaced again, a vision of something beyond the condemned playground in which his own talent had up till then alternately flamed and flickered.

Philip Larkin, 1984

CONTENTS

INTRODUCTION

THE CONDEMNED PLAYGROUND SIGNIFIES FOR ME
the literary scene of the 1930's, the period of ebullience,
mediocrity, frivolity and talent during which I wrote most of
these essays and my first two books. I also chose the title to
refer in a more limited sense to that leafy tranquil cultivated
spielraum of Chelsea, where I worked and wandered. But
there is another sense in which *The Condemned Playground*
refers to Art itself; for Art is man's noblest attempt to preserve
Imagination from Time, to make unbreakable toys of the mind,
mudpies which endure; and yet even the masterpieces whose
permanence grants them a mystical authority over us are
doomed to decay: a word slithers into oblivion, then a phrase,
then an idea. "Le mot vieillit," as Valéry puts it, "devient
très rare, devient opaque, change de forme ou de rôle. La
syntaxe et les tours prennent de l'âge, étonnent et finissent
par rebuter. Tout s'achève en Sorbonne."

This feeling of evanescence has always been with me as a
critic; I feel I am fighting a rearguard action, for although
each generation discovers anew the value of masterpieces,
generations are never quite the same and ours are in fact
coming to prefer the response induced by violent stimuli—
film, radio, press—to the slow permeation of the personality
by great literature. Like most critics I drifted into the profession through a lack of moral stamina: I wanted to be a
poet, and to revive the epic; I wanted to write a novel about
archaic Greece—but my epic and my novel fell so short of
the standards which my reading had set me that I despaired
of them and, despairing, slipped into the interim habit of
writing short-term articles about books. The habit grew and
conquered: many years later, and almost too late, I set out to
conquer it. That is how most of our critics are formed. Not
that I despise criticism: I wish only that I had been a better
critic—for I think that the distinction between true criticism
and creation, as Wilde pointed out in *The Critic as Artist*, is
non-existent and that many a novelist who flatters himself
that he is creative is hanging second-hand ideas on to lifeless

puppets in a mechanical fashion of which a conscientious critic would be ashamed. I have always been heartened by the words of Sainte-Beuve. "Le don de critique . . . devient même du génie lorsqu'au milieu des révolutions du goût, entre les ruines d'un vieux genre qui s'écroule et les innovations qui se tentent, il s'agit de discerner avec netteté, avec certitude, sans aucune mollesse, ce qui est bon et ce qui vivra; *si, dans une œuvre nouvelle, l'originalité réelle suffit à racheter les défauts.*"

But I wish I had been a better critic and that I had not written brightly, because I was asked to, about so many bad books. What merits I have are somewhat practical and earthy. I stay very close to the text—no soaring eagle but a low-swung basset who hunts by scent and keeps his nose to the ground. I am not sure that a critic should have any opinions. Experience develops in the critic an instinct, which, like a water-diviner's, agitates him when near to treasure. He digs and explains afterwards. The authors I most enjoy writing about are first those great, lonely, formal artists who spit in the eye of their century, and after them the wild and exquisitely gifted young writers who come to an untimely end through passion, and lastly those wise epicureans who combine taste with the gossiping good sense of the world, and whose graceful books are but the shadow of their intimate communion with their friends or with nature. And sometimes I don't mind making fun of the pompous and pretentious, the second-rate best-sellers whose word in the thirties was literary law.

I have included in this book some of the earliest things I wrote, such as the article on Sterne which was my first published appearance, aged twenty-three, and *England not my England*, which begins at the same moment. These, and the articles on Joyce [1] and Gide, *Ninety Years of Novel Reviewing* and *Conversations in Berlin*, were all written between the age of twenty-three and twenty-five, and seem to me as good as anything I have managed since. Somehow in the disappointing years which followed I went off the boil—perhaps indeed the thirties were a decadent period and I unconsciously

[1] The first English account of *Finnegans Wake* as told me by him.

was decaying with them, or perhaps, a typical Rimbaud who couldn't write, I was in rebellion against the age and myself. Nevertheless, I have rescued from those years some articles about the eighteenth century; some reflections on novels which hold the flavour of the period; a controversy about A. E. Housman, in which I do not think I come out very well; and some parodies and satires which still convey a little of the thirties' acrimonious *douceur de vivre*. The article *Portrait of an Elizabethan* reveals the dawn of a social conscience (at the moment when it was dawning for so many others), and I have included an account of a revolution in Athens to show the Flaubert, ivory-tower attitude typical of my generation in these occurrences, as a contrast to the politically - minded, if pessimistic, descriptions of the Spanish War which follow. Of the later articles I like best *The Ant-Lion* because it reveals the advance in sensibility which I gained by shedding possessions and living in the South of France; vestiges of this advance remain in one or two other essays, but on the whole the war has turned it into a retreat. The propaganda, the slogans, and the patriotic mouthings of the Margarine Age have taken their toll, and in going through the *Horizon* "Comments" I found that the word "we" is always the prelude to a string of clichés. I have concluded the book with two short pieces on Mr. Maugham and Mr. E. M. Forster because they are typical of my pedestrian critical method, and with a commentary from *Horizon* on the relation of writers to the world in which they now have to live. My thanks are due to the Editors of *Horizon*, *The New Statesman*, *Life and Letters*, *Britain To-day* and to Messrs. Hutchinson for permission to reprint from them, and my warmest gratitude to those two patient, wise, passionate and humane teachers, Mr. Desmond MacCarthy and Mr. Raymond Mortimer, the two Literary Editors of the *New Statesman* for whom it was my happiness to work. They did much to soften a coarse and violent streak in me which was always rebelling against literature, and which took refuge in a mutinous and iconoclastic sloth. Literary Editors seldom expect gratitude and as seldom receive it—so I thank them here once more.

THE POSITION OF JOYCE

JAMES JOYCE HAS BROUGHT OUT A NEW BOOK. IT IS A fragment of a longer one, and is called *Anna Livia Plurabelle*. We are used to the reputations of authors fluctuating from year to year, but Mr. Joyce's also fluctuates from place to place. He is resented in Ireland, neglected in England, admired by a set in America, and idolized by another in France. In every nation there is a general public and a literary public. In Ireland the general public is provincial and priest-ridden. It cannot forgive Joyce his blasphemy nor his contemptuous parodies of Irish jingoism. The other, the smaller public, has chosen escape in a romantic return to the past, characterized by a special lyric note of easy and indefinable melancholy born of self-pity. Joyce is a realist, and out of touch intellectually with that generation. "Michael Roberts remembers forgotten beauty. He presses in his arms the loveliness which has long faded from the world. I desire to press in my arms the loveliness which has not yet come into the world." Thus Joyce's only disciples in Ireland are the young realists of the post-rebellion period. In England the literary public is governed by good taste. Cautious as the cenotaph, the critics decide the value of a book in terms of "delicious" and "charming." The general public is equally conservative, and the fate of a book like *Ulysses* (so hopelessly unpresentable when submitted to the Chelsea canon) is decided in advance. It is in America, where there is a large and less sophisticated general public, and in Paris, where there are a great many young writers anxious to experiment in literary form, that the "Ulysses generation" has grown up.

Mr. Forster, in his lectures on the novel, states perfectly the English attitude to Joyce, the bad bogy-man of letters. "*Ulysses*," he writes, "is a dogged attempt to cover the universe with mud, an inverted Victorianism, an attempt to make coarseness and dirt succeed where sweetness and light failed, a simplification of the human character in the interests of

Hell." It is also an "epic of grubbiness and disillusion . . . a superfetation of fantasies, a monstrous coupling of reminiscences . . . in which smaller mythologies swarm and pullulate, like vermin between the scales of a poisonous snake." "Indignation in literature," adds Mr. Forster, "never quite comes off," and the passage I have quoted does little except to express the general attitude of English culture towards novelty, and to prove that the vocabulary of scandalized vituperation is drawn from the reptile-house in every age.

"Indignation" is not a quality of Joyce's work, but "the raging of Joyce seems essentially fantastic, and lacks the note for which we shall be listening soon," continues Mr. Forster, who proceeds to classify *Ulysses* as belonging to the period of *Zuleika Dobson*. Let us get a clear idea of *Ulysses* before we try to estimate the later work of its author. James Joyce is, by temperament, a medievalist. He has always been in revolt against his two greatest limitations, his Jesuit education and his Celtic romanticism. Each of his books reveals a growing fear of beauty; not because life is not beautiful, but because there is something essentially false and luxurious in the "Celtic Twilight" approach to it. This tinsel element is very strong in Joyce's early poems, and is contrasted with an equally pronounced repulsion from it in "The Portrait of the Artist." In *Ulysses* he has got it in hand, and is experimenting in other approaches to beauty; the pagan simplicity of Mrs. Bloom's reverie, the mathematical austerity of the catechism which precedes it. Only Stephen Dedalus, the Hamlet young man, thinks automatically in the diction of the Celtic Twilight; but in him the remorse, the guilty sense of loneliness which attacks brave but weak men who destroy the religious framework of their youth, has fused with his minor poet melancholy, and gives to his reverie the quality of a Greek chorus. Stephen Dedalus, in fact, equips the Ulysses generation with a fatalism, a dramatization of their own forebodings, and with the medieval quality so rare in America, so reduced in England, so rife in Europe—the Tragic Sense of Life. This is the great link between Joyce and Proust, otherwise so misleadingly compared. Both the Irishman and the Jew possess the tragic intelligence;

the idea that life can only be appreciated, can only be lived even, if the intelligence is used to register all the beauty and all the intimacy which exist in ironic contrast to the unrelieved gloom of squalor and emptiness, mediocrity, disease, and death.

> For all our wit and reading do but bring us
> To a truer sense of sorrow.

The whole climax of *Ulysses* is a single moment of intimacy, when Bloom, the comic character, rescues Stephen in a drunken brawl. Bloom had a son who died, Stephen a father who is alive; but for this instant of spiritual paternity all the swelter of that urban summer, all the mesembrian pub-crawls of Bloom and Stephen, the "vermin" and the "scales" and the "serpents," move into place. The central emotion of *Ulysses* is not indignation, but remorse; and remorse, though perhaps second-rate in life, is an emotion which usually succeeds in literature. Expiation and the sense of doom, which form the essence of Greek tragedy, are only a variation of this feeling; and though in real people remorse seems so feebly static, its very tranquillity and remoteness from action lend it a glassy literary beauty. In *Ulysses* Stephen dwells in the consciousness of having hastened his mother's death by his atheism, Bloom feels obscurely his father's suicide and the troubled history of his people, while all Ireland seems listlessly aware of its destiny. Perhaps the most typical scene in *Ulysses* is that in which Stephen, who has run away from the squalor of his father's house, comes across his young sister also trying to escape her environment without the help he might have given:

"He turned and halted by the slanted book cart. Two-pence each, the huckster said, four for sixpence. Tattered pages. *The Irish Beekeeper. Life and miracles of the Curé of Ars. Pocket Guide to Killarney.*

'I might find there one of my pawned school prizes.'

'What are you doing here, Stephen?'

Dilly's high shoulders and shabby dress.

Shut the book quick. Don't let see.

'What are you doing?' Stephen said.

A Stuart face of nonsuch Charles, lank locks falling at its

sides. It glowed as she crouched feeding the fire with broken boots. I told her of Paris. Late lieabed under a quilt of old overcoats, fingering a pinchbeck bracelet; Dan Kelly's token.

'What have you there?' Stephen asked.

'I bought it from the other cart for a penny,' Dilly said, laughing nervously. 'Is it any good?'

My eyes they say she has. Do others see me so? Quick, far and daring, shadows of my mind.

He took the coverless book from her hand. Chardenal's *French Primer*.

'What did you buy that for?' he asked. 'To learn French?'

She nodded, reddening and closing tight her lips.

Show no surprise, quite natural.

'Here,' Stephen said, 'it's all right. Mind Maggie doesn't pawn it on you. I suppose all my books are gone.'

'Some,' said Dilly, 'we had to.'

She is drowning. Agenbite. Save her, Agenbite. All against us. She will drown me with her, eyes and hair. Lank coils of seaweed hair around me, my heart, my soul. Salt green death.

We.

Agenbite of Inwit. Inwit's Agenbite.

Misery."

This quotation reveals many other aspects of the book; the old word for remorse, for instance, becomes one of those snowball phrases with which *Ulysses* is packed. Appearing continually in the characters' day-dreams, they gather momentum from each association, echoing through the chapters till by the end they are charged with as much personality as the thinkers themselves. Then the drabness of the scene, the halting, trite dialogue, illustrate the other side of *Ulysses*: the attempt to create beauty out of city life, and style out of the demotic English which is spoken in therein. Every year more people's lives are passed in towns than in the country; but while there is a whole vocabulary of rural beauty, there is so far only the slenderest aesthetic of cities, the roughest technique in appreciating them. What Baudelaire and Laforgue did for Paris, or Mr. T. S. Eliot for modern London, Joyce has done for Dublin: and at a time when Yeats and Synge had monopolized the Gaelic side of the Irish, he was able to create a language out of the demotic commercial speech of the anglicized burghers of Dublin itself. Literary English has become very hackneyed, as a glance at any book of essays or a preface to an anthology at once will show, and Joyce in *Ulysses* set out to revive it by introducing the popular colloquial idiom of his own city, by forming new words in the Greek fashion of compound epithets, by telescoping grammar, by using the fresh vocabulary of science manuals, public-houses, or Elizabethan slang. Here, for instance, are two quotations, one to illustrate the city aesthetic, the note of Celtic melancholy introduced into the descriptions of an urban summer sunset by the Hill of Howth, where Bloom had once made love; the other, an example of Joyce's highly latinized English, which produces an effect of austere rhetoric and elaborate original rhythm.

"A long-lost candle wandered up the sky from Myrus' bazaar in search of funds for Mercer's hospital and broke, drooping, and shed a cluster of violet but one white stars. They floated, fell: they faded. The shepherd's hour: the hour of holding: hour of tryst. From house to house, giving his everwelcome double knock, went the nine o'clock postman, the glow-worm's lamp at his belt gleaming here and there through the laurel hedges. And among the fine young trees a hoisted linstock lit the lamp at Leahy's Terrace. By screens of lighted windows, by equal gardens, a shrill voice went crying, wailing, '*Evening Telegraph*—stop press edition! Result of the Gold Cup races!' And from the door of Dignam's house a boy ran out and called. Twittering the bat flew here, flew there. Far out over the sands the coming surf crept, gray. Howth settled for slumber, tired of long days, of yumyum rhododendrons (he was old) and felt gladly the night breeze lift, ruffle his fell of ferns. He lay but opened a red eye unsleeping, deep and slowly breathing,

slumberous but awake.   And far on Kish bank the anchored
lightship twinkled, winked, at Mr. Bloom.

                    *   *   *

What play of forces, inducing inertia, rendered departure
undesirable?

The lateness of the hour, rendering procrastinatory: the
obscurity of the night, rendering invisible: the uncertainty
of Thoroughfares, rendering perilous: the necessity for
repose, obviating movement: the proximity of an occupied
bed, obviating research: the anticipation of warmth [human]
tempered with coolness [linen], obviating desire and rendering desirable: the statue of Narcissus, sound without
echo, desired desire."

Besides this he directed a campaign of parody against the
whimsy and archaism latent in English prose style.   It is
indeed as an enemy of "literature" that Joyce really might
appear to Mr. Forster as working "in the interests of Hell."
Though he did not originate the "stream of consciousness" as
a form of writing, he saw that by recording the thoughts of
each character he could take shorthand liberties with their
syntax as well as get nearer to their selves.   He too, among
those who have used this method, is the only one to have
grasped that people, besides thinking differently, think at a
different pace.   Mrs. Woolf, whose *Mrs. Dalloway* is in many
ways a feminine adaptation of one idea of *Ulysses* to English
good taste, tends to make all her characters think in the same
tempo.   She gives us anatomical slices; not human beings, but
sections of them, which portray the doubts, the tendernesses,
the half-hopes and half-fears of the human mind all conceived in the same mood of genteel despair.   Bloom, Mrs. Bloom,
Stephen, however, and the nameless Cyclops narrator possess
mental processes which are quite incomparable with each other.
Bloom's mean, good-tempered, second-rate, scientific curiosity
colours all his commonplace meditations.   Stephen's bitterness,
imagination, and petulant intellect quicken feverishly the pulse
of his thought.   The racy, cynical and shamelessly prejudiced
gusto of the Nameless One transforms his narrative into the

whirl of the winds of Aeolus that it is meant to symbolize, while elaborate journalese retards the speed of the book for those chapters when the action is at a standstill. Lastly, the even breathing of Mrs. Bloom times with her steady physical reverie, her pagan meditation so free from Stephen's medieval anguish, Bloom's scepticism, or the problems which faced the morning of the one, the evening of the other, and their common night.

The link between the new work of Joyce and *Ulysses* is chiefly one of language; though both are united by the same preoccupation with the aesthetic of cities, with the absurdity of our Jewish-American democracy, and with the capacity for being beautiful which this democracy yet retains.

Here are two quotations, one showing the Hill of Howth again treated in a symbolic manner, the other the praise of Dublin, rhetorical as cities are—Earwicker (the Danish castle) is bragging to his wife, the Liffey, of all he has done for her. I have annotated the text so that the complexity of the portmanteau language may be gauged:

"'Old Whitehowth is speaking again. Pity poor Whiteoath! Deargone mummeries, goby. Tell the woyld I have lived true thousand hells. Pity please, lady, for poor O.W. in this profoundest snobbing I have caught. Nine dirty years mine age, hairs white, mummery failing, deaf as Adder. I askt you, dear lady, to judge on my tree by our fruits. I gave you of the tree. I gave two smells, two eats: my happy blossoms, my all falling fruits of my boom. Pity poor Haveth Children Everywhere with Mudder. That was Communicator a former Colonel.'"

"'. . . And I built in Urbs in Rure for mine elskede, my shiny brows, an earth closet wherewithin to be quit in most convenience from her sabbath needs: did not I festfix my unniverseries, wholly rational and got alike [three Dublin universities national and godlike with Trinity to suggest the holy]; was not I rosetted on two stelas of little Egypt, had not rockcut readers, hieros, gregos, and democriticos [the Rosetta stone]; and by my syvendialed changing charties

Hibernska ulitzas made not I [allusion to superimposing a street map on an older one and rotating it to find what streets lie along a Roman road. Ulitza is the Slav for a street, but in this case is also a prophecy of Ulysses and his labours] to pass through 12 Threadneedles and Newgade and Vicus Veneris to cooinsight. [Allusions to Ulysses, to Newgate prison on the Roman Road.] Oi polled ye many, but my fews were chosen: and I set up twin-minsters, the pro and the con [Christchurch and the pro-Cathedral] woven of peeled wands and attachattouchy floodmud [Italian root, "sticky"] arched for the convenanters and shinner's rifuge; all truant trulls made I comepull, all rubbeling gnomes I pushed, go go; and thirdly for ewigs I did reform and restore for my smuggy piggiesknees her paddy palace on the cross-knoll [St. Patrick's restored] and added there unto a shallow laver to put out her hell fire and posied windows for her oriel house and she saes her nach, chilly-bombom and 40 bonnets, upon the altarstane, may all have mossyhonours!

'I hung up at the Yule my pigmy suns helphelped of Kettil Flashnose [electric lights introduced in Dublin under Kettle, the chief of the electricians and descendant of Kettle Flatnose, an original Dane settler] for the supper hour of my frigid one, coulomba mea, frimosa mia, through all Livania's volted ampire from anods to cathods, and from the topazolites of Mourne by Arcglow's sapphire seamanslure and Waterford's hook and crook lights to the polders of Hy Kinsella [old Danish beacons].'"

The ordinary man of letters, when faced with modern civilization, plays the ostrich with its head in the sand. A very whimsical, arch, mock apologetic, and well-subsidized ostrich too. In fact, they are the paid entertainers of democracy, the jesters who are allowed the licence of bewailing the rattle of hansom cabs, of beginning every sentence with "I must needs avow that I have never seen eye to eye with those who," and ending "nevertheless, to my thinking, when all is said and done. . . ." Of course, there is no law compelling anyone to belong to his period; but not to belong to it, is to take sanctuary, to eke out a whimsical existence and an archaic style in a half-timbered Utopia, visited, like an Elizabethan teashop, by the most insipid of the public one would wish to avoid. If *Ulysses* is largely a parody of literary manners, a dissatisfaction with style, the new work of Joyce is a parody of language, an attempt to create a new vocabulary for literature itself. And both, which readers are unwilling to see, are meant to be funny. After all, the ballad of the Jabberwock has passed into the accepted treasury of English humour; yet when the method Carroll used to reinforce words with double meanings is applied to contemporary prose, which surely needs it, the result is that we label the originator mad.

Literary language in England has become very far removed from conversation, nor is it able to profit, like American, from a rich background of polyglot slang. All literary words in addition tend to be used, especially by Georgian poets, without a due conviction of their meaning, and this depreciates the currency so that most epithets become like the dead notes on an old piano, which go down when they are sounded, but do not come up. The best instance of this is the penultimate passage of *The Oxford Book of English Prose*. The new language of Joyce is only a kind of piano-tuning, whereby he tightens up certain words by grafting fresher foreign equivalents on to them, approximates them to other words to strengthen their own vigour, above all puns with them freely, and gives words a synthetic meaning, with which either to express life, or simply to make a series of academic jokes. The experiment may be a failure, just as Esperanto or phonetic spelling may be a failure, but there is nothing that is contrary to reason in the idea itself. The chief defect of Mr. Joyce's new language is that, so far, it has swamped the lyrical quality of his other prose writings; he has not attempted purple patches in it so much as rhetorical imitations of them. Here is the close of a fable called "The Mookse and the Gripes," which can be compared with Bloom's city sunset, quoted above:

"The shades began to glidder along the banks, dusk unto dusk, and it was as glooming as gloaming could be in the waste of all peaceable wolds. The mookse had a sound eyes right but he could not all hear. The Gripes had light ears left yet he could but ill see. He ceased. And he ceased and it was so dusk of both of them. But still one thought of the deeps he would profound on the morrow and still the other thought of the scrapes he would escape if he had luck enough."

The new book is full of fables, because the whole of the first part is really a *surréaliste* approach to the prehistory of Dublin, the myths and legends of its origin, Duke Humphrey and Anna Livia, the mountain and the river, from a black reach of which the city took its name. The first words "river-run brings us back to Howth Castle and Environs" suggest the melodies to follow. All the urban culture of Ireland is by origin Scandinavian; and, to emphasize this, Joyce has introduced the greatest possible amount of Norse words into his description of it. There are four parts to the new work of Joyce: the first is a kind of air photograph of Irish history, a celebration of the dim past of Dublin, as was *Ulysses* of its grimy present; the second is an interlude in a barn near Chapelizod; some children are playing, and react unconsciously the old stories of the first (Iseult of Ireland linking in the suburb's name); and the third part, jumping from the "past events leave their shadows behind" of the first, to "coming events cast their shadows before," deals in four sections with the four watches of one night. As this is literary criticism, I cannot go into the metaphysics of Joyce's new book, which are based on the history of Vico and on a new philosophy of Time and Space; but two other things emerge, the same preoccupation of the author with his native town, his desire to see all the universe through that small lens, and his poetic feeling for the phases of the dusk, for that twilight which originally gave the Celtic revival its name. The book opens in a museum with a mummified description of the battle of Waterloo:

"'This the way to the museyroom. Mind your hats goan in! Now yiz are in the Willingdone museyroom. This is a Prooshious gun. This is a ffrinch. Tip. This is the flag

of the Prooshious, the Cap and Soracer. This is the bullet
that byng the flag of the Prooshious. This is the ffrinch that
fire on the Bull that bang the flag of the Prooshious. Saloos
the crossgun! up with your pike and fork! Tip. (Bullsfoot!
Fine!) This is the triple-won hat of Lipoleum. Tip.
Lipoleumhat. This is the Willingdone on his same white
harse, the Cokenhape.'"

Monotonous as the tap of a lecturer's pole, rusty, archaic,
the old contraptions of history reveal themselves, the past
lumbers slowly into being under the touch of the chirpy guide.
The museyroom, the sightseers, moving dustily among the
dregs of the forgotten battle, clank into place in the uncouth
language; we are looking at the earth from a long way away,
perhaps as one might look at it by overtaking the light rays—
by turning a telescope on the Dark Ages, from some planet so
far that it still could watch them going on. "Only a fadograph
of a yestern scene."

"So, now idler's winds turning pages on pages, annals
of themselves timing, the cycles bring fassilwise to pass.
how. 1132 A.D. Men like to ants or emmets wondern upon
a groot hwide Whallfisk which lay in a Runnel. Blubby
wares up at Ublanium."

Figures emerge from the chronicle: in this early Dublin,
Irishman meets Norseman, typical of all misunderstanding
since the days of Babel. The Irishman begins:

"'Hop! In the name of Anem this carl on the kopje a
parth alone who the Joebiggar be he? Forshapen his pigmaid
hoagshead, shroonk his plodsfoot, me seemeth a dragon
man. . . . He is almonthst on the kiep fieg by here, is Come-
stipple Sacksounn, be it junipery or febrewery, marracks or
alebill, or the ramping riots of prouriose and froriose. What
a quhare soort of a mahan. It is evident the minchindaddy.
He can prapsposterous the pillowy way to Hirculos pillar.
Scuse us, chorley guy! You tollerday donsk? N. You
tolkatiff scowegian? Nn. You spigotty anglese? Nnn?
You phonio Saxo? Nnnn. Clear all so! Tis a Jute. Let

us swop hats and excheck a few strong verbs weak oach
eather yapyazzard abast the blooty creeks.'
    Jute: Yutah!
    Mutt: Mukk's pleasurad.
    Jute: Are you jeff?
    Mutt: Somehards.
    Jute: But you are not jeffmute?
    Mutt: Noho. Only an utterer.
    Jute: Whoa! Whoat is the matter with you?
    Mutt: I became a stun a stunner."

By and by other heroes appear, Shaun the Rabelaisian
postman, sly Shem, his writer brother, H. C. Earwicker (here
comes everybody) (alias the Hill of Howth), the typical great
man of the new democracy, and his bride, the lovely Anna Livia.

*   *   *

Writers are on safest ground when they confine themselves
to what interests them, and the key to this obscure and difficult
book is the author's *pietas* for his native city. Joyce's life has
been nearer to the classical tradition of great writers than to
the Victorian comfort of the men of letters of to-day. His
existence resembles that of the old Greek poets, a youth spent
in city politics and local revels, then banishment to foreign
places, the publication of a masterpiece after ten years, as
Dedalus promised, with his weapons "silence, exile and
cunning." Now his whole art is applied to celebrating his
native town, though his feeling for Dublin, its squares and
stews and beery streets, its hills and foreshore, seagoing Liffey
and greenbanked Dodder, is very different from the provincial
quality of Irish patriotism and is more akin to the pagan
sentiment of birthplace. There is nothing flamboyant in his
tender attitude to the "poor little brittle magic nation, dim
of mind."

Anna Livia is an episode from this book describing the legend
of the Liffey. Two old washerwomen stand on each side of the
stripling river and gossip away as they pound the clothes.
("O tell me all about Anna Livia.") They talk of Earwicker's
affair with her under his other identity, of Duke Humphrey,

and gradually their language breaks into a melody of water music, a kind of paean, like the praise of the brook Kishon, into which the names of every conceivable river are brought in as onomatopoeic train-bearers.

". . . She sideslipped out by a gap in the devil's glen while Sally her nurse was sound asleep in a shoot, and fell over a spillway before she found her stride and lay and wriggled in all the stagnant black pools of rain under a fallow coo and she laughed with her limbs all aloft and a whole grove of maiden hawthorns blushing and looking askance upon her. . . . And after that she wore a garland for her hair. She pleated it. She plaited it. Of meadow grass and river-flags, the bulrush and the water weed, and of fallen griefs of weeping-willow."

Occasionally the charwomen break in with their own troubles:

"'O my bach! my back! my back! I'd want to go to Aches-les-Pains . . . spread on your bank and I'll spread on mine. It's wat I'm doing. Spread! It's turning chill. Der went is rising.'"

Gradually the widening stream carries them apart as the night falls, for they are standing on the two banks of the infant river as on a moving stairway, and the gap between them has widened as the Liffey leaps, in the words of her song, "to the slobs of the Tolka and the shores of Clontarf to hear the gay aire of my salt troublin' bay and the race of the saywint up my ambushure." When night falls, the old women shouting across in the dark cannot understand each other; still gossiping, they are transformed into an elm and a stone, the strange obscurity of the old myths from which they have emerged gathers about them, and the *motif* of the past of Ireland is re-echoed in their dumb block-like language; for the Mookse and the Gripes had suffered the same fate, mortal beside the immortal river:

"'. . . and it was never so thoughtful of either of them. And there were left now only an elm tree and but a stone. O! Yes! and Nuvoletta, a lass.'"

The end of the *Anna Livia* marks another of Joyce's extraordinary descriptions of dusk:

> "'Whawk? Can't hear with the waters of. The chittering waters of. Flittering bats, fieldmice bawk talk. Ho! Are you not gone ahome? What Tom Malone? Can't hear with the bawk of bats, all the liffeying waters of. Ho, talk save us! My foos wont moos. I feel as old as yonder elm. A tale told of Shaun or Shem? All Livia's daughtersons. Dark hawks hear us. Night! Night! My no head halls. I feel as heavy as yonder stone. Tell me of John or Shem? Who were Shem and Shaun the living sons and daughters of? Night now! Tell me, tell me, tell me, elm! Night night! Tell me tale of stem or stone. Beside the rivering waters of, hitherandthithering waters of. Night!'"

The best way to read Joyce's new book, apart from this rare reprint of *Anna Livia*, is in a quarterly called *transition*, edited by Americans living in Paris. The contents are often as grotesque as the idea is enterprising. But we have no paper for literary experiment in England, and literature is, after all, as technical a business as medicine or engineering. *Transition* is sometimes a silly magazine, and sometimes intensely amusing, for, like most rebel journals, its satire is on safer ground than its originality; but it is the only one which publishes the honest, sometimes fascinating, often incoherent research of those who take new literature seriously in every country. Of course, it is not possible to pronounce a verdict on Joyce's work while it is still fragmentary. The best that this article can hope to prove is that the new work of Joyce is respect-worthy and readable. There is nothing insane in its conception nor bogus in its execution. Though to many a spinster fancy it probably will continue to lack the "note for which we will be listening soon," to others it promises amusement and a most interesting and strange approach to life and beauty. In short, it is an experiment. We are content to accord the wildest tolerance to the latest unintelligible—even uncommercial—pamphlet of Einstein—can we not admit a little of the same tolerance to something in writing which we do not understand? It must be remembered that Joyce, besides being a lover of words, is an Irishman under no obligation whatever to rest content with the English language, and also that, while our Literature, unaware of a decline of the West or a defence of it, grows daily more bucolic and conservative, Continental Letters are nourished on an exhilarating sense of an uncertain future which makes the liberties of their volcano dwellers permissible—and which we are entirely without. Literature is in essence a series of new universes enforced on a tardy public by their creators. This one may be a fake, but it is not from a writer who has previously given us fakes; it may be a failure, but it is surely an absorbing one, and more important than any contemporary success. I, personally, am biased as a critic by nationality, and by the same feeling for geography and Dublin, but still more by the enthusiasm which comes to everyone when they discover themselves through a book—a service which Joyce, Proust, and Gide have rendered generally to almost all our thinking generation; for me any criticism of *Ulysses* will be affected by a wet morning in Florence, when in the empty library of a villa with the smell of wood-smoke, the faint eaves-drip, I held the uncouth volume dazedly open in the big armchair—Narcissus with his pool before him.

April 1929.

LES FAUX-MONNAYEURS

THE COUNTERFEITERS IS THE MOST IMPORTANT WORK of Gide's to be translated into English, and its appearance is an occasion for considering in what the merit of Gide's work consists.

There is probably no French author whose reputation it is harder for an English critic to appreciate; we are accustomed to have our neglect of Racine and Corneille flung in our faces, like that incapacity to appreciate a certain esoteric perfection in La Fontaine which makes French critics think that, however much he is praised in England, he is never praised right. In these cases it is something essentially Gallic that we are supposed not to be able to understand. With Gide, however, it is because his essential quality is so English that we are not more impressed by it, and that the French, who have had no Pater to give an academic twist to the sensuous world or to clarify the distress of adolescence, derive such absorbing and elusive excitement from his work.

Yet Gide is the most creedless of all leaders of French thought. Valéry is an intellectual who can focus his perspicacity like a lens to the problems of metaphysics, or to the most finicky refinements of classical verse. He belongs to the main French tradition, though to a highly rarefied development of it; Gide, though intellectual, would suppress his gifts in favour of a capacity to grasp physical sensations and transmit them in poetry. He would feel that the dilemmas of the intellect do more to wreck a poet than all the temptations of the world, and that he who is master of his emotions is apt to be his reason's slave.

Where there is a rigidly defined tradition, there is an equally defined revolt from it, and this the *Surréalistes* now lead. English literature, being less rigid, drives its prodigals into a hazier and milder opposition; they know nobody will try to chase them, so it is absurd to run away. Gide occupies such a position in France; romantic in outlook, classical in style, with no

16

political background to his work, he has a horror of being taped, of being defined or captured—like Proteus—in his original shape, or killed—like Mercutio—at a battle to which he was not asked. He is the apostle of the Hybrids, a class in England so numerous as not to deserve the name, in France so rare that no provision has yet been made for them in any literary code.

The Hybrid is perpetually haunted by a conviction of exile, his spirit is expended in home-sickness, his intellect in trying to discover what is his home. This central loneliness, this native hue of indecision causes the hybrid to cling desperately to all societies that are at ease in the world; complex himself, he is drawn to the simple, sceptical to the religious, meditative to the men of action, homeless to the homely. Of course, the hybrid, as we are familiar with him, is not so deeply tainted as this; he is usually an aristocrat turned intellectual, an artist who dislikes his art, a Bohemian turned respectable, or someone unable to choose between two values, art or ethics, action or thought. These are the hybrids of circumstance, who have not had the courage to suppress their possible selves, to prune themselves of half the buds that weaken the fruit by being allowed to flower. They are torn between conflicting vocations, not realizing that they have only one vocation, and that is to be torn. With the spiritual hybrids it is worse. Homeless since the loss of Eden, these Cains and Ishmaels acquire a conviction of guilt as profound as their sensation of exile. This leads to a passionate curiosity that sends them experimenting everywhere to find out where they belong, but, dictated as it is by conscience, and not by science, it trails away into sensationalism, or dies on the rich luxurious wail that is the war-cry of these dangerously articulate people, and which, loaded with lyric beauty and self-pity, must surely drown all refrains of hymns and psalm tunes, and acquaint the Creator of the amount of subjects He has left on the earth "erroneous there to wander and forlorn."

M. Gide possesses all these characteristics, and almost every possible combination of hybridity; without his puritan sense of sin he would not read into the physical world so much calculated sensuality; without his classic style he would not be able to carry off so much that is abandoned or sentimental;

and without his intellectual integrity he would not be able to affect a relative indifference as to how people behave. The result of this is a kind of dankness which pervades all his work, something vacillating and ineffectual which proceeds from his sensuous comprehension of so many contradictory schemes of life. Then one feels that he is not naturally a rebel, that he hates young men to read his books and promptly run away from their parents, that he tries to make himself approve, and that the result is a higher degree of morbidity than before, so that he can hardly describe a plate of fruit without making us feel it is indecent, or a noble impulse without suggesting that it is impure.

The peculiar quality of his work is a kind of desultory lyric strain that runs through all English literature, but is very uncommon in French; this, however, is more apparent in his earlier work, and has given way to a loose philosophizing that is the root of his great influence on the young, because he teaches them to dramatize and sentimentalize the values of their own life. This is what Wilde and Pater did for England, and Gide combines the luxuriance of the one with the applied philosophy of the other. There is no scene so typical of Gide as that in *Marius* where Flavian and the young Marius read through *The Golden Ass* in the barn, or where, in *Imaginary Portraits*, the young Sebastian refuses to be painted in the family group because he is under the influence of Spinoza. Gide is, however, an extremely intelligent man with a much wider curiosity than Pater's, and a profounder insight than Wilde's. Moreover, he writes entirely on the side of youth, his mission seems to be to glorify the distress and the idealism of adolescence, and to sound for the first time the depths, if any, of the French schoolboy's reserve. Childhood has long been idealized in England, and we have had a host of public school stories which classify the different shades of prison-house that close round the growing boy. In France, however, adolescence has almost passed unnoticed; there has been no transition in literature from the spoilt, precocious French child to the pale and serious young man. For this reason Gide's romanticism, his sympathy and his restless habit of troubling all the waters where the young

Narcissus sees his face, is invaluable to French thought—both as steering a middle course between the Academy and the "Fauves," and as tapping a new reserve of intelligence and beauty, which is that dawning of intellectual values and sensuous perception that occurs to all youth in all lands. But this, however valuable to France, has long been understood in England, and it is absurd to treat Gide, whom we have in reality fathered, as representing either a new way of life, or of literature, and least of all as one of those mysterious cults from across the Channel which it requires a sixth sense to appreciate, and an intelligence greater than our own to understand. France is still grappling with Butler, Wilde, and Pater; if they are to catch us up, they cannot do better than by thus assimilating them, with a strong dash of Swinburne, and all rolled into one.

The Counterfeiters is a novel about a novelist writing a novel called *The Counterfeiters*; we see the characters through a series of receding mirrors, the nearest reflection being all that we get of their real selves. The novelist is Gide, or a novelist's idea of Gide, and we see him, noble, understanding, helpless, brewing indecision and distress all round. His countertype, or anti-Gide, is another novelist, de Passavant, who is in the true Lord Henry Wotton style, modernized, so as to be a caricature of the rich, slick, amateur, fashionable writer whose book *The Horizontal Bar* and whose epigrams ("what is deepest in man is his skin") point very much to the leaders of the motion for motion's sake, *wagon-lit*, dancing dervish school. Then we have two boys, Olivier and Bernard, who represent the emotional and the intellectual aspects of Gide's approach to a way of life. The novelist is on the whole a disappointing character. He seems, like most hybrids, to lack vitality, or rather to find it tidal, so that he is forced to prey on the spirits of his young friends and becomes easily afflicted with that kind of premature old age which is the punishment of those who are afraid to grow up with their contemporaries. The plot is intricate and absorbing, and this is the kind of book that is very much easier to read in English than in French. There is a large amount of profound criticism and irony scattered through the book, as well as many true observations on the novel itself. Occasionally, however, the sophistication becomes irritating, and in Edouard's long analysis of love one hopes in vain for some Melbourne to break in with "Oh, can't you let it alone!"

What is really preposterous, beyond even the author's morbid sentimentality, is the gang of Borstal boys whom he depicts. The schoolboys, apart from Bernard and Olivier, when not engaged in bringing out a literary manifesto, are discovered organizing a brothel, stealing books, blackmailing their parents with stolen love-letters, passing false coins on a large scale, and finally hounding the weakest to death by means of an extensive suicide pact. Not since Jude's little son hanged himself and his brothers have book-children shown such enterprise in the control of their lives. Granted Gide's preoccupation with suicide, or certain cases like the Loeb murders, the depravity is just credible, but one certainly feels that it shows a decadent necessity for feeding on the extremes of action, for searching out the perverse in nature or the innocent in order to pervert it. His love of life seems a *passion malheureuse*, his curiosity a *soif malsaine*. The book is very well translated and well worth trying to read in spite of the impatience which one is bound to feel. It is an excellent book to have brought out in England because, although it will not influence English intellectual life in any way, it does help us to understand the kind of revolution that is going on in France. Besides, to appreciate an author who is intoxicating the younger generation is always an experience, even if one is not intoxicated.

February 1928.

DISTRESS OF PLENTY [1]

"NOTHING ODD WILL DO LONG," SAID DR. JOHNSON, "WITNESS *Tristram Shandy*," and such is the awful finality of this judgment that one re-reads Sterne almost with a sense of guilt, though indeed no author's reputation has so often survived its own obituary. In his own lifetime he was almost the only writer to alienate both Goldsmith and Johnson on the one hand, and Gray and Walpole on the other, and it is easy to see how the spectacle of the sleek and winning divine arriving in London to reap the success of his annual instalments must have irritated both the hard-working critics of Fleet Street and the fastidious company at Strawberry Hill. Walpole, however, was hardly fitted to condemn Sterne as trivial, and Johnson was unaware of the lesson we learn from Proust, that in years of silence and dissipation a style can mature and an outlook ripen as easily as in a long apprenticeship to letters. Sterne in this respect comes near to his master Cervantes, and his scarcely broken silence of twenty-five years is probably, besides the vigour of his style, responsible for the dense and exasperating character of his mental undergrowth. Walpole was also the first to shy at Yorick's dead donkey and to perceive the terrible flaw which dominated Sterne's sensibility, the habit of luxuriating in emotion he thinks creditable, which turns his sympathy to self-congratulation and sets a smirk on all his tenderness. It is this fault that tainted the effects which Sterne intended to be his finest, as if he had skimmed the cream from comedy and pathos and found it turn overnight. And perhaps the word "sentimental" would not have lost caste so early had not his work exposed so completely its luxurious self-delighting nature. It is this latent insincerity, and not the mischievous indecency by which Coleridge was offended, that has made so many enemies for Sterne and turned nearly every biographer into an apologist. "I blushed in my turn, but from what movements, I leave to the few who feel to

[1] *The Works of Laurence Sterne.* 7 vols. Oxford. Blackwell.

analyse," writes Yorick, and a little afterwards "I burst into a flood of tears—but I am as weak as a woman and I beg the world not to smile but to pity me." One can see that he knew fairly well how the few who feel would react, and it is this irrepressible itch to commend himself, while deploring self-commendation, and to exploit his own humanity which has brought him the wrath of Thackeray, which made Coleridge call *The Sentimental Journey* "poor sickly stuff" and Leslie Stephen anxious to blot out even the Recording Angel's erasing tear.

Certainly *The Sentimental Journey* contains Sterne's most inexcusable lapses, yet in its conception as a book of travel it is absolutely right, though far from being the "quiet journey of the heart in pursuit of nature" that it styles itself. The irresponsibility, the exhilaration, and the frank independence of all its judgments (how right to call the French too serious) make it, however, through all its digressions, a real presentation of movement. Sterne was refreshingly sea-sick; wild with excitement even in Calais, he wished to find the French gallant, and did so. He could repeat "So this is Paris. Crack! Crack! Crack!" as inanely as any traveller rejoicing at the pall of respectability that was lifting from him, he would neither "disdain nor fear to walk up a dark entry," he would be swindled with a good grace rather than witness his host's disappointment, and though he describes but little scenery, he is still friendly to the scantiness which he has created; he seeks for adventure and avoids his compatriots, he ignores the Alps, he understands the French while remaining English, and, what is rare in a book of travel, he enjoys himself, even at a time when Dr. Johnson noted "that there has been of late a strange turn in travellers to be displeased."

Yet Sterne was not a man of deep feelings, and since his profession of sensibility requires him to appear so, there follow his flatteries and exhibitionism and the ill-concealed self-satisfaction that rewards a well-spent tear. His "dear sensibility," however, that lachrymose goddess, was but a Roman sense of *pietas* run to seed, and the final quality of Sterne as a humorist lies in his wide sympathy, when not overstrained, for every creature that is fulfilling its function, or in finding speech for gaping and inarticulate "blind mouths" and enjoying human beings as they are. It is this Latin warmth that links him, apart from style, to Rabelais and Cervantes, and in a lesser degree to Shakespeare, and even Voltaire. Sterne was as fitted as anyone to enjoy the shepherd with his "cold thin drink out of his leathern bottle," but the temptation to make capital out of his own emotions renders him unworthy of their perpetual company. Within his limitations, however, his world is one of the most wayward and serene of all Utopias, and if the quality of his work is taken from the French, its material is as undoubtedly English, the England of peaceful fanatics, and gaunt unpersecuting bigots who have taken refuge from the fogs of the world in the most outrageous sanctuaries of their teeming minds, and who seem to spring up in the peaceful country as naturally as teazels and to live here as happily as rare animals in private parks:

> "This strange irregularity in our climate producing so strange an irregularity in our characters doth thereby in some sort make us amends by giving us somewhat to make us merry with when the weather will not suffer us to go out of doors—that observation is my own—and was struck out by me this very rainy day, March 26th, 1759, and betwixt the hours of nine and ten in the morning."

This "winter's dream when the nights are longest" seems a better summary of *Tristram Shandy* than all the many prefaces, and justifies as well the whimsical and desultory method of Sterne's writing, which leaves the reader "many an entangled skein to wind off in pursuit of him through the many meanders and abrupt turnings of a lover's thorny tracts." Indeed, it is hopeless to approach Sterne except as one who loves him, for no one is more spoilt or more obviously ill at ease and rattled by a hostile reader, while only a lover can really put up with the whole bulk of Sterne's digressions, or endure with patience the "simple propositions, millions of which are every day swimming quietly in the thin juice of a man's understanding," and the majority of which certainly deserve to remain there.

When this is once said there is no further fault to find, and the reader can for ever bid farewell to Walpole irate beside the dead donkey or Thackeray impatient with the polyanthus that blew in December, and enjoy Sterne's beauties at his leisure. The intensity that Sterne lacked in emotion he retrieved in style, and there is hardly any diction in English so perverse and yet so adequately under control. The tempo of *Tristram Shandy*, for instance, must be the slowest of any book on record, and reminds one at times of the youthful occupation of seeing how slowly one can ride a bicycle without falling off; yet such is Sterne's mastery, his ease and grace, that one is always upheld by a verbal expectancy; slow though the action moves, he will always keep his balance and soon there will follow a perfect flow of words that may end with a phrase that rings like a pebble on a frozen pond. He is continually parodying the Elizabethans and using words with a fantastic ingenuity, as when he describes the jolting diligence:

> "the thirstiest soul in the most sandy desert of Arabia could not have wished more for a cup of cold water than mine did for grave and quiet movements,"

or

> "where is Troy and Mycenae and Thebes and Delos and Persepolis and Agrigentum," continued my father, taking up his book of postroads, which he had laid down. "What is become, brother Toby, of Nineveh and Babylon, of Cizicum and Mitylene? The fairest towns that ever the sun rose upon are now no more."

Death, unreal enough here, is parodied once again in the sententious homily, alike redeemed by Sterne's sure command of gesture, that Trim delivers on the same lines in the kitchen. This control of literary emotion, the quality of *Lycidas* and Gray's *Elegy*, is what is most sustaining in Sterne's work to-day. We can enjoy his exquisite handling of eccentricity, and appreciate Walter Shandy's search for the "north-west passage to the intellectual world," with Tristram as a heaven-sent subject for experiment; we can hear him dropping his voice to talk of auxiliary verbs and fixing his listeners as securely as did the ancient mariner; we can see all the paradox of the household living together in uncomprehending amity while their prejudices conflict as uselessly as waves on granite. But it is the strange, bitter-sweet intensity emerging from Sterne's most artificial sentences that forms his particular signature, and which allays our suspicion of him, as it does his own vaunted fears. "I have never felt what the distress of plenty was in any one shape till now," the reader can exclaim with him as he reads of Toby "cast in the rosemary with an air of disconsolation that cries through my ears," or of Sterne's days and hours "flying over our heads like light clouds on a windy day" before his book is finished and ready "to swim down the gutter of time along with them."

There is no understatement in Sterne's style; no "slow, low, dry chat five notes below the natural tone," and his beauties are lost on those who contract intellectual hay-fever from fine writing; yet the dullness of the subject, as in Flaubert, often redeems the style from cloying and enables one more to appreciate the hush of a set-piece like Uncle Toby's falling in love:

"Still—still all went on heavily—the magic left the mind the weaker. Stillness, with Silence at her back, entered the solitary parlour and drew their gauzy mantle over my uncle Toby's head; and Listlessness, with her lax fibre, and undirected eye, sat quietly down beside him in his arm-chair. No longer Amberg, and Rhinberg, and Limbourg, and Huy and Bonn in one year—and the prospect of Landen and Trerebach and Drusen and Dendermond in the next, hurried on the blood; no longer did saps and mines and blinds and gabions and palisadoes keep out this fair enemy of man's repose. No more could my uncle Toby after passing the French lines, as he ate his egg at supper, from thence break into the heart of France—cross over the Oyes and with all Picardie open behind him, march up to the gates of Paris and fall asleep with nothing but ideas of glory . . . softer visions, gentler vibrations, stole sweetly in upon his slumbers; the trumpet of war fell out of his hands—he took up the lute, sweet instrument! of all others the most delicate! The most difficult! How wilt thou touch it, my dear uncle Toby?"

There is no question of how it is touched here, and the haunting somnolence of the whole chapter (6.35) seems almost to approach the tale of Palinurus, while as a lyric it is as complete as some of the short fragments of pastoral in *The Sentimental Journey* or the longer, bird-like raptures on the Town of Abdera.

This edition consists of *Tristram Shandy*, *The Sentimental Journey*, the *Journal*, the fragments, one volume of letters and two of sermons. It is excellently got up and as presentable as it is easy to read. The large print redeems Sterne's tortuous system of asterisks and dashes and without altering their peculiar appearance. The reader indeed plunges into Sterne's work like a prince into an artificial and enchanted forest, "hoc nemus, hos lucos avis incolit, unica Phoenix," and in a moment the path narrows and the boughs thicken, and the sounds of the hunt recede as he struggles through thickets of dusty sycamore, lost in false metallic greenness, before he emerges angrily from the tangled breaks into one of Sterne's perfect sentences that opens before him like a moss-grown ride.

June 1927.

NEW SWIFT LETTERS[1]

THIS BOOK, WHICH IS ADMIRABLY EDITED, CONTAINS FIFTY-ONE letters from Swift to his friend Ford, ten of which were sold to America in 1896, and only one, the last, published in Elrington Ball's edition of the correspondence. The letters run from 1708 to 1737. Ford was an amiable absentee Irish gentleman with a taste for music, travelling, drink, Latin verses, and the Saint James's coffee-houses, where he spent most of his life. He died unmarried in 1743. He was one of those young people whom Swift liked because he had benefited them, and who remained an intimate friend because of his genial temper, his willingness to act for him with the publishers, his hospitality to Stella, and his political views. Though the least formal of Swift's letters, these are mainly taken up with politics and contain no thunderbolts. The most they supply is evidence of the warmth of Swift's friendship and his amiability, and some information about the composition of *Gulliver's Travels* ("They are admirable things and will wonderfully mend the world"). Swift has not much to say about Ireland. "I cannot think or write in this country" (1714). "I do suppose nobody hates and despises this kingdom more than myself" (1729). Already, in 1709, he is complaining that

"I am grown so hard to please that I am offended with every unexpected face I meet where I visit, and the least Tediousness or Impertinence gives me a Shortness of Breath, and a Pain in my Stomack."

The year before he observes

"that men are never more mistaken than when they reflect upon Past things, and from what they retain in their memory, compare them with the present. . . . So I formerly used to envy my own Happiness when I was a Schoolboy, the delicious

[1] *The Letters of Jonathan Swift to Charles Ford*. Edited by David Nichol Smith. Oxford University Press.

Holidays, the Saterday afternoon, and the charming Custards in a blind alley; I never considered the Confinement ten hours a day, to nouns and verbs, the Terror of the Rod, the bloddy Noses, and broken shins."

Except for one or two such sentiments the letters do not further reveal the character of Swift, which, though not likely to become again the bogy of an hysterical Thackeray, remains largely mysterious. For it is obvious that everything which was considered most heartless and cynical in him can be viewed as the attempts of a man with a terrible capacity for suffering to escape from it. He was determined to be tough, to face without euphoria the birthdays that brought Stella nearer ugliness and himself nearer the grave, and his much-disputed "only a woman's hair" is surely an example of the brutality with which a man covers genuine grief; the antithesis, for instance, to the way in which Sterne, a writer who could not be sure of his feelings, would have treated it. The misanthropy of Swift is, in fact, one side of the romantic dichotomy. No one is born a Diogenes, or enters the world complaining of a raw deal. One cannot hate humanity to that extent unless one has believed in it; one must have thought man a little lower than the angels before one can concentrate on the organs of elimination. The problem of Swift arises because we know so much less of the cause of his disillusion, and of what he was like before it, than is the case with other romantics and disappointed idealists. We know, to take some examples, the effect of Lesbia's infidelity on Catullus, of the great war on Céline, of the Catholic Church on Joyce, of disease on Baudelaire, but we do not know what happened to the lovable young man who wrote the charming dedication to the *Tale of a Tub*. The shock of exile, and of losing power, terrible though it was, came late in life; he was not jilted or betrayed, nor was his faith of the kind whose loss would create an upheaval. The causes which turned him against mankind, which made him hate its guts, must, therefore, be sought in his ten years at the upper servants' table as a secretary.

There can be nothing more galling for a young man than to

find himself part of the scheme of auto-suggestion by which an old one justifies his existence. And when the latter was Sir William Temple, the amateur philosopher, the wise old Polonius in retirement, the M. de Norpois of his age, the pressure must have been intolerable. No philosophy is more suspect than the Epicurean, in spite of its attraction for waning powers. For the doctrine that pleasure is the absence of pain, that happiness can only be found by practising moderation in a garden, is contrary to all we know of the nature of the passions, and, like Christianity, is provocative enough to instil a deep contempt for self-deception into those who have to listen to it constantly preached, and to behold it as inconstantly practised. It is interesting to note that Swift wrote his grim "Resolutions when I Come to be Old" at Sir William Temple's, and that he mentions in his obituary of Stella that "she understood the Platonic and Epicurean philosophy and judged very well the defects of the latter." One of the most curious of these is that it is the essayist's creed, favouring mild eccentricities and apologies, the fear of life, and the enumeration of one's possessions. It must have been through too close an acquaintance with the style of Sir William Temple (a style essentially false, for it revealed not what he felt but what he would like to feel) that the prose of Swift was precipitated into its rightful form; vigorous, mature, lucid, and earthy. One wonders how many times he heard the sage repeat "a good plum is certainly better than an ill peach," and the phrase beginning "when all is done, Human Life is, at the greatest and the best, but like a froward child," which still hoaxes so many as it goes ringing down the anthologies.

But if Swift learnt his horror of the *bêtise*, his hatred of pretensions, at Moor Park, he also underwent an emotional disillusionment. It is clear that at first he warmly admired and liked Temple and suffered agony from the slights which that spoilt and peevish mediocrity put upon him. He must at last have felt that he was being deliberately kept down; that Prospero was afraid of Caliban; that the world punished sensibility as unjustly as it repressed intelligence. "Don't you remember," he writes to Stella, "how I used to be in pain when

Sir William Temple would look cold and out of humour for three or four days and I used to suspect a hundred reasons? I have plucked up my spirit since then; faith, he spoiled a fine gentleman." He told Harley of such treatment, that "it was what I would hardly bear from a crowned head."

One thing was needed finally to embitter a man whose youth had been passed in subservience to an inferior in mind and heart, to a Struldbrug, and that was a taste of political power, supreme political power, a drug so potent that it keeps insensitive statesmen sweating and scheming for it till they drop in their tracks, and which, in the slightest quantity, is fatal to the peace of mind of an imaginative writer. It was withdrawn, and the lack of it occasioned "the desiderium which of all things maketh life uneasy." One has only to read a page of the *Journal to Stella* to see in what a state of intoxication the author was at the time; and because of the clumsy boasting, the facetiousness and sentimentality of the messages to Stella (deepening into the frenzied incantations of the little language), it is the most unpleasant, the most morbid of his writings. But even without those moments of triumph the tragedy of Swift would have been that of all those who feel too deeply, yet who cannot tolerate fools and will not mend their ways. What renders it so terrible is the strength, the ingrowing pride of the victim who took twenty years dying "in a rage like a poisoned rat in a hole." In the works of Joyce, Baudelaire, Céline, the hatred of the breath, stench, and complacency of humanity is accompanied by a certain squeamishness, an impression of neurotic weakness; the sufferers escape into night, into satanism, into silence. Even Flaubert, who by the robustness of his mind and his horror of the *bêtise* most resembles Swift (how close *Polite Conversation* and *Directions to Servants* are to *Bouvard et Pécuchet*), is able to fall back on the religion of art for art's sake. But in Swift the fierce indignation never rises into a scream or is mitigated by any consolation. In the loneliness which so frightened Thackeray he continued to the end, punishing and taking punishment.

February 1935.

LORD CHESTERFIELD[1]

ALL OF US WHO ALLOW THE SENSE OF THE PAST A CERTAIN
play in our lives come sooner or later to adopt a special period,
to fall in love with a few decades of history which we cannot
read about without a kind of quickening, an interior voice
affirming "This was the time." For many people it will be
the Elizabethan period, for others the seventeenth century, the
Regency, or the reign of Charles II. For me it is the first half
of the eighteenth century and the few years before it: the
end of Dryden, the flowering of Congreve and Pope, the
beginnings of Horace Walpole and Selwyn, a transitional age
full of a certain beautiful clumsiness such as is found in the
interiors of Hogarth and in the furniture of William Kent.
Compared with it the seventeenth century seems too eccentric
and theological, the high eighteenth century too romantic, too
elegant, and above all too rich, and the Regency frankly vulgar.
Unless you share this feeling (which is so prominent in the
editors of Lord Hervey's memoirs, the Duke of Newcastle's
papers, or in the Thackeray of *English Humorists*), it seems a
pity to write a life of one of its central figures. Above all, this
is no subject for the religious, for it represents the first flowering
in English life of the Roman spirit, with its urbanity, good sense,
and stoical courage, the first reasonable, measured, intelligent
attack which the Augustans launched on the citadel of happiness,
after impregnating themselves with the spirit of Horace, the
city-bred sophistication of Martial and Juvenal, and the solid
qualities of the pagan world rather than the Renaissance's wild
adaptation of them.

But Professor Shellabarger, on religious grounds, disapproves
categorically of Chesterfield—"under the pagan dispensation
his rank would be high; judged by the real not the conventional
Christian practice, he would have no rank at all."

"'I feel the beginning of autumn,' writes the dying
Chesterfield, 'which is already very cold. The leaves are

[1] *Lord Chesterfield.* By Samuel Shellabarger. Macmillan.

withered, fall apace, and seem to intimate that I must follow them; which I shall do without reluctance, being extremely weary of this silly world.'

One cannot help recalling, in contrast to this bleak acquiescence [comments Professor Shellabarger], the humble faith with which Johnson met his death some years later, or the exultant joy of Wesley's final hours in the bare little room near City Road.

Chesterfield is perhaps to be pitied rather than blamed . . . [for not becoming a Wesleyan!]. . . . The smile of a Marivaux or a Chesterfield may be one of life's greatest tragedies."

He even blames all Chesterfield's older friends, "gentleman Congreve ashamed to be thought a writer," Marlborough ("what grace! it secured him the favour of Lady Castle-maine and a tip of five thousand pounds"), Lord Peterborough ("a comic hero . . . a philanderer to the day of his death"), Bolingbroke, Vanbrugh: all are considered the worst possible influences, while meanwhile:

> "In Dartmouth, on Lower Street, a very low fellow, indeed a microscopic fellow from the standpoint of St. James, was tinkering in those days on a mad device for pumping water by fire out of mine pits. It was a blacksmith called Newcomen. . . . About this time, too, was born at a poverty-stricken rectory in Lincolnshire a boy who had as few and as poor expectations as Philip Stanhope had great ones . . . And yet he would change the course of English history," etc.

Wesley, of course, again.

Granted that the author disapproves of Chesterfield, he has written a very interesting book about him, for he is intelligent enough to see that Chesterfield's life represents, as it were, the second line of defence of paganism, just as Rochester's, for instance, is the front line which apologists find almost too hot to hold and which they have often to evacuate. The Cyrenaicism of Rochester killed him in his thirties, the mellow Stoicism of Chesterfield secured him happiness till he was eighty. Even Professor Shellabarger can only find a small measure of misfortune in the long life of one who, despite gambling, was always rich; despite ugliness was always favoured; despite wit was popular; despite political quarrels was Lord Lieutenant of Ireland, Secretary of State, and Knight of the Garter; was famous in three countries on the strength of a few essays, and joked about death when Johnson "with his humble faith" was sweating with fear at the mention of it. Even Chesterfield's deafness I doubt to be the major calamity which the Professor would have us believe. "I make the most of everything I can," he wrote, and it would be hard to discover a more satisfactory recipe for a happy old age.

The truth is that Chesterfield was extraordinarily tough. Swift wrote of his "*âme endurcie*," and the Earl went through life quite complacently, almost without love and almost without friends. It is his one lapse, his one love-affair that has made him famous, and which is dealt with in by far the best section of this book—"The Ordeal of Philip Stanhope." For though Chesterfield lives as a type of Whig aristocrat, as a master of delicate prose, as a father he is a world-character, a person on whom the predicament of paternity has been worked out to its most relentless conclusion.

"'I have now but one anxiety left, which is concerning you. I would have you be, what I know nobody is, perfect. As that is impossible, I would have you as near perfection as possible. I know nobody in a fairer way towards it than yourself, if you please. Never were so much pains taken for anybody's education as for yours; and never had anybody those opportunities of knowledge and improvement which you have had and still have. I hope, I wish, I doubt, and I fear alternately. This only I am sure of, that you will prove either the greatest pain, or the greatest pleasure of

Yours.'"

Anyone who receives such a letter is in for it, and so is anyone who writes it; for to call in the new generation to redress the balance of the old, to exact from our children the success that we have missed ourselves or the love that our contemporaries have not been able to give, is the most pathetic of all ways of making everyone unhappy. As a father Chesterfield is tremendous. The lesson to be learnt from him far outweighs in importance anything Wesley could teach, and yet how few people have learnt it! We see him pushing, moulding, lecturing, spying, piling up the jam round the pill, yet never for a moment leaving alone the miserable little creature whom he has cast to re-enact his own youth for him.

As Professor Shellabarger points out,

> "The casual reader, dipping here and there into the *Letters*, will be charmed by the Earl's gentleness. It is only when the collection is read consecutively and as a whole that the relentless character of the system becomes apparent."

Eventually the son returns home, having been everywhere, done everything and met everyone that his father had. His father waits at Blackheath for the "rattle of hooves and wheels up the Dover Road."

> "At last it came—unmistakable. His son, the hero of his dreams, a figment, indeed, of thought rather than a reality, was at the door—it had been five years. He had last seen Philip as a child, and did not know the young man arriving from Dover in the post-chaise. The child had grown into what? . . .
>
> A gasp, hardly suppressed, answers that question."

It is interesting to think that at the same time another experiment in education was being made by a father who could say, as he watched his son breaking his gold watch, "Well, if you must, you must," and "Let nothing be done to break his spirit, the world will accomplish that business soon enough"— and encouraging to see how the father of Charles James Fox was rewarded.

The author continues with a further account of Philip Stanhope, his failure in Parliament, his secret marriage, how, during a grand dinner at Chesterfield House, he stuffed the corner of the tablecloth in his waistcoat in mistake for his napkin, and walked across the floor pulling down after him the whole service. He concludes with an admirable analysis of the

Letters and their popularity, though again his attitude is unsympathetic. Of Chesterfield's suggestion that his son should have an affair with a married· woman of the Faubourg, he writes: "The abscess suppurates at this point."

It is a pity that Professor Shellabarger does not devote more space to an analysis of the style of the *Letters*. A man who could write such a phrase as "Cunning is the dark sanctuary of incapacity" deserves something more than moral condemnation, and he is hard also on the famous poem to Lady Hervey, saying "his rather lame muse burst into doggerel"— yet it is better than doggerel. The clumsy freshness of the period appears again:

> Had I Hanover, Bremen and Verden,
>   And also the Duchy of Zell,
> I would part with them all for a farthing
>   To enjoy my dear Molly Lepel.

Those who are going to write about men of the world ought, I think, to like the world, but apart from this, there is much that is interesting, understanding, and well put in this biography, which has, indeed, a certain mournful epigraphic quality, appearing at a time when we seem about to bid a final farewell to the life of reason, and in a year that has witnessed the demolition of Chesterfield House, and the death of the last Earl of Chesterfield.

November 1935.

IMITATIONS OF HORACE [1]

THIS IS THE FIRST VOLUME TO APPEAR OF THIS EAGERLY awaited edition, and includes some of the least known work of Pope. As other volumes will be devoted to his major poems and presumably will include a biographical sketch, a general consideration of Pope had better be left to their reviewers; Mr. Butt confines himself to elucidating as many allusions and borrowings as possible, and leaves the character of the great Borrower to be explained by others.

One would have enjoyed an account of the influence of Horace on English poetry, an influence which seems to have grown with the growth of London as a metropolitan city. For though Milton imitated Horace, as he has never since been imitated ("Lawrence, of virtuous father"), it was round the Court of Charles II that the impact of the Horace of the *Epistles* and *Satires* first made itself felt. The Horace of the *Odes* is one of the great lyric poets of all time, but the Horace of the longer poems is the poet of a clique, a clique which is always reproducing itself, and which rises constantly to power in highly civilized urban communities at the hub of great empires. Because this clique is reactionary, concerned with the eternal values of power, rank, fortitude, elegance, and common sense, and opposed to the eternal truths of genius, whether spiritual or revolutionary, Horace has made many enemies, and more than once among romantic critics appears the ridiculous statement (also applied to his disciple Pope) that nobody who admires him can admire poetry at all. To-day the attack has somewhat shifted. Horace was a Perfectionist, and Perfection, as the imperfect are proud of telling us, is Dead. The Perfectionist is sterile, a figure, according to Mr. Day Lewis, "embalmed in a glacier."

What did the imitators of Horace imitate? It is clear from reading Rochester, Roscommon, Dryden, Cowley, that what

---

[1] *Imitations of Horace.* Edited by John Butt. (The Twickenham Edition of the Poems of Alexander Pope.) Methuen.

appealed to them was sophistication, the new possibilities of
personal relations, the improvement in critical values, the
discoveries in Taste, which were afforded by the increased
security, wealth, artificiality, and centralization of the London of
Wren and of the Court of Charles II, a civilization which owed
much to France, to Saint-Evremond, Boileau, Molière. They
were fascinated by the mechanism of clique life, by conversation
without brawls, disinterested friendship, criticism without
duels, unpunished sex. They were modern in the sense in
which Pepys is modern; early products of an urban culture,
with a newly developed city sense, and an interest in the more
mundane ethics, in friendship, or the use of riches, in the value
of moderation or the follies and rewards of youth and age. In
Rochester the freshness of these discoveries gives to his
adaptations a vitality, a clumsy naïvety which is lacking in
Pope, and which is the difference between the Londons of
Charles II and George II; and Dryden, being both a lyric poet
and a genius, is also a greater translator, because he compre-
hends diversities of the original which escape his more talented,
but more limited, successor. His translation ("Descended from
an Ancient Line") is one of the great poems in English. But it
is not in translation that the influence of a writer is felt so much
as in work indirectly inspired by him, and it is in Pope's *Moral
Essays*, in his *Epistle to Lord Burlington*, or his *Characters
of Women* that his debt to Horace is repaid, repaid by the depth
and variety of observation, the perfection of form, and by that
manliness which was the Roman contribution to poetry, and
which, present for so long in English verse, has in our time
degenerated into heartiness, and now disappeared.

When Pope comes to translate Horace, in spite of his enormous
verbal felicity (no tight rope has been more delicately walked),
one is conscious of three defects which intrude themselves. One
because the heroic couplet is not the natural medium for translating the hexameter, and hence, although the colloquial and
broken conversational effects of Horace are exquisitely done,
there arises a certain reproach as one compares the splendid
and sullen force of the original with Pope's urbane numbers.
Another and graver defect is that, while we take Horace's

estimate of himself on trust, we cannot do the same with Pope, for while Pope in these poems is in love with his own moderation, loyalty, and devotion to virtue, these qualities appear illusions which sharply engender an awareness of their opposite, when we compare them with the rude avowals of the original. Moreover, Horace, although eighteenth century in much of his thought, was an ancient Roman, and Pope seems too anxious to fit him, as he had fitted Doctor Donne, into the *dixhuitième* mould. On the lecherous, irritable, and prematurely bald man of genius the periwig does not quite fit, and it is his lyricism which must suffer. Thus, even as Swift translates "O rus quando ego te aspiciam," "Oh could I see my Country Seat," so Pope makes:

> O noctes coenaeque deum, quibus ipse meique,
> Ante larem proprium vescor,

into

> O charming Moons, and Nights divine
> Or when I sup, or when I dine.

and one feels that his translation is inadequate, because it lacks nostalgia, just as his most beautiful lines are those in which nostalgia appears. Mr. Butt quotes a sentence of Addison, an epitaph on the Augustans:

> "It is impossible for us, who live in the latter ages of the world, to make observations in criticism, morality, or in any art or science, which have not been touched upon by others. We have little else left us, but to represent the common sense of mankind in more strong, more beautiful, or more uncommon lights."

Yet at his best Pope leaves common sense far behind, as in his expansion of the lovely "Singula de nobis anni praedantur euntes Eripuere jocos, venerem, convivia, ludum."

> Years foll'wing years, steal something every day,
> At last they steal us from our selves away.
> In one our Frolicks, one Amusements end,
> In one a Mistress drops, in one a Friend :
> This subtle Thief of Life, this Paltry Time,
> What will it leave me, if it snatch my Rhime ?

and

> Long, as to him who works for debt, the Day;
> Long as the Night to her whose love's away;
> Long as the year's dull circle seems to run,
> When the brisk Minor pants for twenty-one;
> So slow the unprofitable Moments roll
> That lock up all the Functions of my soul;
> That keep me from Myself; and still delay
> Life's instant business to a future day.

"Sic mihi tarda fluunt ingrataque tempora"—if there had been a little bit more of Johnson in Pope, Horace would have been born again.

This volume includes the *Epistle to Dr. Arbuthnot*, which has always struck me as a priggish and even vindictive poem wherein Pope's inferiority complex is unhappily at work, and where, though the invective to which it rises is unique, his fragments of self-justification and self-flattery undermine the whole. In Pope, as in Tennyson, sensuality was more rewarding than a moral sense.

Mr. Butt's notes follow through the poems like a handrail in a subterranean passage, and one comes to lean on them heavily. He makes the political significance clear, and a parallel emerges with our own time, for Walpole, with his appeasement, was not unlike Mr. Chamberlain, and Bolingbroke, the lion in opposition, not unlike Mr. Churchill. Could not these lines be ironically applied to the Hero of Munich?

> Oh! could I mount on the Maeonian wing,
> Your Arms, your Actions, your Repose to sing!
> What seas you travers'd! And what fields you fought!
> Your Country's Peace, how oft, how dearly bought!
> How barb'rous rage subsided at your word,
> And Nations wonder'd while they dropped the sword!

But the appeal of Pope must always be to lovers of poetry, to those who appreciate the subtlest arrangements of which the language is capable, and they will look forward to the remaining volumes of this admirable edition, perhaps regretting that the old spelling was not preserved, but more concerned with the mysteries of versification, the technique of a great artist:

> O you! whom Vanity's light bark conveys
> On Fame's mad voyage by the wind of Praise . . .

Such lines seem all air, yet the structure is rigid, and each word has weight.

July 1939.

ILLUSIONS OF LIKENESS [1]

TRANSLATING FROM ONE LANGUAGE TO ANOTHER IS THE finest of all intellectual exercises; compared to it, all other puzzles, from the bridge problem to the crossword, seem footling and vulgar. To take a piece of Greek and put it into English without spilling a drop, what pleasurable dexterity! And there is no doubt that the many hands who have been called upon, from Pope to the present day, for the translations now published as the English version of *The Oxford Book of Greek Verse* represent a sum of enjoyment seldom found in one volume. But if the enjoyment of the translators is obvious, how much of that enjoyment do they pass on to the reader?

I think a great deal. The last ten years have witnessed a welcome decay in pedantic snobbery about dead languages. A knowledge of Greek is no longer the hallmark of a powerful intellectual caste, who visit with Housmanly scorn any solecism from the climbers outside it. The dons who jeer at men of letters for getting their accents wrong command no more sympathy than doctors who make fun of psychiatrists or osteopaths; the vast vindictive rages which scholars used to vent on those who knew rather less than themselves seem no longer so admirable, like the contempt which those people who at some time learned how to pronounce Buccleuch and Harewood have for those who are still learning. The don-in-the-manger is no longer formidable. There was a time when most people were ashamed to say that *The Oxford Book of Greek Verse* required a translation. That time is over. We shall not refer to it again except to say that if people as teachable as ourselves couldn't be taught enough Greek in ten years to construe any piece unseen, as we can with French, or with any other modern language, then that system by which we were taught should be scrapped, and those stern nincompoops by whom we were instructed

---

[1] *The Oxford Book of Greek Verse in Translation.* Edited by T. F. Higham and C. M. Bowra. Oxford University Press.

should come before us, like the burghers of Calais, in sackcloth and ashes with halters round their necks.

The book opens with an analysis of Greek poetry by C. M. Bowra which is both compressed and lucid. T. F. Higham follows with an admirable essay on translation. He points out that there have always been two schools of translators whom he calls "Hellenizers" and "Modernists."

> "Hellenizers are those who would bring us nearer to the Greek, preserving its more 'literal' sense and also, as far as possible, its idiom and metrical character. They win approval, one suspects, not from the wholly Greekless, but from readers who look for guidance rather than for poetry, and are well content if the English avoids offence.
>
> 'A poem for a poem' is the creed of the Modernists. English analogues govern their choice of metre, or where none exist, they credit their author, if alive to-day, with a preference similar to their own. . . . Their popularity is more general than that of the Hellenizers, but varies with the fashions of poetic taste."

Higham quotes Browning and Bridges as examples of Hellenists, and FitzGerald and Samuel Butler as Modernists. Cory's *Heraclitus*, which doubles everything that the Greek says once on the grounds that English poetry requires more colour and personality than the original, was modernist at the time, and so was Professor Gilbert Murray.

There is, of course, right on both sides. One point of view does not exclude the other. One of the most exquisite lyrics in English is Milton's "What slender youth bedewed with liquid odours," which is a literal word-for-word translation from the Latin, with in addition a very close attention to the original metre. One of the most magnificent odes, on the other hand, is Dryden's "Descended from an Ancient Line," which he "intended to make his masterpiece in English," and which is a somewhat free and cursive rendering of Horace. The value of a translation must in the end depend on the poetical power of the translator, on that quality in him which is capable of digesting the emotional content of the original and re-creating it again.

Such value is found in the translations of Milton, Dryden, Pope, Cowper, and Tennyson, in Byron when he takes the trouble, in Eliot when he recasts Dante or Laforgue into lines of *The Waste Land* and *Prufrock*. Yet poets can indulge in huge fallacies, like the fatal idea which deceived Lang and Butcher, and to a less extent Hallam Tennyson, and then Lang again, and Leaf and Myers—the idea that the language in which Homer could be made real to us was the archaic prose of the Bible, of Malory's *Morte D'Arthur* and the Scandinavian sagas. The result was that generations of schoolboys grew up to whom the racy Mediterranean world of Homer was visible only through a Pre-Raphaelite fog in which with archaic unreality moved the Wagnerian shapes of Nordic gods and goddesses. Helen's beauty was easily confused with the Holy Grail; Penelope was a kind of sacred cow and Odysseus a very Christian gentleman. There was an indulgent smile for those scallywags, Samuel Butler and Lawrence of Arabia. Yet, as Higham reminds us,

> "translators whose names are familiar beyond the scholastic world—Walter Pater, Samuel Butler, T. E. Lawrence—are all modernizers, and careful to regard the genius of the language into which they translate. One may group them roughly under the title of 'men of letters' as opposed to 'scholastics.'"

One result of the Butcher-Lang-Mackail tradition has been slightly to discredit, in the eyes of the editors, translation of Greek poetry into English prose. (The Mackail renderings in this book are all in verse.) "Greek epigrams in prose-translation have been excluded on more debatable grounds," writes Mr. Higham, but he doesn't say what these are. Undoubtedly there is a certain lush monotony in Professor Mackail's prose translations, but the fact remains that prose is surely the best medium, with free verse, for the translation of short lyrics and verse epigrams from Greek. Let us take an example, a drinking catch, No. 234:

Σύν μοι πῖνε, συνήβα, συνέρα, συστεφανηφόρει,
σύν μοι μαινομένῳ μαίνεο, σὺν σώφρονι σωφρόνει.

> When I am drinking, drink with me,
> With me spend youth's gay hours :
> My lover equal-hearted be,
> Go crowned, like me, with flowers.
> When I am merry and mad,
> Merry and mad be you :
> When I am sober and sad,
> Be sad and sober, too.

Two lines are expanded into a jingle of eight which one wouldn't bother to read if one found them in a cracker—but what is completely missing in the English is the pulse and beat of the original, the echoing "soon" sound. "Drink with me, be young with me, love with me, wear flowers with me, be mad with me in my madness, reasonable when I see reason." The two lines have in reality a solemn, friendly, fuddled trochaic ring. "Comrades, leave me here a little"—if it must be in verse, let it be the verse of *Locksley Hall*. To my mind, the mistake of most translators is that they ignore the real nature of the elegiac couplet, especially in its most common form, the two-line and the four-line epigram. The elegiac couplet does not consist of two lines of equal length, it is a kind of curve, a parabola like those ejaculatory religious poems the Spanish call *saetas*, arrows fired from the human heart up to God. Tennyson said that the best lyrics had a double curve, like a piece of S-shaped apple rind flung down, or a tress of women's hair; the elegiac couplet has only one, the hexameter rushes forward with desire, the pentameter subsides in appeasement, the hexameter breaks like a wave, the pentameter is the backwash ebbing away. Consequently, translations of the elegiac couplet into blank verse or into the heroic couplet or the octosyllabic quatrain, by equalizing the length of the lines, destroy the rhythm of the poem. Mr. Higham devotes six very interesting pages to a discussion on how to translate the famous :

> Ω ξεῖν' ἄγγειλον Λακεδαιμονίοις ὅτι τῇδε
> κείμεθα, τοῖς κείνων ῥήμασι πειθόμενοι.

Eventually, after an exhaustive analysis of what all the words meant at the time and what they mean now, he arrives at:

> Take Lakedaimon tidings, passer-by,
> That here abiding by her word we lie.

In leaving the subject he mentions Bowles' translation:

> Go tell the Spartans, thou who passest by,
> That here obedient to their laws we lie.

It will be noticed that while Mr. Higham's couplet is reversible, Bowles has a cadence not unlike an elegiac by reason of the emphatic monosyllables of the first line, and the pause after "Spartans," which lengthen it to resemble a hexameter. The couplet is not reversible. Most lyrics are distinguished by a kind of tumescence, a note of longing which is there in the poet, and which is absent from epic, choral, or didactic verse. The structure of the elegiac couplet is perhaps the purest expression of it, and such quatrains as "O western wind" or the Spanish *coplas* are the modern verse forms which most resemble them. Where verse does not bring out this curve it is better to use prose. Anyone who feels interested might try to translate that couplet of Theognis which is hardly more than a few words breathed in and out, an involuntary sigh:

> Οἴμοι ἐγὼν ἥβης καὶ γήραος οὐλομένοιο
> τοῦ μεν ἐπερχομένου, τῆς δ'ἀπονισσομένης.

I have not read anything like all the translations, but even so certain facts are apparent. There is the excellence of that young translator, Gilbert Highet, who combines what is best in the Hellenizing and Modernist schools, finding the vocabulary of Hopkins convenient for the extravagance of Timotheus, attempting to render the elegiac quality in free verse:

> The oriental tree distilling balsam,
> The last waft of a drooping saffron bloom.

He does the archaistic Oppian into Anglo-Saxon rhythms, translating odes of Alcman and Simonides with grace and a sure precision. He is clearly a translator of genius. C. M. Bowra's versions become soon recognizable by their style. He has treated the death of Lycaon admirably as a Border ballad, and in general when we come upon the verses of Alcaeus, Sappho,

Archilochus or Pindar and suddenly feel the presence, not of some schoolroom wraith, some vague Sir Galahad, but of a sensual, fiery, aristocratic Mediterranean poet, full of wrongs and passion, breathing over our shoulder, we shall know that it is Dr. Bowra who has so expertly conveyed him there.

The translations of Mr. Higham are varied and workmanlike, experimental but lacking in poetic intensity. Sir William Marris is also more of a stand-by than an inspiration. I am sorry none of Mr. Yeats' *Oedipus at Colonus* is included, grateful for the interesting fragment from Mr. MacNeice's *Agamemnon*, for R. C. Trevelyan's charming version of Theocritus in the metre of Blake's Prophetical Books, for the delicious prose passage from Pater. *The Oxford Book of Greek Verse* is like a great museum of antiquities. Here is the catalogue, and with it one may wander as one wishes past pieces of archaic charm or ferocity, through halls where lie the friezes and pediments of the great period, into grave portrait galleries, rooms of bronzes and funeral vases, and finally discover, among much late bric-à-brac of incidental beauty, the last examples of Byzantine virtuosity or graceful Hellenistic decay.

February 1938.

A. E. HOUSMAN:
A CONTROVERSY

I

THE OBITUARIES OF PROFESSOR HOUSMAN HAVE GIVEN US THE picture of a fascinating personality and have made real, to an unscholarly public, the labours of an unrivalled scholar. But in one respect they seem to me misleading, that they all defer to him as a fine lyric poet, the equal of Gray according to some, acclaimed by Sir Walter Raleigh as the greatest living poet according to others. Now there are so few people who care about poetry in England, and fewer still who are critical of it, that one is tempted at first to make no comment. But in case there are some fellow waverers, and in case we can be of small comfort to those whose ideas about poetry are the opposite of Professor Housman's, and whose success also varies inversely to that of the Shropshire Bard, I have made a few notes on his lyrics that may be of use to them.

It is the unanimous verdict of his admirers that Housman is essentially a classical poet. Master of the Latin language, he has introduced into English poetry the economy, the precision, the severity of that terse and lucid tongue. His verses are highly finished, deeply pagan; they stand outside the ordinary current of modern poetry, the inheritors, not of the romantic age, but of the poignancy and stateliness, the lapidary quality of the poems of Catullus, Horace, and Virgil, or of the flowers of the Greek Anthology. This impression is heightened by the smallness of Professor Housman's output and by the years he devoted to finishing and polishing it, and, not least, by the stern and cryptic hints in the prefaces, with their allusions to profound emotions rigidly controlled, to a creative impulse ruthlessly disciplined and checked. This theory seems to have hoodwinked all his admirers; their awe of Housman as a scholar has blinded them to his imperfections as a poet, just as the pessimism and platonism of Dean Inge have sanctified

47

his opinion on topics which, in other hands, might suggest silly season journalism. The truth is that many of Housman's poems are of a triteness of technique equalled only by the banality of the thought; others are slovenly, and a quantity are derivative—not from the classics, but from Heine, or from popular trends—imperialism, place-nostalgia, games, beer—common to the poetry of his time. *A Shropshire Lad* includes with some poems that are unworthy of Kipling others that are unworthy of Belloc, without the excuse of over-production through economic necessity which those writers might have urged. Horace produced, in the *Odes* and *Carmen Seculare*, a hundred and four poems; Housman, not I think without intention, confined his two volumes to the same number. Yet a moment's silent comparison should settle his position once and for all. To quote single lines, to measure a poet by his mistakes, is sometimes unfair; in the case of a writer with such a minute output it seems justified. Here are a few lines from *A Shropshire Lad*, a book in which, incidentally, the word "lad" (one of the most vapid in the language) occurs sixty-seven times in sixty-three poems.

Each quotation is from a separate poem.

(a) Because 'tis fifty years to-night
That God has saved the Queen.

(b) Clay lies still, but blood's a rover ;
Breath's a ware that will not keep.
Up, lad . . . .

(c) I will go where I am wanted, for the sergeant does not mind ;
He may be sick to see me but he treats me very kind.

(d) The goal stands up, the keeper
Stands up to keep the goal.

(e) And since to look at things in bloom
Fifty springs are little room.

(f) You and I must keep from shame
In London streets the Shropshire name ;

(g) They put arsenic in his meat
And stared aghast to watch him eat.
They poured strychnine in his cup
And shook to see him drink it up.

These are some of the verses that, we are told, could not be
entrusted to anthologies because of the author's fears that they
would suffer through incorrect punctuation! (a), (b), and (c)
suggest barrack-room Kipling, (d) old-boys'-day Newbolt, (e) and
(f) are typical of Georgian sham-pastoral, and (g) suggests
non-vintage Belloc.

So much for a few of the bad poems. Let us now examine the better ones. There are two themes in Housman:
man's mortality, which intensifies for him the beauty of
Nature, and man's rebellion against his lot. On his treatment of these themes subsists his reputation for classicism.
But his presentation of both is hopelessly romantic and
sentimental, the sentiment of his poems, in fact, is that of
Omar Khayyám, which perhaps accounts for their popularity;
he takes over the pagan concept of death and oblivion as
the natural end of life and even as a not inappropriate end
of youth, and lards it with a purely Christian self-pity and
a romantic indulgence in the pathetic fallacy. By the same
treatment his hero becomes a picturesque outlaw, raising his
pint-pot in defiance of the laws of God and man, running away to enlist with the tacit approval of his pawky
Shropshire scoutmaster, and suitably lamented by him when
he makes his final escape from society, on the gallows. In
the last few poems it is his own mortality that he mourns,
not that of his patrol, but here again his use of rhythm is
peculiarly sentimental and artful, as in his metrically morbid
experiments in the five-line stanza:

> For she and I were long acquainted
> And I knew all her ways

or

> Well went the dances
> At evening to the flute.

It must be remembered, also, that classical poetry is essentially
aristocratic; such writers as Gray or Horace address themselves
to their own friends and would be incapable of using Maurice,
Terence, and the other rustics as anything but the material
for a few general images.

> The boast of heraldry, the pomp of power
> And all that beauty, all that wealth e'er gave,
> Awaits alike the inevitable hour :
> The paths of glory lead but to the grave.

That is classical in spirit.

> Too full already is the grave
> Of fellows that were good and brave
> And died because they were

is not.

There are about half a dozen important poems of Housman, of which I think only the astronomical one (*Last Poems*, 36) is a complete success. Two were given us at my school to turn into Latin verses.

> Into my heart an air that kills
> From yon far country blows

was one, which would suggest to a Roman only a miasma; one has to put it beside "There is a land of pure delight" to realize its imperfection in English, and the other was

> With rue my heart is laden
> For golden friends I had, .
> For many a rose-lipt maiden
> And many a lightfoot lad.
>
> By brooks too broad for leaping
> The lightfoot boys are laid ;
> The rose-lipt girls are sleeping
> In fields where roses fade.

This I have been told is the purest expression in English poetry of the spirit of the Greek Anthology—one of the few things that might actually have been written by a Greek. Yet the first line is Pre-Raphaelite; "golden friends" could not go straight into a classical language, "lightfoot lad" is arch and insipid. The antithesis in the last two lines is obscure. Once again it is a poem in which not a pagan is talking, but someone looking back at paganism from a Christian standpoint, just as the feelings of an animal are not the same as the feelings of an animal as imagined by a human being. The other important verses are in *Last Poems*. There is the bombastic epigram on the army of mercenaries, again with its adolescent anti-God gibe, and the poem which in texture seems most Horatian of all;

> The chestnut casts his flambeaux, and the flowers
> Stream from the hawthorn on the wind away,
> The doors clap to, the pane is blind with showers.
> Pass me the can, lad ; there's an end of May.

The first verse, indeed, except for that plebeian "can," has an authentic Thaliarchus quality—but at once he is off again on his denunciations of the Master Potter—"Whatever brute and blackguard made the world." Even the famous last stanza,

> The troubles of our proud and angry dust
> Are from eternity and shall not fail.
> Bear them we can, and if we can we must.
> Shoulder the sky, my lad, and drink your ale

suffers from the two "pass the cans" that have preceded it, and from the insincerity of pretending that drinking ale is a stoical gesture identical with shouldering the sky instead of with escaping from it. The poem does, however, reveal Housman at his poetical best—as a first-rate rhetorician. The pity is that he should nearly always have sacrificed rhetoric in quest of simplicity. Unfortunately his criterion of poetry was, as he explained, a tremor in the solar plexus, an organ which is seldom the same in two people, which writes poetry at midnight and burns it at midday, which experiences the sudden chill, the hint of tears, as easily at a bad film as at a good verse. Rhetoric is safer.

The Waste Land appeared at the same time as *Last Poems*, and the Phlebas episode may be compared, as something genuinely classical, with them. The fate which Housman's poems deserve, of course, is to be set to music by English composers and sung by English singers, and it has already overtaken them. He will live as long as the B.B.C. Otherwise, by temporarily killing the place-name lyric, his effect was to render more severe and guarded the new poetry of the Pylon school. His own farewell to the Muse reveals him at his weakest, with his peculiar use of "poetical" words:

> To-morrow, more's the pity,
> Away we both must hie,
> To air the ditty
> And to earth I.

This is not on a level with Gray: it contains one cliché and two archaisms (*hie* and *ditty*), nor does it bear any resemblance to a classical farewell, such as Horace's:

> Vivere si recte nescis, decede peritis :
> Lusisti satis, edisti satis atque bibisti.
> Tempus abire tibi est, ne potum largius aequo
> Rideat et pulset lasciva decentius aetas.

II [1]

SIR,—Debate about the merits of poetry produces not light, but merely heat. But certain *facts* in Mr. Cyril Connolly's article on Housman seem open to question.

"The unanimous verdict of the Housman admirers is that he is essentially a classical poet." It is surely fatal to go on using terms like "classical" and "romantic" without defining which of their many meanings one intends. But if Heine be a "romantic" poet, as most would agree, then so is Housman. He has "classical" qualities, also; but he clearly remains more nearly akin by far to Heine than to Horace. What is Mr. Connolly's evidence for this "unanimous verdict"?

"He takes over the pagan concept of death and oblivion . . . and lards it with a purely Christian self-pity and a romantic indulgence in the pathetic fallacy." Why are we to believe self-pity peculiar to Christians? Has Mr. Connolly never read Homer or Greek tragedy or Theocritus or the Greek Anthology or Lucretius or Virgil or Horace, with all their lamentations? And if "the pathetic fallacy" be a fault, how much of the world's poetry is free from it, from the "lonely-hearted crag" of Aeschylus to the winds that answer Lear?

"Metrically morbid experiments in the five-line stanza"—why is a five-line stanza "morbid"?

"Classical poetry is essentially aristocratic; such writers as Gray or Horace . . . would be incapable of using Maurice, Terence, and the other rustics as anything but the material for a few general images." Yet Homer could call a swineherd

---

[1] The four letters which follow appeared in *The New Statesman and Nation* in response to the foregoing review.

"divine" and devote pages to him; a Greek, Theocritus, took shepherds for his heroes and founded European pastoral; and the Greek Anthology is full of "the huts where poor men lie." Why in any case blame Housman for not being "classical"? Is *all* romanticism bad?

"The insincerity of pretending that drinking ale is a stoical gesture identical with shouldering the sky instead of with escaping from it"—why "insincerity"?

> The feather pate of folly
> Bears the falling sky.

Here is no pretence of heroism; it is a commonly observable fact of human psychology.

> To-morrow, more's the pity,
> Away we both must hie,
> To air the ditty
> And to earth I.

"This," we are told, "is not on a level with Gray; it contains one cliché and two pedantries (*hie* and *ditty*), nor does it bear any resemblance to a classical farewell." Why should it? And if "more's the pity" is a forbidden cliché, are we to understand that no poet must ever use a phrase from ordinary speech? And why is it "pedantic" to call a song a "ditty"? The pedantry may well seem to some to lie elsewhere. In a word, "Why pass an Act of Uniformity against poets?"

F. L. LUCAS.

King's College, Cambridge.

[Mr. Lucas read "archaism" as "pedantry."—C. C.]

SIR,—As a regular reader of *The New Statesman and Nation* I often get a great deal of pleasure and amusement from Mr. Cyril Connolly's articles. They are *par excellence* the voice of the Opposition; but they have a certain antiseptic quality and act as an effective antidote to our national drug of complacency. In your last week's number, however, I felt that Mr. Connolly had overstepped himself and joined the ranks of the professional denigrators, those often disappointed carpers to whom it is painful to hear praise of anyone or anything. I understand and share Mr. Connolly's objection to the Housman cult; I believe that both Housman and T. E. Lawrence gained false reputations by the persistent silence and mystery with which they surrounded themselves. I agree with Mr. Connolly again when he dismisses the claim of classicism made for Housman's poetry by many of his admirers—though never, so far as I know, by himself. It is only when Mr. Connolly extends his objections to the whole of Housman's work, except "about half a dozen" poems, that I part company with him. Here, surely, the mania for debunking accepted masters has gone too far, and there is an ungenerousness and a pettiness in Mr. Connolly's attack—not rendered less ungenerous or less petty by the moment chosen for its launching—which recalls Yeats' eight lines "On those that hated *The Playboy of the Western World*."

Mr. Connolly chose seven quotations from Housman's most unfortunate poems, lines which in many, but not all, cases not even the poet's greatest admirers would defend, and he analysed these passages as examples of Housman's "triteness and banality" and his essentially unclassical outlook. To deal with the last charge first, I admit that Housman was not a classical poet, but I cannot see that to have been influenced by Heine rather than (or as well as) by Horace or Catullus makes anyone a bad writer. It surely does no more than make those who called him an essentially classical poet bad critics. The charge of "triteness and banality" is linked with that of being under the influence of "the popular trends—imperialism, place-nostalgia, games, beer." Now I will not deny that many poems written under these influences have been bad, nor that some of Housman's in this category are very bad. But the influences themselves, which have been popular in other days besides Housman's, do not always make for bad poetry. Virgil was inspired by imperialism, I suppose, when he wrote the *Aeneid*, and it was place-nostalgia that moved Euripides to write in *Iphigenia in Tauris* the chorus beginning

Ορνις, ἁ παρὰ πετρίνας
πόντου δειράδας, ἀλκυών

and prompted Catullus' "Paene insularum, Sirmio, insula-rumque." The Greeks were not unmoved by games, and

Pindar's Olympiads do not bear a merely formal title, while
the pleasures of drink have inspired almost as many and as
good poems—Anacreon and Horace, without thinking—as the
pleasures of love. It would have been possible for Mr. Connolly
to pick seven unfortunate passages from any poet, however
great, and the reason for their badness would in most cases, as
in Housman, lie not in their subject-matter, but in a flaw or
lapse in the poet himself.

When Mr. Connolly turns to what he calls the "better"
poems of Housman, he finds them "romantic and sentimental."
Let us grant him that they are often enough romantic; this
is surely not a crime in itself. The charge of sentimentality
seems to reduce itself to a repetition of the charge of being
unclassical. Is not the five-line stanza unclassical rather than
"metrically morbid"? And is it a serious criticism of any
aspect of a poem except its classicality to say that

> Into my heart an air that kills
> From yon far country blows

—lines worthy of Emily Brontë at her best—"would suggest
only a miasma to a Roman"? They suggest something very
different to the twentieth-century Englishman, by and for whom
they were written; but it is something which at least rests on
a background of Christian culture and is therefore strictly
unclassical. Mr. Connolly attacks Housman on this same
religious issue, and points, as with derision, at his position
half-way between Christianity and Paganism. I find it rather
perverse to magnify the line

> What God abandoned these defended

in the "Epitaph on an Army of Mercenaries" into an "adolescent
anti-God gibe"; and the line

> Whatever brute and blackguard made the world

in *Last Poems* is surely negatived, as a serious expression of
Housman's own feeling, by the lines in a preceding verse—

> May will be fine next year as like as not.
> Oh ay, but then we shall be twenty-four.

Young men of twenty-three must be allowed to feel bitter with
the world occasionally (and perhaps Mr. Connolly must be

allowed to call them adolescent); the rightness of the line in
its context seems unassailable.

The other scholar-poet and pessimist whom Housman
resembles in many ways, Giacomo Leopardi, wrote at the age
of thirty-five of

> . . . Il brutto
> Poter che, ascoso, a commun danno impera

—the hideous power which, hidden, orders all things to the
common woe, and yet, like Housman, he could never forget or
step outside the Christian civilization into which he was born.
Many of the greatest European poets have held a position half-
way between the two worlds, and it has lent a breadth of
sympathy and often a certain pathos to their works. It would
be foolish to compare Housman even with Leopardi, to mention
no greater names; but it was certainly neither his religious
feelings nor his dependence or independence of classical models
which made him a lesser poet—limited, but within those
limitations a master. It would be more generous at the time
of his death to dwell on his mastery rather than the limits
of the field in which he showed it.

MARTIN COOPER.

Chelsea.

Sir,—Mr. Cyril Connolly, in his eccentric note on Housman's
poetry, asserts that "golden friends" could not go straight into
a classical language. Why not? Socrates could exclaim in
Plato's *Phaedrus* (235 E): φίλτατος εἶ καὶ ὡς ἀληθῶς χρυσοῦς,
ὦ Φαῖδρε, "you are a dear, Phaedrus, and golden indeed." And
even if this be discounted because their talk has been of golden
statues, the word occurs in the same sense elsewhere in Greek—
in Lucian, for instance, and later in Synesius. But the usage is
still more familiar in Latin. Tibullus (I, 6, 58) refers to Delia's
mother as *aurea anus*. Or take a poet whom Mr. Connolly
seems to know; he need only read as far as the fifth Ode of
Horace to find the word applied to Pyrrha in a well-known
passage—"qui nunc te fruitur credulus aurea"—from which
Dryden introduced it into English:

> To her hard yoke you must hereafter bow,
> Howe'er she shines all golden to you now.

Housman's use of the word is nearer to the classical than to
Shakespeare's. For the "golden lads and girls" in *Cymbeline*
are gilded primarily with *wealth* as contrasted with the chimney-
sweepers, and elsewhere Shakespeare points the same contrast:

> 'Tis better to be lowly born
> Than wear a golden sorrow.

About Housman's "lads" there is no such suggestion.

L. P. WILKINSON.

King's College, Cambridge.

SIR,—Late for the funeral, Mr. Connolly at least had the
satisfaction of arriving in time to spit upon the grave before
the mourners had departed. His article on Professor Housman,
with its reference to the "pawky Shropshire scoutmaster" and
"his patrol," appearing when it did, was a brilliant piece of
journalistic opportunism; but, as criticism, it suffered from an
evident desire on the writer's part to display his dissent from
popular opinion at a time when that display would attract
the maximum of attention. This was a pity, because Mr.
Connolly's criticism is usually admirably balanced, and a
balanced criticism of Housman's verse is to be desired, for his
reputation suffers from the indiscriminating adulation of many
of his admirers.

In his haste, Mr. Connolly made one or two mistakes, and
it is to correct these that I write.

Labouring to prove that the spirit of Housman's verse is
different from the "classical" spirit, Mr. Connolly says that
classical writers being "essentially aristocratic" would be
"incapable of using rustics as anything but the material for
a few general images." Has he never read Idyll XIV of
Theocritus? Or does he think that no one else has? Does he
forget that Virgil was marked for the realism of the dialect he
put into the mouths of his peasants? Is he unfamiliar with the
gibe "nostri sic rure loquuntur"?

Again, Mr. Connolly says that the line "Into my heart an air that kills," "would suggest only a miasma to a Roman." Those who know a great deal more of the classics than either Mr. Connolly or I assure me that this is nonsense.

But it was quite unnecessary for Mr. Connolly to venture thus into the classical field, for no discriminating person will deny for a moment that the spirit of Housman's verse is not classical, but romantic. Space spent (as Mr. Connolly spends it) in declaring that the spirit of "With rue my heart is laden" is alien to that of the Greek Anthology is wasted. Its spirit is utterly different, but the poetry itself is none the worse for that. (I observe, with reference to that particular example, that it is merely pretty, and one of the worst poems that Housman ever wrote; Mr. Connolly with remarkable innocence, or remarkable astuteness, quotes it in full as one of his "half-dozen important poems." Several of Mr. Connolly's other quotations are similarly misleading.)

Housman's verse combined, in a most unusual manner, classical form and romantic feeling. Mr. Connolly might have written a valuable article showing where he thought that Housman fell below his classical models in point of form, and where his feeling lapsed into the merely sentimental.

It is a pity that he left that article to be written by someone with greater knowledge and a more balanced judgment, and wrote instead the article that he did.

JOHN SPARROW.

III

SIR,—I did not know that in the Sacred Wood of English Literature the poetry of Housman was a ju-ju tree, to touch which is punishable with torture and death. Nor that it was, as my two Wykehamist opponents have not delayed to point out, gross bad taste to find fault with it. The death of any writer is always followed by a revaluation of his work, and the *advocatus diaboli* can surely be allowed a hearing. To suppose that there are degrees of being dead, that after three weeks one cannot pass judgment on an author, and that at some unspecified moment afterwards one can, is too nice an interpretation of the etiquette of the grave. There was nothing in my article that Housman would not have said, with far greater venom, of a living adversary, and nothing in it as unbalanced as the panegyrics which preceded.

> "The poems of A. E. Housman will endure as long as English poetry is read, his work as a scholar as long as there are people who wish to appreciate the finest shades of language and the obscurest references in the less-known Latin poets. But Housman was not merely an unrivalled Latin scholar, not merely the author of immortal verse, he was perhaps the most remarkable man among all the distinguished figures of his time."

If Mr. Sparrow, who admits that "Housman's reputation suffers from indiscriminating adulation," can write this, is it in such execrable taste to contradict it?

Mr. Cooper goes on to object to my finding only half a dozen good poems in Housman. Is that so few? There are no more in Collins. In his charge that I blame imperialism, place-nostalgia, games, and beer for Housman's "triteness and banality" and not Housman himself he misunderstands me. Great poetry has been written on those themes, but not between 1896 and 1922. I mentioned them only to show how close Housman was to the poetical fashions of his time. As to the anti-God lines, I find they betray something undigested and unassimilated in his work. Mr. Cooper defends "whatever brute and blackguard made the world" as being appropriate to young men of twenty-three, but nothing else in the poem is; we know he was between thirty-six and sixty when he wrote it, and he should either have brought the diction and philosophy of the rest of the poem down to it, or matured the line to suit them. I do not agree that nothing is to be gained by comparing Housman to Leopardi. Leopardi was a classical scholar, a recluse, and a pessimist, but also one of the supreme poets of all time; when one compares his laments for his youth or for the untimely deaths of Silvia and Nerina with Housman's Threnodies one is exactly able to isolate the element of hurdy-gurdy in the latter. There is, for instance, the subtlety and fine restraint

of the *Sabato del villaggio* when Leopardi reflects on how much
happier the villagers are on the eve of the fête than they will
be on the fête itself, and compares them to a boy looking
forward to the feast of life. "Do not be sorry that your *festa*
is slow in coming—more I will not say," he concludes—far
from the crudities of Ludlow Fair.

Here I should like to answer Mr. Cooper's last objection, which
is also made by Mr. Lucas. I do not mind anyone standing
half-way between the Christian and pagan worlds, but since the
handling of the pagan concept of life should be a very delicate
one, and since it is a position still capable of giving great artistic
results, I do mind the insincere use Housman made of it, constantly overdoing the notion of mortality and exaggerating it
into a cloying graveyard poetry and a *succès de larmes*. In the
same way I like the "pathetic fallacy," but, because I like it,
I resent Housman's constant indulgence in it, especially in the
form of lamenting that he will not be there to witness some
natural phenomenon, or that, if he has been there, no one
will know.

Mr. Lucas and Mr. Sparrow also object to my point about
Housman and his rustics. I know how Homer, Theocritus, and
Virgil made use of them. Homer is detached from his swineherd, the shepherds of Virgil and Theocritus are either genuine,
or the poet and his friends playing at being them, not both in
the same poem. Now, in the case of Housman there is an
uneasy and variable relationship; he is not quite sure whether
he is a peasant himself; with some his relations are more than
friendly, at other times he becomes a distant monitor—or are
they all Cambridge professors? I maintain there is a deep
confusion here, "meliusne hic rusticus infans?" We come once
more on one of those unresolved situations, as if Homer were
suddenly to say, "You're a better man than I am, Eumaeus,"
or Virgil to interfere between Alexis and Corydon. It was to
try and pin down this shifting social status that I used the
image of the scoutmaster and his patrol.

Mr. Lucas and Mr. Cooper both inquire about the five-line
stanza. Now, Housman generally wrote in four-lined rhyming
stanzas, a metre which he often allowed to lapse into a jingle, for

he had not the ear of Mr. Eliot or Mr. Yeats. In one of his earlier and in several of his later poems he added a line to this stanza, using it to impart something particularly bitter and poignant, and having thus three similar open rhymes to each verse.

> O let not men remember
> The soul that God forgot
> But fetch the county kerchief
> And noose me in the knot
> And I will rot

is an example. Surely there is something overloaded and over-artful about this stanza, especially when the last line is given such emphasis. I therefore called the extra rhyme metrically morbid. I do not object, either, to poets using contemporary speech, as Mr. Lucas thinks, but I do not feel that "more's the pity," "lief would I," "Ay, lad," or

> Then the world seemed none so bad
> And I myself a sterling lad
> And down in lovely muck I've lain
> Happy till I woke again

succeed as colloquialisms. "Ditty" and "hie," I think, are rather feeble words. When Mr. Sparrow says that I might have written a valuable article showing where Housman fell below his models instead of leaving it to someone with greater knowledge and judgment, he leaves out the other qualification— a far greater certainty that Housman's poetry is permanently important. Also to say "my friends tell me this is nonsense" is not criticism. I should have preferred to hear from Mr. Sparrow more about Housman and Gray. Speaking of Nature, and Gray and Bentley, he wrote: "to make a third [Professor Housman], she joined the other two." This was a claim I contested; may I hope he will substantiate it?

Mr. Wilkinson's letter I think admirable; I only wish I knew the classics well enough to correct other people with the ferocity such knowledge always permits. I admire his examples, but still timidly contend that they are not quite the same as Hous-man's more sentimental "for golden friends I had." But I think his point is won. May I ask anyone else who feels like writing a letter to consider first how long it is since they read Housman, and what age they were at the time, for he is a poet who appeals especially to adolescence, and adolescence is a period when one's reaction to a writer is often dictated by what one is looking for, rather than what is there? At least let them read a few consecutive poems over and see if they are as good as they once seemed. I think Housman wrote a certain quantity of admirable rhetorical verse, a few beautiful lyrics, and some lovely occasional lines and stanzas, but I still think there is about him something emotionally vulgar and shallow which is reflected in the monotony of his versification and the poverty of his diction. I think he will always have a place, for his good things, in late Victorian poetry, but I shall continue to maintain that he is greatly overrated.

CYRIL CONNOLLY.

Chelsea, *May-June* 1936.

THOMAS MANN [1]

IT IS EXTRAORDINARY, AS ONE GETS INTO THESE STORIES, HOW soon one forgets that Thomas Mann is a German. For the Germany he represents is like the lost continent of Atlantis of which he seems one of the few survivors, a Germany full of people like ourselves. Not a breath of politics disturbs these five hundred and fifty pages; the war occurs casually between *Death in Venice* and a dog story; the inflation gives rise to a study of a grandfather's feelings for his grandchild—even *Mario the Magician* will easily stand without its allegorical significance. Yes, here is a great artist writing for thirty years about a vanished and submerged race, a people who are as if they had never been, writing in exile of an enormous cultivated bourgeoisie, dignified, liberal, art-loving; bringing forth a certain amount of juvenile and morbid delinquents, but apparently for thirty years secure in the saddle, and now quite extinct, extinct as those early films, *Destiny*, *Dr. Caligari*, *Warning Shadows*, *Dr. Mabuse*, which once thrilled us with their hints of macabre patrician vices. There has even lately been talk of an English company making a film of *Death in Venice* in which the Polish boy is changed to a girl—or von Aschenbach could be changed to a woman!

What makes the world of Thomas Mann so particularly remote is his own cultural background, the formative influences of his early years. These influences are clearly of the 'nineties, that is to say, they derive from the Flaubertian conception of art and the artist. Writing is a high calling exacting great labour and patience and a certain self-sacrifice from those who profess it. One can't expect to make much money, and one must be content to remain an observer of life and of one's own life, often deprived of the experiences which render more rounded and full those of other human beings. The artist is a being naturally isolated who cannot or should not seek admission to the

[1] *Stories of Three Decades*. By Thomas Mann. Secker and Warburg, London.

63

organized body of society, he is an aristocratic ivory-towering
hermit vowed from his birth to sensibility, austerity, loneliness,
and fame. To this ideal of the 'seventies and 'eighties the next
decade added a delicious *art nouveau* touch. The artist should
travel. And so there grew up a literature of these travelling
artists; the romance of the liner and the *wagon-lit* appears, and a
nostalgia for villages seen from trains, or for certain hotels, which
increases among the writers of the nineteen-hundreds—till after
Firbank, Larbaud, Morand the new restrictions and the new
currencies put an end to the travelling epoch. We now "read
most of the night, and go march on Sundays." It is interesting
to compare the Venice of the *Aspern Papers* with that of *Tod
in Venedig*, the latter so full of hotels and *l'affreux lido*, of
carefully-built-up local colour exaggerated in a *fin de siècle*
manner. Henry James' long short story of the 'eighties, on
the other hand, is scrupulously reticent about the obvious
charms of Venice, and is confined to the existence of two old
ladies in a shabby palazzo in an unfashionable quarter—without
the poster quality of Thomas Mann's story of 1914.

"He did not like to be aware of the hour or of the day of
the week, and, moreover, he had no truck with the calendars.
Some time ago he had lost the habit of knowing the day of
the month or even the month of the year. Everything must
be in the air—so he put it in his mind, and the phrase was
comprehensive though rather vague. After all, was it not
enough for him to know more or less what season it was?
'It is more or less autumn,' he thought, gazing out into the
damp and gloomy train-shed. 'More I do not know. Do
I even know where I am?'"

In this delicious aestheticism of 1899 we are at once reminded
of the early Gide and the early Valéry. As the stories grow
(although there are trains in nearly all of them), two themes
emerge as those most congenial to his talent: studies of the
nature of the artist—that being who, for Thomas Mann, combines the integrity and self-discipline of a puritan banker with
the emotional depravity of a criminal—and studies of adolescence,
often on a note of idealized homosexuality. In the best stories

these two themes are combined, as in *Tonio Krüger*, *Death in Venice*, or *Felix Krull* which is their satirical counterpart. They thus illustrate the extraordinary affinity which exists between his work and Gide's and, in a lesser degree, between him and the Henry James of the short stories, and Mr. E. M. Forster, and the earlier Lawrence.

Landscape, Denmark, 1903.

"Sometimes it was still and summery there. The sea lay idle and smooth, in stripes of blue and russet and bottle green, played all across with glittering silvery lights. The seaweed shrivelled in the sun and the jellyfish lay steaming. Then grey stormy days would come. The waves lowered their heads like bulls and charged against the beach; they ran and ramped high up the sands and left them strewn with shining wet sea-grass, driftwood and mussels. He went landward by lonely meadow-paths, and was swallowed up in the beech-groves that clothed the rolling landscape near and far. Here he sat down on the moss, against a tree, and gazed at the strip of water he could see between the trunks. Sometimes the sound of surf came on the wind—a noise like boards collapsing at a distance."

Death in Venice, 1914.

"His head burned, his body was wet with clammy sweat, he was plagued by intolerable thirst. He looked about for refreshment, of whatever sort, and found a little fruit-shop where he bought some strawberries. They were overripe and soft; he ate them as he went. The street he was on opened out into a little square, one of those charmed, forsaken spots he liked. Grass grew between the stones and rubbish lay about. A waft of carbolic acid was borne on a warm gust of wind.

There he sat, the master: this was he who had found a way to reconcile art with honours, who had written *The Abject*, and in a style of classic purity renounced bohemianism and all its works, all sympathy with the abyss and the troubled depths of the outcast human soul. His eyelids were closed, there was only a swift sidelong glint of the eyeballs now and again, something between a question and a leer; while the

rouged and flabby mouth uttered single words of the dis-
ordered sentences shaped in his brain by the fantastic logic
that governs our dreams."

Dog-days, 1918.

"Certainly the meeting in the open of two dogs, strangers
to each other, is one of the most painful, thrilling, and
pregnant of all conceivable encounters; it is surrounded by
an atmosphere of the last uncanniness, presided over by a
constraint for which I have no preciser name; they simply
cannot pass each other, their mutual embarrassment is
frightful to behold. . . . 'Go away,' I repeat in a lower voice.
But Bashan does not go away, he sticks in his distress the
closer to me, making as brief a pause as he can at a tree trunk
to perform the accustomed rite. I can see the other dog doing
the same. We are now within twenty paces, the suspense
is frightful. The strange dog is crawling on his belly, like
a cat, his head thrust out. He is under a spell; he is bound
to the other dog; they are bound to each other with some
obscure and equivocal bond which may not be denied. We
are now within two paces. They cannot pass each other,
they probably want to, they turn away their heads, rolling
their eyes sideways; evidently the same sense of guilt weighs
on them both."

These two quotations may show something of the many-
sidedness of this great, vigorous, and sensitive writer. It is
obvious that the later stories are the best; *Mario the Magician*,
Disorder and Early Sorrow, are little masterpieces; *A Man and
his Dog* is remarkable. *Death in Venice* is a borderline case. For
one thing, alone among these stories, it is not very well translated. Nothing can be got out of an expression like "with closed
lids Aschenbach listened to this poesy hymning itself silently
within him, and anon he thought it was good to be here and
that he would stop awhile." I am inclined to think that though
perfect in many details, and in form especially, there is something a little artificial, almost arty, about the homosexual
element—which is not deep and honest enough—and something
a little vulgar about the thick palette which is used to describe

the plague in Venice—but how, if one can't read German, can one lay down the law?

Death in Venice is based on a fundamental but neglected principle of tragedy: the sequence of cause and effect. When von Aschenbach, the austere great writer, is suddenly prompted to go to Venice by the appearance of a wayfarer in a Munich cemetery, we feel that he is doomed as any bull that enters the arena, creature of equal dignity or fire. All von Aschenbach's elaborate spartanism crumbles under the strain of his passion for a Polish boy whom he sees when he arrives on the Lido. During the whole book they never speak, but Aschenbach goes through all the stages of a desperate and irremediable passion, blundering through Venice in pursuit of his idol as the bull blunders after the sword that will kill it, and as the one sinks down to die, its back planted with absurd streamers, so Aschenbach, now painted, powdered, and rejuvenated by dyed hair, is carried off by the plague. The plague in Venice forms the background, as if the author had understood that the city's essential spirit, torrid, sinister, pagan and decayed, could reveal itself only in such a décor. Death appears in many shapes through the book which, in spite of the Wagnerian union of love and death and the heavy quality of German Hellenism, has the frozen completeness of a work of art, a classic example of the tragic breaking-up of a fine character through the fatal abandon of age to its "sola et sera voluptas"—love for what Proust called "la jeunesse féroce et légère."

Stories of Three Decades is not really a book to recommend to writers, for to those who wish to write well it is disheartening to find so much of themselves already expressed thirty years ago and in another language, and to those who don't care, Thomas Mann will prove only too easy to imitate. But for the disinterested this book presents, in the most readable way possible, the picture of a fine writer and his time, a writer who may lack the emotions which sweep over us to-day, but who stands master of a complete world and of his attitude to it, an attitude of great fertility, that of the artist, in all his sensuality, in all his distinction.

November 1936.

ONUS VALLIS VISIONIS[1]

THIS IS THE MOST COMPLETE AND BEST INFORMED LIFE OF
Rimbaud that I have read. Miss Starkie has had access to new
material and brought a critical sense unhampered by precon-
ceived ideas to the understanding of it. Everyone has his
"theory" about Rimbaud. That of Miss Starkie is that Rimbaud
was a mystic who for a period really thought that he was God,
that he had found the key to existence, had reconciled good
and evil, and risen superior to life; this was the period of
Bateau Ivre, *Les Illuminations*, of his friendship with Verlaine,
and of his missing work, *La Chasse Spirituelle*. But Rimbaud
had, in imitation of Baudelaire, used too many short cuts, and
his relations with Verlaine made it hard for him to sustain the
illusion. In the "dark night of the soul" which followed, the
Saison en Enfer, he wrestled with doubt about his inspiration,
about the nature of his influence on Verlaine (*Délires* I) and
of his "alchemy of the word" (*Délires* II). Unlike other
mystics, he did not emerge from the "dark night" more
conscious of the authenticity of his vision. There was no one
to cry "This is my beloved son in whom I am well pleased"—
on the contrary, he was shattered by it, and the victory which
he thought he had won was only the acceptance of his position
in life, the return to reality, "Esclaves, ne maudissons pas la
vie"—a victory which was impoverishing and worthless to the
victor. From that moment his life, in so far as it was possible,
became based on conventional values, or his conception of them.
He became an adventurer determined to grow rich, kind to
his subordinates, quarrelsome with his superiors, anxious for
news of home, ambitious to save money, to return to France,
to marry and settle down—and his life was a double tragedy—
because in the material struggle he failed as completely as in
the spiritual. The long agony of his last illness, when, after
the amputation of his poisoned leg, he tried in vain to return to
Abyssinia, seems to parallel the anguish of the *Saison en Enfer*
when he tried to return to childhood purity and adolescent

[1] *Arthur Rimbaud*. By Enid Starkie. Faber and Faber, London.

omnipotence, despite common sense. Miss Starkie does good
service in discrediting the accepted idea, that Rimbaud, after
Verlaine stabbed him and went to prison, wrote *Une Saison en
Enfer* as his farewell to literature and then at once rushed off to
Abyssinia to make money, never putting pen to paper again
and hating all his old associates. What is the truth? Rimbaud
took great pains over *Une Saison en Enfer*; it is the only considerable work of his which he saw through the press and carefully revised. He sent off presentation copies and regarded it
as the beginning of his literary career, not as the end of it.

"There is no evidence that Rimbaud intended to say
a final and definitive farewell to art; it was only to be a
farewell to frenzied inspiration, to the *Théorie du Voyant*,
to *L'Alchimie du Verbe*. 'Cela s'est passé,' he said at the
end of *L'Alchimie du Verbe*, referring to his previous attitude
to art. 'Je sais aujourd'hui saluer la beauté.' Delahaye tells
us that Rimbaud had spoken to him during the winter of
1872-3 of the new prose poems he was going to compose, not
the short prose poems of the previous year, but poems on a
grandiose scale, something more vivid than Michelet. The
general title was to be *L'Histoire Magnifique*, and it was to
open with scenes called *Photographies des Temps Passées.*"

It is clear from this (*Photographies* is the operative word) that
Rimbaud was moving towards a less personal form, a literary
realism. Disappointment at the reception of *Une Saison en
Enfer might*, but the life he led during the next six years
must have made it harder for him to go on. For it was six
years before he abandoned Europe—six years in which he lost
his looks, began to grow grey at twenty-five, in which he lived
in London with Germain Nouveau, threatened Verlaine,
became interpreter to a circus, and year after year set out for
the East, only to be repatriated by a French consul, back to
Charleville. "Verses of his?" wrote Delahaye to Verlaine in
1875. "His inspiration has long run dry." The Rimbaud of
these six years is still the Rimbaud of before, the boy genius,
the "époux infernal," but now abandoned by the Muses, with
only his faults remaining; while Rimbaud of Harar, proud of

his business reputation, his word, his efficiency, his industry and parsimony, is no longer the dead husk of inspiration, but the new kernel of reality. Miss Starkie goes very fully into Rimbaud's Abyssinian life and shows how, in the rude society of Harar, Rimbaud was still famous for his wit, his erudition, and his anecdotes. The intellect which made him the prize pupil of Charleville continued to mature, as his handwriting showed, independently of the vicissitudes of genius. If his leg had not been poisoned, he might easily have become an important figure, a wielder of French influence in the complicated struggle for Abyssinia, a great administrator. The letter from Ras Makonnen to Rimbaud's sister on his death shows his hold on one great chieftain. Miss Starkie has chapters on Baudelaire's influence on Rimbaud, on Rimbaud "le voyant" and Rimbaud "le voyou," on the Cabbala, and the mysticism of Ballanches, and on the curious moving poem, *Le Cœur Supplicié*, which she claims was the result of an unfortunate experience in the barracks of the National Guard which was to colour his whole life. Its symbolism substantiates this. There are some interesting illustrations, one a photograph of the young Rimbaud which we can compare with Fantin Latour's delicious *Coin de Table*. The Rimbaud in the painting looks like a pensive Botticelli angel beside Verlaine's correct, weak, ninety-ish schoolmaster figure; the Rimbaud in the photograph is a spiritual Dillinger. There is a full bibliography. The faults of the book, besides a misquoting of the title of Mr. Waugh's *Remote People* and *le* for *la* on page 182, are iteration, amplification, and digression—a lack of distinction in the writing and a somewhat harsh summing-up. At the age when English writers are still qualifying for the school magazine, Rimbaud had created at least six works of absolute genius and raised problems which critics of all nations are still trying to answer. Miss Starkie has most intelligently stated them.

But everyone, as I said, has his theory about Rimbaud; I continue with some reflections after reading Miss Starkie, and re-reading him.

The three great artist-writers of the nineteenth century, Baudelaire, Flaubert, Rimbaud, are all French. Beside them, as beside Tolstoy, Dostoievsky, Tchehov, English authors—Tennyson, Browning, Thackeray, Dickens—appear amateur; incomplete and immature talents hamstrung by respectability. Keats, Shelley, Byron were the last European geniuses which England produced. They represent the romantic heyday. English literature of the nineteenth century could not improve on them. They were to dominate our poetry. English writers were not prepared to sacrifice their lives to the dictates of their artistic conscience, to be celibate like Flaubert, or to be debauched like Baudelaire and Rimbaud: they would not stand up to the matador. They represented romanticism in decay, shielded from its logical consequences by good mixing, Anglican ethics, Victorianism. Baudelaire, Rimbaud, and Flaubert are important because they made a synthesis out of romanticism and realism. Thus a hundred years after Keats we have Rupert Brooke, who is still blending a washy Keatsian romanticism with a dash of Byron. English poetry in the nineteenth century did not, except for Hopkins, in any way *progress*—but in French poetry Baudelaire had carried the romantic movement a step beyond Hugo and Lamartine, and Rimbaud taken it a step beyond Baudelaire.

Romantic poetry is the poetry of the Fall, poetry in which childhood represents a state of grace, a period of innocence, of the apprehension of beauty, and hence maturity a period of disillusion, when the sense of guilt, the knowledge of good and evil, of the conflict between soul and body, poisons everything. Romanticism is an aesthetic consequence of Platonism and Christianity, and Romantics who accept the Fall but reject Redemption take refuge in Satanism as their defeatist cult. Baudelaire tried "les paradis artificiels," Rimbaud saw that it was necessary to get outside Christianity altogether, and so introduced the cult of the negro, who was untarnished by the sense of sin; his original title for *Une Saison en Enfer* was *Livre Païen ou Livre Nègre*. And the blame for his romanticism he placed on his forebears, the servile Gauls, easy prey of the Church, and on "cette sale éducation de mon enfance." He saw the true nature of the problem. Romanticism is a state of mind which has been suggested to humanity by Christian morality and which is tragic when not supported by Christian belief, for it is the idea of Eden and the Fall, without Paradise to round it off. It is aesthetic Calvinism. Why go through life looking always back to childhood, why tolerate a philosophy which envisages life as a paradise before puberty, a series of ecstatic moments in early youth, and a disastrous anticlimax, a gradation of decay after the age of twenty-six? Why carry a burden of guilt for sins never committed, why split oneself up into two people, an angel and a baboon? Who cares about the childhood of Voltaire? Of Horace, Lenin, Newton, or Julius Caesar? Why reject maturity, and be afraid to grow up? The English pre-Romantics, Vaughan, Traherne, Jeremy Taylor, balanced their love of childhood by their hope of heaven. To accept the Fall and reject Redemption is to be a scapegoat of Christianity, victim of a confidence trick. Aware of this, and of the need for a religion, Rimbaud had staked everything on his personal vision, and worn himself out in the process. Had he possessed *any* money with which to mitigate his hardships and privations, or the leisure to gain disciples without the necessity of admitting defeat by returning home—home where his failure to rise above his surroundings was always rubbed in—he might have lasted out longer, and so have made contributions to realistic literature as valuable as *Les Illuminations* have been to romantic. One cause of Rimbaud's silence was that he was literally too poor to write, for the poverty that is tolerable to a boy becomes for a young man a cause of self-reproach.

Technically, the English writer who most resembles Rimbaud is Blake. How curious is the parallel between Rimbaud's poetry and *The Songs of Innocence* and *Songs of Experience*; between some of his prose and *The Marriage of Heaven and Hell*, between Swedenborg and the Cabbala! How alike their attitudes to Christianity! Even their poetic beginnings are similar, one starting at the age of fifteen with

> How sweet I roamed from field to field
> And tasted all the summer's pride ;

the other with

> Par les soirs bleus d'été j'irai dans les sentiers
> Picoté par les blés, fouler l'herbe menue.

Another cause contributing to Rimbaud's rejection of his art which could be more deeply gone into is his use of drugs. We know he and Verlaine experimented with drugs, but how much, and when? Did he use opium as well as hashish? Has some competent opium-poet, like Cocteau, ever gone over Rimbaud's work, noticing what images and what poems suggest the influence of the drug to him? I have heard that opium-smokers develop an exquisite lyrical sense, that they are capable of writing short lyrics of great beauty, but of no sustained effort—opium-smoking painters, for instance, tend to produce fashion-drawings. Cannot one detect three kinds of effect in the later work—the Hit, when the drug has liberated some subconscious memory of childhood, and the artificial paradise held the key to the "vert paradis"; the Miss, when the drug sets up images which, as communication, are meaningless, like jokes in dreams; and thirdly, the conscious effort, written without external stimulus, the descriptive prose poem, in which one is more conscious of talent than of magic? Examples:

(1) *Hit.* "Une matinée couverte en juillet. Un goût de cendres vole dans l'air;—une odeur de bois suant dans l'âtre,—les fleurs rouies—le saccage des promenades—la bruine des canaux par les champs."

(2) *Hit.* The whole of *Enfance*—which seems, especially sections 2, 3, 4, to be influenced by opium or hashish. "O les calvaires et les moulins du désert, les îles et les meules!" "Il y a enfin, quand l'on a faim et soif, quelqu'un qui vous chasse." "Des fleurs magiques bourdonnaient," etc.

(3) *Miss.* All such poems as *Nocturne Vulgaire* with its clinical comment, "Un vert et un bleu très foncés envahissent l'image"—or such impressions as "Oh—le pavillon en viande sanglante sur la soie des mers et des fleurs arctiques; (elles n'existent pas)—"

(4) *Straight.* The longer prose poems, *Villes*, *Conte*, etc., which seem written in a different language.

If the *Illuminations* were written under the influence of drugs, then *Une Saison en Enfer* might have been written during a disintoxication, for Rimbaud could hardly obtain such things at Charleville. The depression of the cure would then form an ingredient in his despair, and the disgust at a clumsy and fallible stimulant contribute to his disillusion with the inspiration which it produced.

Verlaine and Rimbaud, the caterpillar and the ichneumon!— Verlaine's face: authority waiting to be depraved, "que de larmes! et que de larmes encore plus tard, j'espère!''; Rimbaud's, the destroying angel. There is an element of masochism in cultured liberal society—from time to time it generates such high-powered scavengers, and when they have done their work and eaten out the decaying tissue, it turns on them.

Rimbaud's influence. Alas, it has been tardy and misdirected! If only the *jeune ménage* of Howland Street had been presented with letters of introduction in the early 'seventies to young Mr. Gosse, or Pater of B.N.C., how much ink and paper would have been saved! There might have been no Georgian poetry.

For the lesson to be learnt from Rimbaud is that, after him, romanticism can go no farther, a reaction is necessary, inevitable. Rimbaud himself knew this, hence his plan for the *Photographies*. Those who have been influenced by him, being romantics, have refused to see it, and used him to sanction their short cuts and excesses. They accept the lovely ejaculations and suspiria of *Les Illuminations* and ignore the concentrated realism of *Une Saison en Enfer*, like guests who look away when the bill arrives. Thus the conception of the poet as the seer opens the field to the charlatan. Surrealist poetry ignores the conclusions which Rimbaud drew from this theory, and in consequence it has not produced anything to equal him. However much Rimbaud raided the subconscious and the world of dreams, it must be remembered that he was a first-rate intellect and a ruthlessly conscious artist; his alchemy of the word was paid for in a gruelling apprenticeship, and if he took short cuts they were afterwards repudiated. Those whom he has influenced, with hardly an exception, have only ended where he began, instead of beginning where he left off. Baudelaire, Flaubert, Rimbaud, were romantic writers who were intelligent enough to purge their medium. Though occupied with problems of guilt and sin, they eliminated romantic traces from their technique, they permitted no luxuriance, vagueness, inflation, or verbosity; their sentiment is never false. To jot down nostalgic dreams, to flaunt a private damnation, a Delphic obscurity, will no more make a Rimbaud than an arrangement of dots will produce a Seurat. What must remain supreme in Rimbaud is the fusion of romantic imagination, militant thought and verbal mastery into, in his best passages, a precision of inspiration.

> C'est le repos éclairé, ni fièvre, ni langueur, sur le lit ou sur le pré.
> C'est l'ami ni ardent ni faible. L'ami.
> C'est l'aimée ni tourmentante ni tourmentée. L'aimée.
> L'air et le monde point cherchés. La vie.

August 1938.

FRENCH AND ENGLISH CULTURAL RELATIONS [1]

J'aime les auteurs qui ont un mérite susceptible d'être d'autant plus goûté que le monde sera plus civilisé et plus spirituel.

SAINTE-BEUVE.

IF WE LOOK UP THE WORD INTELLECTUAL IN THE NEWEST AND cheapest English dictionary, *The Everyman*, we find it means an enlightened person. For me "Enlightened Person" is not quite enough, and so, since the word will have to be used more than once, I would like to say that I mean, by this new word intellectual, one who believes in the intellect, one who feels that it is the dark lantern given us to penetrate the blackness of the world we live in, and so our main hope of understanding and improving it. But since I am to talk about culture, and since culture is made by artists and writers who are not all in that sense intellectual, we must allow the word to include those whose lantern-beam proceeds not only from the intelligence but from intuitive flashes of the imagination, and I do not think that this extension of the meaning presents any difficulty, because the intellect includes so much more than the mere faculty of reason and introspection. What we mean by genius is only the intellect proceeding by stages which are too sudden and rapid for conscious thought to follow: as is the case with those athletes and Everest climbers of the mind, the physicists, who are at their best when very young, and who after long hours of concentration in the anti-human and almost unbreathable atmosphere of their science find their minds taking, as Clerk-Maxwell has described, mysterious leaps forward into the unknown. We can measure the powers of the conscious mind, but the powers of an unconscious mind such as that of a profound, noble, and original genius, like the Douanier Rousseau, we cannot measure; we know that they are there,

[1] A lecture delivered to the Franco-Scottish House in Edinburgh under the auspices of the British Council.

and that they belong to the intellect as a submerged mountain range belongs to the islands that dot the Aegean sea.

Not only, then, do I believe in the intellect, but I believe that all occupations which do not serve the greatness of the intellect are so much waste of time. If the way in which we occupy ourselves, apart from necessary relaxation, is a way which provides no data for the mind in its struggle to master the conditions of life, the nature of happiness, and the meaning of existence, then we had better give it up. I believe in the absolute validity of Pascal's axiom: "Penser fait la grandeur de l'homme."

There are four types of intellectual who have helped the evolutionary process of humanity: the philosopher, the scientist, the artist, and the mystic. They are the true creative beings, and all rulers and administrators of mankind, however much they may have alleviated the common lot, are only in the long run important for having provided or not provided the conditions favourable for such creators to arise. So different have been the political systems of the world, so different the climates, the faiths, the racial characteristics, and the opportunities of human beings, that in certain parts of the world only have these four kinds of intellectuals been permitted to flourish. Scientists, for example, are confined almost exclusively to Western Europe, Russia in Europe, and North America; philosophers have much the same range, and that of artists is not much wider, though here China and India have made a great contribution, and in the case of mystics a preponderant one. But when we come down to what the Western mind accepts as the supreme level in art, literature, philosophy, and science; that is, the great men of the last fifty years, our map of genius becomes still smaller. In England and Scotland we have had the great physicists and Sir James Frazer; we have had some considerable and perhaps great writers, like Moore and Hardy, Lawrence, Strachey, and Mrs. Woolf; we have one artist in Sickert and one poet in Hopkins, and we have acclimatized some valuable Americans: T. S. Eliot, Whistler, and Henry James. Ireland produced the poet Yeats, the dramatist Shaw, and his contemporary, Oscar Wilde, and the philosopher-novelist, James Joyce; from Vienna came Freud and the other analysts; from Russia, Tchehov, Tolstoy, Stravinsky, and Diaghilev, and a philosopher in action, Lenin; from Central Europe, Rilke and Kafka; from Germany, Einstein and Thomas Mann, Wittgenstein, with his logical positivism, which took root at Cambridge; from Italy, Croce and Pareto, D'Annunzio and Toscanini; from Catalonia, Dali and Miro; from Andalusia, Picasso and Lorca; from Finland, Sibelius; from Denmark, but a long time ago, Kierkegaard; from Norway, Ibsen; and from Sweden, Strindberg; from Switzerland, Klee and Corbusier; from Holland, Van Gogh; from Belgium, Maeterlinck.

But our map is still ragged and vacant; true, a map of the Americas would be much emptier, but the countries of Europe seem not to produce more than one genius, at the most two or three. And then we come to France. Here we find such an astounding collection of great painters and writers in the last fifty years, as well as scientists like Curie, and philosophers like Bergson, with half a dozen migrants from the list just given, that at once our map fills up and we feel like elephant hunters who have been stalking a solitary animal and who suddenly discover, browsing by their favourite river, the majestic herd. And here for the moment we will leave them, to approach them by a long way round, down the centuries.

*　　*　　*

Let us now compare two pieces of prose.
Here is the first.

"Not until you have been away from it do you realize how friendly, how beautiful is the meanest English town. Not the most magnificent scenery, misty mountains, raging seas, desert sunsets, or groves of orange can compensate for the loss of the Corn Exchange, the doctor's house, tennis in suburban gardens, the bank and the bank manager's house, the rural garages, the arid municipal park, the church clock and the jubilee drinking fountain. Even a town like Wolverhampton looks splendid through memory's telescope, while tears of homesickness blur the focus of Blandford's market square and the grey, shut-in climb of Bodmin's main street.

Sitting here, remembering the provincial towns of England, I wonder why it is that they hold me, as they do thousands of my countrymen, with a spell that not all their obvious faults can break. Why is it that they are so attractive?"

And the second.

"I am approaching a little town, and I am already on a hill from where I can see it. It lies half-way down; a stream bathes its walls on its way to flow through some lovely meadows, a thick wood shelters it from cold winds and the North. I see it on such a beautiful day that I can count its towers and church spires; it looks as if it were painted on to the side of the hill, and I am tempted to cry out and say 'What happiness to live under such a fair sky and in such a charming place.' I go down into the town, where I haven't stayed two nights before I am like the people who live there, and long to get away.

There is something which has never been seen yet, and which, to all appearances, never will be, and that is a little town which isn't divided into cliques, where the families are united, and the cousins trust each other; where a marriage doesn't start a civil war, and where quarrels about precedence don't arise every time that a service, a ceremony, a procession or a funeral are held; where gossip and lying and malice have been outlawed, where the Landlord and the Corporation are on speaking terms, or the Ratepayers and their Assessors; where the Dean is friendly with the canons, and the canons don't despise the chaplains, and the chaplains tolerate the men in the choir."

The first piece is from John Betjeman's *English Cities and Small Towns*, Collins, 1943. The second from the *Caractères* of La Bruyère, first published in 1687. The keynote of the first piece is romantic nostalgia, "tears of homesickness" for places which the author is quite willing to admit are ruined or hideous, and of which he gives a detailed description in the hope that accuracy will lend them charm. The keynote of the second is a sense of reality—a classical vagueness of detail about the picture, but a complete refusal to be taken in by it;

the eye observes the little town of Richelieu, and is delighted with it, but immediately the intellect starts to operate, and says NO. In these two passages (and many other examples could have been chosen) it seems to me that we see the difference between the culture of the two countries, the characteristic of English literature being Imagination, of French, Intellect; the vice of the one Unreality, and of the other Sterility, and both requiring the intervention of each other's influences, the interplay of each other's masterpieces, so that the luxuriance of the Anglo-Saxon intermingles with the lucidity of the Gallo-Latin and both are fortified.

Here we should say at once that in all literatures there is room for everything; that France has produced its quota of inspired madmen, and England its natural Parisians, like Hume or Horace Walpole. It is absurd to generalize—all we can say is that Anglo-French culture exists, that Byron and Constable have intoxicated Paris, as Voltaire and Rousseau have shaken London, but that, if we are to understand what Anglo-French cultural relations are going to mean, we must try to isolate the particular element with which French culture has enriched us, which we cannot do without, and which we pine for when deprived of; and this I would identify as the sense of intellectual reality.

We can trace this sense through all the French masterpieces, from Villon to the Surrealists, but if I were to arrange a row of busts around a library and crown them with sacred myrtle, I would begin with Montaigne. This great writer, whom Shakespeare studied, grows in stature in times like ours, because as we taste something of the passion and bitterness and fear and tyranny of ideological wars, so we come more to appreciate the courage and deep, robust, clear-headed gaiety with which Montaigne, "sitting in the sun under the dove-house wall," proclaimed his dangerous creed of tolerance, scepticism, and self-respect. This creed was not just a sprawling egotism, as the lazy mediocrity of his imitators might lead us to imagine, but a heroic affirmation of humanism at a time when his country was racked with civil war and religious persecution. "The public good requires us to betray, and to lie, and to massacre," he writes, "let us resign this commission to those who are more pliable, and more obedient." While as to his egotism he says, "The worst of my actions do not seem as ugly to me as it would seem ugly and cowardly not to confess them," and I know no finer expression of the Renaissance sentiment of human dignity than his recommendation that we should live a quiet and unpretentious life on the grounds that the whole of moral philosophy can be in the reach of an ordinary existence, because "chaque homme en soi porte la forme entière de l'humaine condition"—this is his real philosophy, which he sums up in his unforgettable final paragraph, when he says that the absolute and as if divine perfection is to know how fully to realize our nature, to "jouir loyalement de son être."

If Montaigne is a man in the prime of life sitting in his study on a warm morning and putting down the sum of his experience in his rich, sinewy prose, then Pascal is that same man lying awake in the small hours of the night when death seems very close and every thought is heightened by the apprehension that it may be his last. We live in an age of such terror and despair that it is only those whose emotional experiences have been as tragic and as despairing who are our real contemporaries, and when we come in our reading upon some room with the blinds down where a man is in agony, we know that we are at home.

> "Let us imagine a number of men in chains, and all condemned to death, and some of these men having their throats cut every day in the sight of the others, and those who remain recognizing their own condition in those of their companions, and, as they wait their turn, staring at each other with anguish and without hope. Such is the picture of the condition of man."

That sentence of Pascal's, so clear and so rapid, so desperately true of Europe to-day, and containing as it were a whole school of modern realism, crystallizes that heroism of the imagination which is the mark of genius.

I have already mentioned La Bruyère, but I would like to say again that he seems to me to possess all the virtues of the French outlook, that sense of formal perfection allied to a passionate love

of truth, that profound melancholy, that surprising insight
which we glimpse in La Fontaine, and find perhaps rather
overdone in La Rochefoucauld, and which is the reward of
exploring the human heart without bitterness and without
fear. There is no time to seek for it in all the great names of
the seventeenth century, though I should like to point out, in
case I seem to be over-valuing French literature, that a visitor
to Paris in 1650 could meet then, and, in all but three cases, for
the next thirty years, the following group of people: Descartes,
Corneille, Pascal, the Cardinal de Retz, La Rochefoucauld,
Mme de Lafayette, Mme de Sévigné, Molière, Racine, Boileau,
La Fontaine, Bossuet, La Bruyère, and Saint-Evremond.

When we reach the eighteenth century we find a certain
optimism comes to be mixed with that sense of reality whose
course we are tracing; to the sombre and exquisite writers of
the seventeenth century succeed the long-lived philosophers,
of whom Saint-Evremond, Master of the Duck Island in St.
James's Park, was the precursor. It is the age of Voltaire,
Diderot, Fontenelle, Montesquieu, Buffon, Saint-Simon, and
Rousseau. A taint of journalism and Brains Trust uplift affects
some of these writers, but nevertheless two, Voltaire and
Rousseau, are outstanding. Voltaire's genius wells up in a
perpetual radiant fountain of inspired good sense. He may not,
perhaps, have been the most intelligent man who has ever lived,
but certainly he is the one in whom intelligence has best
combined with vitality; his mind moves in everlasting daylight. The courage of the seventeenth-century moralists lay
in their awareness of the tragedy of *La condition humaine*, but
the courage of Voltaire went, not into analysis of the tragedy,
but into the building up of an aggressive, rich, active life in
the service of reason; he was a mental man of action and
decided to behave as if the tragedy were not there. He of all
French writers is the best tonic against intellectual defeatism,
against the lion under the bed, and his gayest and cruellest
laughter is directed against the errors and fallacies and bogies
that have now returned to plague us, and which it can still
help to drive away. "O divine Voltaire, ora pro nobis,"
Frederick the Great used to say, and his prayer should be

inscribed on the doors of all who persecute out of stupidity and fear, or from love of power and superstition.

It is one of the advantages of living now that we can make a synthesis out of Voltaire and Rousseau, that when the glare of Voltaire's reason gets in our eyes, we can retire to the other's contemplative shade. This shade is seen to perfection in the *Confessions*, and in the *Rêveries d'un Promeneur Solitaire*. The fifth of these is a description of his life botanizing on the uninhabited island of Saint-Pierre on the Lake of Neuchâtel, and it is, I think, the purest, as it is almost the earliest, statement of that absolute and mystical love of Nature, that union through contemplation which Wordsworth was to develop fifty years later, and which has remained one of the most valid spiritual experiences of which we can avail ourselves.

When we reach the nineteenth century (with Stendhal and Chateaubriand providing the transition) we find the moral realism of the French genius applied to a new problem and one for which no solution has been found. Whatever the earlier writers felt about the human situation, they saw it in its relationship to the inhuman world; it was not till the middle of the nineteenth century that the monstrous way of living that mankind had made for itself out of the industrial revolution became a problem, that De Quincey cursed stony-hearted Oxford Street, and Baudelaire and Nerval wrestled with, and were defeated by, the wasting disease of large cities. So much has this infection spread that in our day we have seen the spirit of angry futile urban boredom, the vicious emptiness of slums and suburbs, take shape in widening circles of death and destruction, because the few who invented the machines have not provided a life with true values for the masses whom the machines have begotten. To meet such an emergency Baudelaire flung his powers against the city, and was destroyed, leaving his terrible diary of the battle, and his sheaf of poems, which are still uniquely modern because they go so far to analyse the peculiar misery of living in large towns, with no Rousseau's island to retire to, with no spiritual values, with only work, drink, and sex, and their excesses, to animate the industrial scene. It was Madame du Deffand, in the eighteenth century, who called boredom the tapeworm which devoured everything, but it was Baudelaire who proclaimed that this boredom was contagious, and that it arose from a spiritual vacuum, a consciousness of wasted potentialities, before in his turn he was devoured.

So far I have only spoken of such of the French who have a definite message for English writers, and by mentioning few poets and dramatists or novelists I have inferred that in these fields we need no help; that Dryden and Swift, Pope and Johnson, and the Romantics are able to look after themselves. But when we compare the nineteenth century in the two countries the situation is different. In spite of all the scientific and philosophic achievements of the Victorian age, it stands condemned of Unreality in the world of art. It had its poets and novelists, and they were born into their world with a wealth of talent, but they suffered from a worse disease than boredom, that of complacency. They flinched from poverty and unpopularity, from the tragic implication and the dangerous thought. They ran away from the city terror, and the fearful human enigma, to cling to the folds of their stupid, cosy Victorian Nanny, the Upper Middle Class. Flaubert and Baudelaire, giants of prose and poetry, were contemporaries of Matthew Arnold; they were some ten years younger than Dickens, Thackeray, Tennyson, and Browning, as Hugo and Balzac were some ten years older. When we compare Balzac and Flaubert to Dickens and Thackeray, Baudelaire to Tennyson, Sainte-Beuve to Hazlitt, we must lower our eyes. There is nothing to say; the Frenchmen are adults: beside them, the English, for all their natural advantages, have not grown up.[1]

A few years later the French produce Rimbaud, Verlaine,

[1] I owe this observation to an essay of Mr. F. L. Lucas. Spoken in a Georgian house in Edinburgh, it sounded almost blasphemous, and the angry bearded ghosts of Browning, Tennyson, Arnold, Carlyle, and Ruskin seemed to rise to reproach me. " How could you ! " Yet this was the city where, in the name of infant Victorianism, Jeffrey and North had mauled the Romantics and Tennyson. One should say rather that Browning, Arnold, and Tennyson all made some contribution to the battle, but refused to die in it. Their contemporaries in France faced facts longer, and took their punishment.

Mallarmé. Against the by now even more impregnable
fortress of materialist urban civilization the boy genius of
Rimbaud flings itself, as some half-naked young savage, greased
with magic charms, would hurl himself with a wild cry against
the frontier machine-guns, and fall dead under the concrete
fortress of the Bourgeoisie. And in all this long nineteenth-
and twentieth-century struggle between the poetic French
realism which seeks for spiritual values and the obdurate
philistine materialism of bourgeois society what part did we
play? We buried Byron and Shelley, and let Wordsworth bury
himself, we helped the great Victorians to become peers and
clubmen, and handsomely rewarded our artists with the pension
of respectability; some of them may have pined and grumbled,
while others even were too stupid to know that a battle was on
and that they had run away. We had, of course, Hopkins, and
Butler, and Pater hinting at heresy in an Oxford common
room, we had Swinburne, Doughty, and poor Wilde, to whom
we taught Degeneration through Suffering. But we stood aside
from the conflict, with the result that in the twentieth century
our art and literature became even more unreal: the fanciful
pastime of well-to-do middle-aged children who had refused to
grow up, and who could never hurt themselves because whenever they fell it was always on a thick green lawn. I think, in
fact, that around 1900 to 1910 art and literature in this country
were in a fair way to vanish, and depended on a very few
people, Henry James, Thomas Hardy, Bridges, Moore, Yeats,
and the Bloomsbury group (who were just beginning), to save
them from extinction. In the 'twenties and the 'thirties we
have paid for this.[1]

And now we have stalked up behind the herd of great
Frenchmen and come upon the moderns, who belonged to their
age, upon the writers who were never satisfied: Mallarmé,
Proust, Valéry, Gide, Claudel; upon the innovators: Apol-

[1] One of the great differences between France and England in the
nineteenth century was that French writers had no American market.
After Byron English writers ceased to be continental and looked westward. They made money from American lecture tours, and both the
American money and the American taste exercised a censorship on
them.

linaire, Cocteau, Aragon, Eluard, Malraux; and upon those great living artists who inherit from Cézanne, Renoir, Degas: Bonnard, Rouault, Maillol, Dufy, Picasso, Braque, Matisse.

How can they help us, and how, if at all, can we be of use to them?

Firstly, we can make their books more accessible. We can publish more translations, and reprint more originals; we can have an *Edition des Introuvables*, we can bring authors who are only names, Germain Nouveau, Tristan Corbière, René Ghil, Laurent Tailhade, Albert Jarry, that fine poet Guillaume Apollinaire,[1] before our public; those living writers of whom we know so little, Aragon, Eluard, Jouve, Jouhandeau, Fargue, Péret, Sartre, and strange new poets like Patrice de la Tour du Pin. And even the classics are unprocurable, as any of us know who have sought a Rimbaud, a copy of *Flaubert's Letters*, or of the *Goncourt Journals*. Then we can try to import one or two Frenchmen. America has received many, and needs them certainly as much as we do, but if the talent of Europe is going to seep slowly away across the Atlantic, as has been the trend for the last few years, then each one of us will be the loser. We must make an England which gives a welcome to artists, and is not a country to be by-passed by the European talent on its way to the U.S.A. A beginning can be made now. Aragon is reputed to be in Switzerland; wherever he is he is in danger; let us fetch him out. Eluard and his family should be rescued. Malraux would be invaluable; and Valéry. And in Tunis we have come upon our greatest prize, that old nugget of radio-active cerebration, M. André Gide, who wrote in 1941, in the German-controlled *Nouvelle Revue Française*, "Every time I dip into English literature again, it is with delight. What variety! What abundance! This is the literature whose disappearance will most im-

---

[1] Every June, since 1940, I am haunted by a verse of Apollinaire's which returns like hay-fever, and which I first read in that hot, implacable sunshine in which Paris fell.

> Juin, ton soleil, ardente lyre,
> Brûle mes doigts endoloris,
> Triste et mélodieux délire
> J'erre à travers mon beau Paris
> Sans avoir le cœur d'y mourir.

poverish humanity." I would like to feel that he is going to be rewarded.

But it is after the war that the opportunity to benefit from French Culture will arise. Whatever may be the political relationship between England and France, and I am certain it will be very close (for it is through alliance with France that England can be again united with Europe, and Europe become a great power), I hope their cultural relationship will be one of absolute union. The future of Europe will belong to intellectuals, because it must belong to them. For intellectuals are the only group in society who are fundamentally international. Everyone who believes in the intellect takes his place in the great family tree of the human intelligence in which those who have influenced him are his true ancestors, and these ancestors are from every race, every creed, and every condition. I am all for regionalism, for decentralization, for the "goût du terroir" in our artists, but I think that nationalism, though it has proved the soundest and deepest instinct in this war, and is beyond praise as a sentiment when our country is in danger, is not one of the most forward-looking of human creeds. It has won wars, but it has also made them, and it is to that love of truth which unites artists and scientists, that common belief in virtue and reason, that we must look for the perpetuation of peace and the prevention of wars to come.

So far we have attempted no explanation for the presence in France of so many great writers and painters. I think it is largely due to its climate, or rather its combination of climates, Atlantic, Continental, and Mediterranean, and to its central position as a market for ideas; but I think it is also because in no other country is Art so highly considered, and artists left so benevolently alone. An English artist is always conscious of responsibilities—to his family, to his tutors, to his public, to society and to the State. We have produced the greatest poets, but somehow in spite of ourselves. That is why France must remain a place where everyone can go, and where everyone can, if he wishes, live, and live without guilt and without a feeling of expatriation. The great blessing France confers on the artist is anonymity. When an English writer goes there, one by one

the layers of his social personality peel off, he finds there are
more and more things he can do without, and more and more
he comes to be preoccupied with his central situation, his
creative possibilities. For in France he is not an ordinary
nobody. This nobody, who leaves behind his old social or
academic skin, is offered all that is most rare and delightful in
life: masterpieces of painting and architecture, natural beauty,
congenial climate, cheap food, good wine, a room to write in,
a café to talk in, and a well-wishing atmosphere in which
everything is simplified. For the painter there is outdoor
light at all seasons and the world's centre for pictures. For the
writer, health and constant exhilaration. He has the Mediterranean for a sun-lamp, and Paris as his oxygen-tent. I don't
think any writer can live in France without acquiring something
of that serious and lucid power which we have been discussing,
and lacking which, so much English work is a salad without
a dressing, a nostalgic left-over from the Victorian age.

I know in my own case how much the thought sustains me of
my first visit to France after the war, so that I can be decon-
taminated from all the newspapers I have read, the unnecessary
people I have met, the stupid things I have said and the woolly
opinions I have held. I shall land at Bordeaux or La Rochelle
and go first to the valley of the Dordogne, that beautiful
temperate Romanesque corner of France where Montaigne
came from, where in the Virgilian countryside white oxen
move about the maize-fields, and where, in the oakwoods above,
the edible truffle mysteriously propagates itself, a connoisseur
of geese and men. From there I will make my way over the
Massif Central, across the heather and granite of the Margeride,
and over the pine forests and volcanic cones of the high plateau
of the Vivarais, to that extraordinary road which descends, by
a little stream marked in huge letters, *Ardèche*, to the Rhone
valley. Thence I shall take the Route Nationale Sept, un-
winding like a black liquorice stick through the plane trees, to
Aix en Provence, and then branch off over the Maures, through
the chestnut forests and the cork woods, till by Saint-Tropez
I reach the sea. There for several months I shall lie on the
beach without moving, like a lump of driftwood, until I have

regained what Rousseau called the "sensation of existence stripped of every other feeling which is in itself a precious sense of contentment and peace," and without which we cannot develop the best that is in us, and then, when the cicadas are silent and the nights turn cold, it will be time to think of Paris.

*   *   *

Man evolves through a perpetual spiritual conflict whose issues vary, but in which at any given time the artist must take part. The sixteenth century established the individual's right to his personality, the seventeenth the dignity of that personality in relation to society, and to its tragic destiny. The eighteenth century saw the struggle for liberty and the life of reason, for freedom from persecution and fear, and the nineteenth that for man's right (in spite of having bound himself in his own chains of ugliness and hate) to beauty and love. All these struggles still continue; but if the intellectuals of the twentieth century can obtain an armistice, then the greatest struggle, the struggle to understand the nature of life, and of our fate, which the new sciences, physics, biology, and psychology, are attempting, and where the artist can help by dropping his depth-charges, may become the preoccupation of all the intellectuals of Europe, and come a little nearer to being solved. England must provide the security which alone can help the patient, passionate, inquiring genius of our tiny continent to create and soar.

I would like to end with one more dark saying of Gide's, which he published in Paris in 1940, a definition which is highly subversive were it not so unlikely ever to apply to us!

"Our literature is being incriminated these days. People are reproaching it for its refinement and for having worked to weaken rather than galvanize our energies. Would it not be wiser to realize that every advanced literature, whatever its character, tends to exhaust what produces it? This flower of civilization develops and opens at the expense of the plant, which surrenders, gives, sacrifices itself to the flower. If Germany were in richer bloom, she would have been less strong."

June 1943.

II

NINETY YEARS OF NOVEL-REVIEWING

THE REVIEWING OF NOVELS IS THE WHITE MAN'S GRAVE OF journalism; it corresponds, in letters, to building bridges in some impossible tropical climate. The work is gruelling, unhealthy, and ill-paid, and for each scant clearing made wearily among the springing vegetation the jungle overnight encroaches twice as far. A novel-reviewer is too old at thirty; early retirement is inevitable, "les femmes soignent ces infirmes féroces au retour des pays chauds," and their later writings all exhibit a bitter and splenetic brilliance whose secret is only learnt in the ravages on the liver made by their terrible school. What a hard-boiled, what a Congo quality informs their soured romanticism! Invalided out only in February, my memory is still fresh with the last burgeoning of prolific and uniform shrubs and bushes. Those leathery weeds, so hard to kill, at first attract through the beauty of their flowers—the blurb or puff "splurging," as a botanist has described it, "its gross trumpet out of the gaudy wrapper." Wiry, yet insipid, characterless, though bright, these first-flowering blooms of Girtonia or Ballioli are more oppressive in their profusion, most reviewers will agree, than the forest giants, the Galsworthys and Walpoleworthys, whose creeper-clad trunks defy attempts to fell them.

An unpleasant sight in the jungle is the reviewer who goes native. Instead of fighting the vegetation, he succumbs to it, and, running perpetually from flower to flower, he welcomes each with cries of "genius!" "What grace, what irony and distinction, what passionate sincerity!" he exclaims as the beaming masterpieces reproduce themselves rapidly, and only from the banned amorphophallus, "unpleasant, dreary, difficult, un-English," he turns away his eyes.

Another sight for the cynic is the arrival of the tenderfoot who comes fresh from the university and determined, "above all, to be just—to judge every book on its merits—not to be

90

led astray by the airs and graces of writing, the temptations to score off a book in reviewing, but primarily to try and help the author while advising the reader as well." "The great thing," he begins, "is never to forget one's standards—and never to grow stale." I remember very well sitting round the camp fire one night when Tenderfoot and "Goo-Goo" (who was then going native) were "doing" a book. The date escapes me, but it should be easily traceable, for I remember there was some talk of the *Mercury* falling off, and the *Criterion* getting dull.

"This book," said Goo-Goo, "has genius, and not only is it a work of genius—of passionate intellectual sincerity and emotional directness—but it comes very near to being the best novel of the month, or at least of the latter part of it."

"Although I would willingly give an earnest," interrupted the Tenderfoot, "that this is Miss Bumfiddle's first novel, she seems to be a writer of very delicate intention, and has brought to a difficult subject a restraint, a distinction, that, to my thinking, makes *Goosegrass or Cleavers* remarkable not only as a novel, which, if not of the very first order (remember my standards), does at least attempt to state the series of reactions which a young woman of keener sensibility and more vulnerable perception than the common must inevitably receive in the conflict between genius—I use the word in all circumspection—and what, for want of a better definition, we must call life. I should like, however, to suggest to Miss Bumfiddle, in all fairness—"

"*Goosegrass or Cleavers*," broke in Goo-Goo, beaming tipsily, "is modern, as the name implies—as modern as Matisse or Murasaki. It is bold, and confronts the critic in all the perishable flamework of youth—of post-war youth burning fitfully in all its incandescent ardour. Take the scene where Alimony leaves her parents:

"Midway between springsummer and summerautumn falls the old-fashioned month of August-come-July—season of gross yellow moons, brown grass, and lousy yearnings. Alimony lay awake counting the slats of the blind that

seemed to scab viciously across the rich broth of evening
sunlight like the splayed fingers of a crucified neargod, a
flayed Marsyas. She hated bed by daylight. Through the
windows came the noise of the party and her parents' voices.
'Now try and rush the red down to the next hoop—with
luck you might perhaps push her through it. O dear! You
should have poked her more.' 'But I did poke her.' Alimony
cringed involuntarily. To think she ever would be one with
the ungainly old—and yet to-morrow was her birthday! It
was hot, stifling—out in the fields perhaps. . . . She opened
the introduction to a novel beside her. 'A short while ago
a friend of mine put into my hands an object which I had
little difficulty in recognizing—Sir James Buchan and
Mr. John Barrie, whom I consulted, soon confirmed me.
"Yes," they said, "it is a book, but only identifiable as such
by a few discriminating people."' Idly she turned the pages.
'Girt slough of cloud lay cast upon the jannock mere.
Weaver, be th'art there—weaver, I'm drained with love of
you among the drule scrobs, though in the village they call
me a hard woman.' 'Ah, to write—to write like that,'
thought Alimony—'to write like Mary Webb. But how,
without experience? Out in the fields perhaps.' . . . She
rose and collected a few scattered belongings. Tiptoeing
down the stairs, she saw it was not yet past seven. Suddenly
she imagined herself tiptoeing through life, a broken stalk
embalmed of this day's roses—like her own equivocal youth,
now cast behind for ever. 'Alimony! go back to bed.' It
was her mother. Something in Alimony seemed to snap.
She turned, her face transfigured. 'For crap's sake leave
me alone, mother. I will not be run by people; all my life
people have been trying to run me and all my life I've been
escaping them. I damn will continue to. I guess my life
is my own, even if it is a mess, isn't it? And you presume
to speak to me when I have to listen to you and Poppa
fighting on the lawn like a pair of alley cats. Hell and all
it gripes me so I guess I could upchuck.' 'Dearest mine o'
mine, my own ownest, my octopet.' 'Oh, go sit on a tack,
mother—can't you see I've had enough of it?' She flung

out, past the front door, with its friendly knocker, on to the gravel, by the dining-room windows. She turned to look through them. Her birthday presents were there for the morning; on the table was the solemn cake with its eleven candles. The click of croquet balls sounded faint on the lawn. 'Weâver,' she sighed again; and something told her the old Alimony was dying—would be dead, perhaps, before the night was past—before even the moon of metroland had risen on the filling stations."

"A strong book," resumed Goo-Goo. "This is no work for those who prefer—"

"One has to be on one's guard, of course," said Tenderfoot, "against being too sympathetic to a writer simply because she provides a restatement of one's own problems."

"One of the few modern masterpieces," continued the other, "a book for the library rather than the linen room—for those who like to find, between a Bradshaw and a breviary, between a gold and a glister, a modern-ancient trifle that will fulfil Milton's definition of the novel as something slow, sinuous, and sexy. A work, in fact, a work of— But be it not mine to deface our lovely currency by stressing that most distressful word. Simply I will say—slowly, sinuously, but not, I hope, sexily, 'Welcome, Miss Bumfiddle! welcome, Alimony!'"

And yet, looking back on those evenings when the fates of so many unreadable books, and so many more unread ones, were brilliantly decided, I can't help feeling regret and tenderness rather than relief at being free of them. It is easy to forget the nerve-strain and the nausea, the cynical hopelessness with which we strove to quench the indefatigable authors. There is something so clean and surprising about a parcel of review copies that one cannot but feel pleasure in opening them. The sense of getting something for nothing, though short-lived, is pleasant while it lasts, and the early expectations one had of discovering a new writer are perhaps less keen a pleasure than one's later hopes of being able to discredit an old one. The real fault of English fiction is that it has ceased to be readable. If novels were only this, it would matter much less that they were bad. American writers are readable; in general, a second-rate American book carries a reader along with it. He may resent this afterwards, but it is desirable at the time. The English novel doesn't, and never will so long as it consists either of arranged emotional autobiography or a carefully detached description of stupid people to show that the author is too clever to be clever. But I am getting into my stride again. Meanwhile a new generation of novel-reviewers is growing up, and this thought brings me to the real tragedy of reviewing—to that ironical and irrevocable law of poetic justice which ennobles the humdrum work and allows the broken journalist to feel in his very ruin something of the divine. For all the novels that he scotches the novel will in time scotch him; like the King at Nemi, the slayer shall himself be slain. Brave and agile, the reviewer enters the ring. He rushes blindly at the red wrappers. He disembowels a few old hacks. But his onsets eventually grow futile, his weapons are blunted, his words are stale. He may go under nobly, a Croker facing his Keats; he may simply wear out in praising or abusing—(it matters not which)—the never-ceasing flow of second-rate and worthy productions—but eventually the jungle claims him.

What advice, then, would I give to someone forced—for no one could be willing—to become a reviewer? Firstly, never praise; praise dates you. In reviewing a book you like, write for the author; in reviewing any other, write for the public. Read the books you review, but you should need only to skim a page to settle if they are worth reviewing. Never touch novels written by your friends. Remember that the object of the critic is to revenge himself on the creator, and his method must depend on whether the book is good or bad, whether he dare condemn it himself or must lie quiet and let it blow over. Every good reviewer has a subject. He specializes in that subject on which he has not been able to write a book, and his aim is to see that no one else does. He stands behind the ticket-queue of fame, banging his rivals on the head as they bend low before the guichet. When he has laid out enough he becomes an authority, which is more than they will. And had I stood the climate, this was what I might have been!

The problem of the retiring age has long bewildered economists. Wandering, as I now do, among other finished critics, broken in health and temper by the rigours of the service, or the censure of authors, publishers, and public, I can't help wondering, in the shabby watering-places, the *petits trous pas chers* near Portsmouth or the Riviera that the retired inhabit, if we are really down and out. Can a reviewer come back? Is he too old at twenty-five? Could he find a place, with younger men, in the front lines where they stem the advance of autumn novels—and die in harness? I know it is foolish to dream, to think on these possibilities. I should face facts as bravely as I once faced fiction.

> miser Cyrille desinas ineptire
> et quod vides perisse perditum ducas—

And yet these secret heartburns are only human. The other day, languishing among the back numbers in a French hotel, I received a letter from New York which almost gave me hope again. "When," demanded the writer—"when will you tell the public that Mr. Compton Mackenzie, in his last three novels, has not only recaptured the prose style of Congreve, but also Congreve's attitude to life?" "When," I breathed—and there were tears in my eyes—"when shall I?"

August 1929.

MORE ABOUT THE MODERN NOVEL

SIXTY BOOKS OUT OF EVERY HUNDRED PUBLISHED ARE NOVELS, nine out of those sixty are here, three out of that nine are readable, none out of the three worth seven and sixpence. This type of remark is a reviewer's platitude by now. There are several obvious but impracticable remedies. One author thinks that novels, like poetry, shouldn't be reviewed any more. Then only the best work would struggle occasionally into print. But if novels are not reviewed, then the publishers complain (for sixty books out of every hundred, etc.), and if they complain they will not advertise, and consequently there wouldn't be a paper left in which to review the good ones. I would prefer to have a close season, no new novels to be published for three years, their sale forbidden like that of plovers' eggs. And nobody under thirty should be allowed to write one—it is amusing to apply this age-canon and see how well it works out, how little would be lost to us. But above all, I should like to see an enormous extension of the censorship—not simply libel and obscenity would be taboo, but whole landscapes, whole strata of our civilization would become unmentionable. Schools and universities, all homes with incomes of between three thousand and three hundred a year, words like Daddy, love, marriage, baby, birth, death, mother, buses, shops—I particularly dislike both the shopping expedition ("she looked at her list, let me see, two bars of soap, three bars of chocolate, but already the huge store had overwhelmed her with its Oriental mystery—it was an Arab bazaar, Eunice decided rapidly as she paused before a chinchilla mantilla. Seven yards of demi-rep the list continued")—and those horrible bus-rides, when the stars are so close, and the young man treads on air ("he was getting nearer, Pimlico was a forgotten dream, Fulham and West Brompton passed unheeded—supposing she should be out? 'Fares please,' shouted the conductor for the third time. 'Fourpenny to heaven,' he answered unthinking"), and picnics,

and going for walks, and conversations in pubs, and all novels
dealing with more than one generation or with any period
before 1918 or with brilliant impoverished children in rectories
or with the following regions, which I understand are going
to be preserved from novelists by the National Trust: the Isle
of Wight, the Isle of Purbeck, Hampshire, Sussex, Oxford,
Cambridge, the Essex coast, Wiltshire, Cornwall, Kensington,
Chelsea, Hampstead, Hyde Park, and Hammersmith. Many
situations should be forbidden, all getting and losing of jobs,
proposals of marriage, reception of love-letters by either sex
(especially if they are hugged closely and taken up to attics or
the familiar seat in the apple tree), all allusion to illness or
suicide (except insanity), all quotations, all mentions of genius,
promise, writing, painting, sculpting, art, poetry, and the
phrases "I like your stuff," "What's his stuff like?" "Damned
good," "Let me make you some coffee," all young men with
ambition or young women with emotion, all remarks like
"Darling, I've found the most wonderful cottage" (flat, castle),
"Ask me any other time, dearest, only please—just this once—
not now," "Love you—of course I love you" (don't love you)—
and "It's not that, it's only that I feel so terribly tired."

Forbidden names: Hugo, Peter, Sebastian, Adrian, Ivor,
Julian, Pamela, Chloe, Enid, Inez, Miranda, Joanna, Jill,
Felicity, Phyllis.

Forbidden faces: all young men with curly hair or remarkable eyes, all gaunt haggard thinkers' faces, all faunlike
characters, anybody over six feet, or with any distinction
whatever, and all women with a nape to their neck (he loved
the way her hair curled in the little hollow at the nape of
her neck).

Really good novels excepted, the rest fall into two kinds,
English and American; the one will probably be written by a
woman, the other by a man. The English novel certainly, the
American probably, will begin with childhood. This insistence
on childhood is the radical defect of most ordinary novels of
to-day. There are three reasons for this. Childhood is not
in itself interesting, the great accounts of childhood are of
abnormal childhoods, and the reader is now too wary to be

caught with this familiar bait—which permits the novelist to meander about among the past, confident of hiding his egotism under a thin coating of squalid charm, and behind a tender appeal to the universal experience of the race. Secondly, childhoods are nearly all wholly irrelevant to any plot; memoirs, essays, poems are the proper place for accounts of childhood; at the beginning of novels they only hold up the action, while giving a very poor idea of the characters. And lastly, the novelist is usually clever, and the childhoods of the clever are invariably unpleasant, a record of grievances and snubs, of too brutal perception and too smart replies. Then the childhood theme is often introduced to show up the parents, a dreary device. Formerly the most touching feature of Victorian novels lay in such a situation as "Mother, why have those men taken father away?" "There has been a dreadful mistake, my darling, but he will soon come back, for the law will put it right." This has changed, however, to the child complaining with all the pained malice of the habitual eavesdropper or commenting brutally, with the penetration of self-pity, on the defects of the parents' conjugal relations.

The American novel will only not begin with childhood if the hero is a group hero (a family, a factory, a small town, a business, or the American nation). In these cases it usually begins several generations farther back with matter which is as irrelevant as childhood, but which yields that dazzling sequence of births and deaths which enables the book to appear an "epic." The typical 100 per cent. American novel has almost invariably a group hero, and is usually a monument of wasted energy, sentimentality striving after realism, and an admirable talent for description being thrown away on life that is quite unworthy to be described. This vigorous material confidence provokes many exceptions, and these in turn fall into three classes, for the romantic revolt against success in life and realism in literature has but a very narrow path of escape. If the novelist hates business, births and deaths and prosperity, he falls a victim to minority worship and writes about Indians, Mexicans, negroes, or subject populations of America, finding in them the idealism which is his goal. If

he is too reflective for those, he falls back on the past—tales
of a grandmother, the old days on the farm, the novel of the
orchard. If he is interested as well in style, he is swallowed up
by Europe. This type of American is invariably a culture snob.
These uprooted self-exiled Americans, however, are mostly
taking refuge from a life for which they were unfitted rather
than seceding in passionate rebellion; hence a limpness in all
their work, for the soft spot that caused their failures in their
native land becomes a defiant timidity when they are landed on
an indifferent Europe; hence the tepid quality of the expatriate
American novel, which has escaped vulgarity to become insipid
instead. Many more American novels are half-way towards
Europe, with a dullness about things American similar to that
in caterpillars, which, when about to enter their chrysalis,
go off their feed. The culture applauded in these American
novels is nearly always the French literature of the end of the
last century, the art for art's sake movement which reveals the
timidity rather than the defiance at the heart of these emigrants
religiously escaping for the sake of their style. Flaubert,
Verlaine, Huysmans, Baudelaire, Pater, Henry James, and
George Moore are alluded to most frequently by these intending
fugitives, and a mention of one of them should place the book
at once for the reader, just as that of an American real-life
writer will betray the fake epic, the ruthless saga about the
most commonplace world.

With the English novel we are in a different universe, the
realm of the egotist, and of the most dangerous kind of egotists,
those who, for self-protection, have developed the gland of
charm. Having so often bewailed the glut of feminine autobiographies, there is little more to say about this except to warn
the reader against the day-dream which, always abused in
these novels, leaves a sickening taste behind. The day-dream
is an immense discovery for the novel's technique, but an
innate capacity for luxurious wish-fulfilment makes it an
instrument to be handled with the greatest reluctance and care.
The day-dream should be crisp, terse, and relevant to the plot,
or else an exquisite and impersonal lyric like a simile from
Homer or *Paradise Lost*. When the reader experiences a

muzzy and unpleasantly tipsy feeling, it means the passage is autobiographical, and probably the most trying form of auto-biography, the arrangement which self-worship dictates of how something might have happened could we have it all over again. These English autobiographies, however, at least end in marriage, while the American epics seldom end at all. They are, moreover, tender, graceful, and humorous books, and their zeal for understatement saves them from the terrible American faults of style ("powerful" passages in the epic, rhetorical epigrams in the Europeanized form). The English cake is plain and eatable except for the dank spots where the mildew of childhood day-dreams and school friendships has left its shadowy web; while the American is either massively stodgy and commemorative, thick with icing, or, like tea-cake on a railway train, cut into thin, tasteless slices, not indigestible, but a little stale. If the reader can apply this classification to the main body of novels he will need no reviewer at all; only he must keep in mind the possibility of the grace of England, the vitality of America, or the enterprise of the Rive Gauche, producing at any moment a great work.

1935.

DEFECTS OF
ENGLISH NOVELS

THERE ARE THREE, COLOSSAL, ALMOST IRREMEDIABLE.

1. *Thinness of Material*. English life is on the whole without adventure or variety, 90 per cent. of English authors come from the mandarin class, the experiences from which both sexes can draw are limited to three or four—a peaceful childhood, a public school education, a university, a few years in London or the provinces in which to get a job, a wife, a house, and some children. Material for one book, perhaps, which publishers and the need to earn one's living will drag out to three or four. A rigorous class system blankets down all attempts to enlarge these barriers. The English mandarin simply can't get at pugilists, gangsters, speakeasies, negroes, and even if he should he would find them absolutely without the force and colour of the American equivalent.

2. *Poverty of Style*. There are only about two ways to write a novel in English, one by using the moderately intelligent, rather academic language of the mandarin class, a style which depends for its force on the combination of adjective and noun or two adjectives and noun:

> "With his practised and professional eye, Mr. Cardan thought he could detect in his host's expression certain hardly perceptible symptoms of incipient tipsiness."

That style is the typical instrument of English fiction, and it badly needs tuning. The other seeks to avoid the Oxford, consciously intellectual, attitude by extreme simplicity. E. M. Forster, David Garnett, Dorothy Edwards write in this way, but in other hands it easily becomes whimsical and mousy. English novels seem absolutely chained to these two forms, there is no *lingua franca* to correspond to the "tough" colloquial American style, which is not so much the slang of crooks and bootleggers, but the vigorous workaday speech of the reporters,

journalists, and advertising men who turn out so many of the
best American novels. We, however, have no novels in spoken
English—that of Eliot's *Sweeny Agonistes*.

3. *Lack of Power*. This is hard to define, but I mean lack
both of intellectual power, of any mastery of the situation, any
real maturity (such as is found in all great novelists, although
as different as Tolstoy or Henry James), and of narrative power,
of punch, concision, dramatic sense. This is the most serious
shortage in the English novelist—one hardly ever finds a trace
of it in the younger writers, although we are almost bowled
over by it, for instance, in the longer stories of Maugham.
I think one reason for its absence is that the English novelist
never establishes a respect-worthy relationship with his reader.
The American novelists, Hemingway, Hamnett, Faulkner,
Fitzgerald, O'Hara, for instance, write instinctively for men
of their own age, men who enjoy the same things; "Look, go
slow, don't miss this," they seem to say, "this will interest
you—maybe you've been to this actual place or had the same
thing happen to you"—it is an intimacy which at its worst
degenerates into dogginess, but which in general brings out
everything that is natural, easy, and unrepressed in the author
as only can friendly communion with a contemporary. English
novels seem always to be written for superiors or inferiors, older
or younger people, or for the opposite sex. Of the books I have
reviewed this year, only *Mr. Norris Changes Trains*, by
Christopher Isherwood, and George Orwell's *Burmese Days* have
got that decent and inspiring intimation of equality. I suppose
the climate is to blame, there seems something in it that gelds
and arranges all English writers, substituting timidity and
caution for freedom and curiosity, hence all the flatness, dullness, and feebleness of the novel—hence also, above all, the
stagnation. For English fiction is stagnant; a wide bog inter-
spersed with sparse tufts and pools of tepid water. Occasionally
the reviewer espies a light and plunges after it. It leads him
on for a while, even seems to burn brighter, then flickers away
in an odour of marsh gas and goes out.

And every bad book he reviews is a nail in the reviewer's

coffin. As with the queen bee and the worker, it is the quality of his nourishment that determines whether he is to be a critic or a hack. He may have every conceivable talent, but if he has only bad books to write about, he is doomed. He can sidestep, improvise, but he must go under. There are three kinds of reviewers: the cynical, who know they are beaten, who turn out consistently adequate copy, and are completely reliable, having sacrificed the critical sense for a certain knack of amiable appraisal or polite disappointment; those who are still fighting, who are on the whole unsatisfactory, since they turn and twist, go off the deep end or become unpunctual with their copy, from psychological reasons; and those who are not aware of any problem, who go cheerily on for thirty or forty years and are bitterly hurt to find that they have long been the innocent dupes of publishers and the laughing-stock of the public. The difficulties of the reviewer are increased because there are only four or five weekly posts that carry any dignity, whose occupiers need write on only one book or on none with the knowledge that their articles can be included in their collected works, that they inherit the mantle of Arnold, Pater, Hazlitt, or Sainte-Beuve. The remaining consolations of the novel-reviewer are that if he reads two books a day and writes for at least three papers he can make four hundred a year, that, anyhow, he appears regularly, and since everyone sooner or later writes a novel he will always be treated with consideration.

I have just received Old Boor's Almanack for 1936. Who sends one these things? "Books for the next five years will have a 'national' flavour. You can't mistake it. Like a prize marrow at a harvest festival, they will be long, prosperous, vapid, and seedy. Great years for bannings and backslidings, the ivy of indifference will creep higher up the trunk of talent, increasing neglect of E. M. Forster because his excellence is inconvenient, of Norman Douglas, Max Beerbohm, and those who live abroad non-politically." Appeal to expatriates: "Come home. There's no happiness outside the telephone book. We are approaching what the mystics term 'the Sunday luncheon of the soul.'"

December 1935.

REVIEWERS

REVIEWERS CAN BE DIVIDED INTO TWO CLASSES. FOR ONE literature cannot be too esoteric, too much a preoccupation with style and imagination. I like only two kinds of novel, the work of art or slim volume, and the novel of entertainment. The other kind of reviewer prefers didactic fiction; for him the novels I admire most are merely full of pretty writing, frivolous, amusing, or egotistic. The novel, he feels, is not an end in itself, but a means to redress injustice, to present information or tabulate theories. *Wuthering Heights* may claim thousands, but *Uncle Tom's Cabin* claims tens of thousands. The novel of political propaganda, more than any other, I find as unpalatable as a cannon ball in a plum pudding.

After struggling with such a book it was sad to read Mr. Sean O'Casey's attack on reviewers in *Time and Tide's* "Notes on the Way." He considers all reviewers, except those on the Sunday papers, to be timid and contaminated to the last degree. It is possible, with hard work and a bit of luck, for a highbrow reviewer to earn fifteen pounds a month, but nine to eleven would be more like it. And on that he expects them to give as spirited a performance as that of the Sunday novel-reviewers, who have always been famous for their savage and incorruptible assaults on author and publisher! And anyhow, "reviews never sell a book," as the publishers are never tired of telling us. No, it is farther than that that he must look for the causes of the decline of the novel, even if the sycophantic torpor of reviewers contributes to it. There is, for instance, the indigence of authors who are forced through journalism or over-production to deny themselves the gestation which their talent demands; and the intransigence of libraries and of all other book-societies which cater to the public, and which in turn use pressure on the publisher to make him exact the longest and dullest contribution from the safest writers, an omnibus if possible, and failing an omnibus a saga; and failing a saga a hundred-and-twenty-five-thousand-word cavalcade. And then there is the ignorance of the publishers themselves, their lack of standards. Of how many books can you say "It must be good—So-and-so published it"—as you could say it of the work of architects or painters or film-producers? And then their hopeless ambition to publish a best-seller which will pay for the masterpiece—which results in confusion: the verdict of posterity obsessing the popular writer; the writer of master-pieces dreaming of Hollywood; the publisher himself com-bining vague leanings towards creation with the desire to double his capital; a middleman of talent anxiously deleting words like "rape" in novels that are in any case unreadable. And one might add the imbecility of collectors, who (caring only for rarity, condition, and some incomplete experience of their childhood) take one look at *Howard's End*, *Prufrock*, or *Inclina-tions*, and go hurrying on in search of Mary Webb, and *Winnie the Pooh*, *Beau Geste*, and *The Tale of the Flopsy Bunnies*.

One might conclude by mentioning the ox-like indifference of the reading public which cannot bring to its activity even the discrimination of the chewing one, and thus we have six interlocking causes of the dullness of our current fiction. They do not seem easy of remedy, and meanwhile the English novel must descend to the barathrum of incompetence in company with those twin horrors, the English hotel and the English nursing home.

Reviewing is a whole-time job with a half-time salary, a job in which our best work is always submerged in the criticism of someone else's, where all triumphs are ephemeral and only the drudgery is permanent, and where no future is secure except the certainty of turning into a hack. There are days when a reviewer approximates more and more to that robot figure on Brighton pier, who wheedles the passers-by in a brassy subhuman voice, and when they put down a coin hands out a cardboard square of commonplace and irrelevant criticism. He can say of his books like the sundial of the hours, "vulnerant omnes; ultima necat." Who would not rather than the best of reviewers be the worst of novelists and contrive between November and April a novel from the excesses which he has committed from May to October?

1935-36.

MR. MOSSBROSS
TAKES THE CLASS

AND NOW FOR MR. LINKLATER'S *Ripeness is All*.

"What are the characteristics of middlebrow satire?"

"Sanity, sir."

"Not bad; MacDonnell?"

"Being Scotch, sir."

"That's not funny; Collier?"

"Topicality."   "Ribaldry."   "Tolerance."

"Don't speak at once, one at a time—you, Agate?"

"Splendidly virile, robust, immensely readable, sir."

"Mackenzie?"

"Full-throated laughter, sir, a rousing bumper."

"And you, Priestley?"

"Zest and gusto, sir, the high spirits of a clever man."

"Very good, all of you, you avoided the trap. And you are quite right—for if you put irony, indignation, feeling—in short, wit—into this sort of thing you overdo it, like Swift, or merely irritate the public, like Joyce and Lawrence. You must be careful not to offend anybody. How are you going to manage? First: don't let your characters come to life—they must be types, you can abuse them freely. How do you create a type? You take a character and say he is a bridge bore or a golf bore or a poet or a colonel—and then whenever he appears he talks about bridge or golf or poetry or the army. Then you create a comic situation. You shut the poet and the colonel up in a stuck lift, you put the bridge bore on the golf links, or you let loose a pig at the vicarage garden party, like Linklater here. And then you put in the satire."

"How do you do that, sir?"

"The golden rule, I find, is to avoid the personal. Go in for something you really feel about and you endanger sanity. Endanger sanity and where is gusto? And, without gusto, what are royalties? No! Read the newspapers, and satirize what they satirize. Foreigners, Americans, D.O.R.A., Fascists, and spinsters. Never write a word you'd be ashamed to write for the *Daily Express*."

"And zest, virility, sir?"

"Get that eighteenth-century feeling. Study sturdy common sense. Become a good trencherman. Make a few jokes about the way of a man with a maid. Remember — the frankness of Fielding with the slyness of Sterne! And plenty of generalization about humanity! Style? That will come with *Tom Jones* and practice. Show them, Linklater."

"Bugler Bliss's tongue was imperfectly taught, and that poignant call, that may summon the heart to a loneliness like the outer stars, brayed with his breath like a tinker's moke.

Major Gander's life had not been happy, and the ceremonies attendant on his death were correspondingly mismanaged."

"Got the knack? If the major's life had been happier would the bugler have known the Last Post? No—but don't you smell the eighteenth century? Now once more, please, here's the chalk—and put some poetry into it."

"But the Silver Trumpets sang:

> Blow, northern wind,
> Send thou me my sweeting.

and a pizzicato, like the pin-prick pattern of April rain, softened all hearts and all desired that Daisy and Katherine and Bolivia should have twenty pink-bottomed babies a-piece, a festoon of them, wreaths of them, troops of them, with no thought of prizes but simply to match May and fulfil the turning of the year. The triumph of all who'd begotten, and the travail of all who'd borne, were as warp and weft in their lot, and flute and fiddle, brass and drum, would join in a great cry, 'Ripeness is All.'"

"Thank you very much. Time's up. Good night, boys. Happy Pens!"

"Yes, sir." "Thank you, sir." "Happy Pen, sir!"

1935.

FELICITY

AS THERE SEEMS A LITTLE SPACE LEFT OVER, I AM UTILIZING it to thank those correspondents who have submitted unfinished manuscripts to me for advice and help. I am afraid they cannot be returned; for instance, I have lost all of Kip Streatham's novel, except the page beginning, "It felt pretty good to be out there under the moon with the gin running round in me like an electric hare and my arm as far as it would go round Myrtle." He will have to write another.

Hedda Bedales, who is "five feet ten and a half in her hikers," she tells me, has sent in a tale of primitive passion on a Hertfordshire farm somewhere up near the North Circular. Thirza, the heroine, refuses to take her bicycle out in the rain, and narrowly escapes a larruping. The second two hundred pages show a falling off.

But it is with real joy that I print some of the manuscript of Miss Aglae ("three syllables please, but it's not my real name anyhow") Oakenshaw's unpublished novel, "Absent from Felicity"—publishers, those lean subfusc creatures with rolled umbrellas and little blue engagement books, must keep a look-out for Aglae $(- \smile \smile)$:

Felicity was dressing for dinner. A cosy gas-fire burned in the grate towards which she held out her bare foot while she held out (in her hand I mean) a slinky open-mesh gold stocking. She loved to crinkle her toes in the firelight. Her foot didn't seem to belong to her, it was a little pink animal or something. She loved her bedroom, which had been her nursery, with its dado of beasts and its view out on the Hampstead garden. There was a knock at the door. "Come in." It was Dads! "Hello, old chap," he said. "How's tricks?" She looked up lovingly at the curly head, tanned face, and open smile of her father. Dads was wonderful, only he worked so terribly hard. He was a blurb-writer, and April was coming on so that he was absolutely indispensable. "Not been overdoing it, skipper?" she asked anxiously. "Only the Golding omnibus," he smiled back, but she thought he looked worried all the same. "Don't fret about me—I'm strong as a Steen." He laughed. It was one of their favourite jokes. "May there be no Cronin' at the Bar," she capped. "Hurry up now, old boy," he cried. "Don't keep your mother waiting." For Felicity's mother, Mrs. Arquebus, was a very special person. She pulled on her stocking and took a last look at the room. A bowl of hyacinths, her white bed with the green eiderdown, and very few pictures. A small oils by Barribal called "Green Chartreuse" hung over the mantel-piece, with its plaster gargoyles from the little shop near Notre Dame, and there were one or two etchings with masts and a choice Steggles of Rosebery Avenue that she had got, in an austere mood, out of the Picture Library when she took the Edward Wolfe back. And her books! She loved the little cabinet with its glass doors. There was just room for her favourite authors, Phyllis Bentley, Phyllis Bottome, Helen Waddell, Helen Simpson, G. B. Storm, Beverley, and Theodora Benson—and poetry, too, Humbert Wolfe of course, and some of the new writers who left one rather breathless, and whose books had lovely cold names like *Open the Sky* and *Armed October*. The door opened again. This time it was Mums. "Hurry up, daughter o' mine, there's a good fellow!" she cried. "Fellow" was Felicity's favourite nickname. She had brown curly hair, rather special brown eyes, and a nose with the weeniest tilt to it, "just room for a deck quoit," as Dads put it, and a very pretty figure. She loved green, smoked lots of cigarettes, adored dancing, but knew there were other things beside it, and was altogether a heathery honeyish brackeny kind of Hampstead Piskie, alternately the joy and tribulation of her family, servants, nanny, teachers, friends, and taxi-drivers, in fact of everyone whose delight and misfortune it was to know her. Phew! She was just grown up. As Dads had said the other day, "Fellow used to be a drawing by Shepperton. Now she's a Gouache by Lewis Baumer." She repeated it to herself on her way down to the hall and cocktails. To-night it was a party. There were two other successful blurb-writers and their wives, Mr. Goulash the publisher, and two very nice young men for Felicity. A "poet" and a "thinker." "Mr.

Beastly may drop in afterwards," said Mums, who looked almost
regal. "I'm thinking," said the thinker, "he has the root of
the matter in him." "I've always found him charming myself,"
said Mr. Goulash; "the only realist in Flask Walk," said a blurb-
writer. "Is his new book *John Hanbury, Ironmaster*, or *John
Hanbury, Ironmonger*?" whispered the other—"in writing the
blurb that's going to be rather important; one used to be able
to go by the picture on the wrapper, but with these beastly
yellow-jacks one never can tell." They had out the silver
fish-knives and napkin rings "with two k's!" as Dads put it.
That meant one of their grand parties.

Outside in the spring night the laburnums were hanging
their golden bodkins over the wall, and the laurustinus loomed
evilly out of the shadow. "Scrumptious, Sacred, and Profane!"
cried one of the blurbies. "The moment I saw it I said,
'This is NOT a detective story.'" "I don't know what you
mean by that word," said Miss Gibbon, who was a stickler for
etymology. "And I don't know which word you mean either,"
riposted the blurbie. "And does Miss Felicity," he laughingly
added, "inherit the family talent for 'appreciation'?" "Don't
talk cocker," laughed Fellow—and she smiled secretly to
herself at the idea of *Her* writing blurbs. For she was going
to do something creative. A biography of her father, perhaps,
with all the family jokes in it. Not that she wanted—she
looked across at him, handsome, healthy, shaggy, smiling—
still, you never knew, these athletes cracked up sooner than you
expected, and blurb-writing carried with it, she had heard, a
high mortality. First the dedication—*to the memory of the
dearest of Dads*—then the preface, "*I have not hesitated to
set down the other side of the picture. Gilbert Arquebus was,
in many ways, a very tiresome man. . . .*" Good heavens, what
was she thinking! She smiled brightly at him, and reassuringly
he smiled back. "Absent thee from Felicity," he reflected,
"awhile." Yes. But why not for ever? More money all
round. Conceited little bore. Expensive, too. Trying that
grin on me now. All right! This evening she should have
her first glass of port. More money all round! And then,
maybe, he could get at that actress, the one who was playing

the governess, a big fat bouncing creature who looked as if she had a temper. He began to hum "Singing in the Rain" to himself. Macking in my whack, I'm whacking in my mac, 'cos I'm glad to be back. . . . "Elia," he cried suddenly. "My adorable Elia! Who reads him now?" "Oh, Dads!" and Mums beamed loyally down the table. Special Person indeed! he thought. If they knew what a drag a writer's wife can be. The woman who shares your early struggles is very different from the one you would choose to share your later success. And why the hell should she? Port for her too. "I saw the first caterpillar to-day," Mums went on, "it was a looper." "You might really be in the depths of the country," said Mr. Goulash. The poet was telling a story, "'And what do *you* do?' I asked her. 'Paint.' 'And what do you paint?' 'Fans.' 'What fun—like Conder, I suppose; do you get a lot of fan-mail?' 'Not fans, you idiot, vans. I don't paint silly fans, I paint useful vans.' She's a girl from the Tottenham cell." Tiresome young cub, thought Dads—and that dreary thinker, with his Scotch face hanging over the savoury. A glass of port all round. "A very special bin," he said, when the time came. "Not a has-bin, I hope," said Mr. Goulash. Dads scowled. "I want you all to drink a health," he said. "It's my birthday, don't forget!" The blurbies were still whispering. "Who wrote the last Charles Morgan?" said one—"I don't know who did the front; as a matter of fact, I did the back." "I did the front," said Dads, "if you still want to know." They didn't, for the cyanide was doing its work. "You were quite right not to like the laurustinus, Felicity," laughed Dads—"but my biography will have to wait." The way they fell they reminded him of a skittle alley, only quieter; each seemed to knock against the next one, there would be a wobble, and over they'd go. Last went the thinker, and Dads drummed impatiently on the mahogany with his cigar-cutter while he was "passing." Soon all, with varying grace, had made the fatal exit, and it was a very lonely man indeed who, five minutes later, was speeding down Haverstock Hill on his way to the stage door.

June 1936,

THE NOVEL-ADDICT'S
CUPBOARD

"OTHER PEOPLE'S HOBBIES," AS ONE BOOK-COLLECTOR HAS remarked, "are always ridiculous," so I will do no more than say that about two years ago the printed words "Second edition, second issue, seventh thousand, first published in . . . reprinted in . . ." suddenly became to me the most horrible stains and blots on a book imaginable. And cheap editions, travellers' libraries, anti-travellers' libraries; ghastly! There is some point in collecting ancient first editions, for in the seventeenth and eighteenth centuries they differed often very considerably from succeeding texts, and were, also, lovely objects. But I collect modern ones, the seven-and-sixpenny poisons. They are cheaper and one has the pleasure of backing one's judgment, generally wrongly, against the whole weight of middlebrow, sentimental, childhood-loving, and pedantic opinion represented by booksellers' catalogues. I still do not collect books unless I think I shall enjoy reading them, but I do not expect that phase to last. Reading, in book-collectors, is replaced by a kind of fidgeting motion, balancing the book in the left hand, opening it and shutting it with the right, and exclaiming "But that's not really his first book at all, you know," or some other holy rubric. But as a good many of my books are novels, it may be of interest to recall a few in the hope of suggesting some new titles for the novel-addict or reminding him of some old ones. Incidentally, it will be proof that there was once a time when I enjoyed fiction. Where the authors are American, I try to get the American editions, as the English are so often altered, but there is no book I am going to mention that is not in some form cheaply and easily procurable. I can't afford *South Wind*, *The Way of All Flesh*, *Human Bondage*, or the *Old Wives' Tale*, so you must imagine them filling shadowy blanks to begin with, and there are some publishers whom I refuse to collect, because all their novels look exactly alike, and destroy my conception of a book-shelf, which should be a mass of gaudy variety.

E. M. Forster, *Howard's End*, *Room with a View* (Arnold). *Howard's End*, written in 1910, introduces the first post-war young highbrow, with a post-war name (Sebastian), and a simplified form of writing in full revolt against Henry James. But an artist's revolt—not a philistine's, like Wells'. The themes of Forster's novels are always the breaking down of bridges and barriers—between English and Indian, between the intelligentsia and the bourgeoisie (*Howard's End*), between soldier and scholar (*Longest Journey*)—he is really anti-highbrow, in the sense that he dislikes nothing more than intellectual presumption and spiritual pride. He is consequently a revolutionary writer, one of the first to attack the individualism of the 'nineties, to find the crack in the ivory tower; his heroes are plain men and plainer women, his motto "only connect"—yet as a writer he is an artist always. I think *Howard's End* is his best book, the *Longest Journey* (which started the Wiltshire trek) second. He has written only one book since 1910, and is still waiting for English fiction to catch up.

Henry James, semi-complete. I get an inconceivable pleasure from a Henry James book when I am able to finish it, but too often I can only flounder out a few yards and then have to retreat. For others in this plight I recommend his long short stories, particularly *The Lesson of the Master*, *The Aspern Papers*, and *The Death of the Lion*. They enshrine the subtlest vanities and disappointments of the pursuit of letters for all time. Another remedy is to read anecdotes of Henry James. He is the last of the great writers to be a great man, and even the dirtiest pens take on a new quality when they write about him—enough to send one back to his books again. Or read his letters—that one in which he so pathetically reminds Gosse that he is "insurmountably unsaleable" and says of his collected edition, like Ozymandias, "look on my works, ye mortals, and despair."

A great critic has described Mrs. Wharton as the Sargent of the modern novel, and it is on her accomplished, rich interiors that it gives me most pleasure to gaze. She has been fortunate enough to belong to a class—the super-rich, the super-philistine, the super-cosmopolitan—that can as a rule be observed only from outside and consequently is misrepresented. Therefore the studies of these jewelled and inaccessible analphabetics by one who is pre-eminently a serious and intelligent writer may become valuable documents. *The Custom of the Country* and *Glimpses of the Moon* are the brightest.

Maurice Baring, semi-complete. *Passing By* and *Daphne Adeane* seem to me his best books, which are all variations on a theme—the rivalry of sacred and profane love. One knows that sacred love will always win, and profane love be always on the point of winning, and the consequent order, regularity, and logic of the treatment, resembling a Greek tragedy, is his greatest power. Like those Spanish *aficionados* who watch a series of dancers repeating the same steps, singing the same song, one resents any alteration in structure as keenly as one derives pleasure from the variations of the performers in tempo, grace, and style. "It seduces one. And then it seduces one again."

Aldous Huxley, complete. David Garnett, complete. Lawrence, *passim*. Mr. Huxley tells a story of Firbank meeting him in the Café Royal: "He gave his usual agonized wriggle of embarrassment and said, 'Aldous—always my *torture*.'" I think I feel the same way about him. At school I borrowed *Limbo* from one master only to have it confiscated by another, while the Frenchman who let me read Mallarmé's *Après-Midi d'un Faune* for extra studies had to turn repeatedly to Huxley's translation to find out what it meant. I bought *Crome Yellow* out of some prize money. After that his novels and stories continued to dominate my horizon, so enormously competent, so clever, sympathetic, and on the spot. During the 'twenties it was almost impossible for the average clever young man not to imitate him—just as he once had imitated Norman Douglas, Firbank, and Eliot. Now that I have been free for a few years I see *Crome Yellow* as his best book, backed up by *Limbo*, *Antic Hay*, and his short stories. His early work had a natural gaiety, his satire lacked the heavy hand of the moralist; Science, with its horrible plausibility, had not yet walked off with Art.

The first forty years of Aldous Huxley's literary career have been marred by over-production, for which the present economic system is to blame. Conventionality of thought and diction, fatigue of style result—but his long silence since *Brave New World* is the most hopeful augury for the remaining three-score. David Garnett's books remain a standing argument in favour of the short novel, for, though equally bound to his publisher by golden cords, he has resisted Aldous Huxley's temptation to long novels, pamphlets, essays, and philosophical journalism. As for Lawrence, I really believe he is asleep at last, and I think nothing should be done to disturb him. If you must approach him, do it lightly, and by way of his early books, those like *The White Peacock*, with its creamy pastoral descriptions of the English countryside, full of a sentiment that has not yet been muddied by dogma.

Firbank, complete. Every critic, however roughly he may seem to wisecrack away the achievements of his enemies, the creators, will sooner or later shyly unlock his playbox and produce his few treasures. Then woe betide the reader who does not express a proper admiration. For my part, I am secretly a lyricist; the works to which I lose my heart are those that attempt, with a purity and a kind of dewy elegance, to portray the beauty of the moment, the gaiety and sadness, the fugitive distress of hedonism; the poetry of Horace and Tibullus, the plays of Congreve, the paintings of Watteau and Degas, the music of Mozart and the prose of Flaubert affect me like this, and of recent books, the novels of Ronald Firbank. That doesn't mean I think he is as good as Mozart, I hasten to say, but that in him more than in any contemporary writer I find that taste. He and the early Eliot seem to me the pure artists of the 'twenties, Lawrence and Huxley the philosopher-artists, the explainers. His thin black books are incidentally some of the few which it is a pleasure to collect. Of course, it is quite useless to write about Firbank—nobody who doesn't like him is going to like him, and he can be extremely aggravating and silly—but he was a true innovator, and his air of ephemerality is treacherous in the extreme.

Hemingway, complete. Waugh, complete. Powell, complete. Scott Fitzgerald, complete. Now we are among the Firbank derivatives. Great Hemingway is under a cloudlet, partly owing to the increasing truculence of his subject matter, partly owing to the spate of imitations of him, and his boom. Yet he has created the American style: no other transatlantic novelist so combines native force with mastery of form. Scott Fitzgerald represents a more literary compromise between the American qualities (generosity, courage, open-mindedness, and immoderation) and the English technique. His *The Great Gatsby* and *Tender is the Night* (Chatto) are also, incidentally, two of the novels most typical of the Boom, as is the charming *Gentlemen Prefer Blondes*. Evelyn Waugh, as a novelist, seems also to me to be in a predicament. I regard him as the most naturally gifted novelist of his generation (the round-about-thirty). He has a fresh, crisp style, a gift for creating character, a mastery of dialogue, a melancholy and dramatic sense of life—but his development has taken him steadily from the Left towards the Right, and Right Wing Satire is always weak—and he is a satirist. The anarchist charm of his books (of which *Black Mischief* is the best example) was altered in *A Handful of Dust* to a savage attack on Mayfair from a Tory angle. And though there on safe ground, it is going to be difficult for him to continue, since Tory satire, directed at people on a moving staircase from a stationary one, is doomed to ultimate peevishness [Example, Beachcomber]. *A Handful of Dust* is a very fine novel, but it is the first of Evelyn Waugh's to have a bore for a hero.

The novels of Antony Powell are unaffected monochromes of realism. Anything which might heighten the colouring is scrupulously omitted. They deal in nuances of boredom, seediness, and squalor—"the artist is recognizable by the particular unpleasantness of his life" is his creed, and since he gaily accepts it his novels have a delightful quality, containing much of the purest comedy that is now being written. I recommend especially *Afternoon Men* and *From a View to a Death* (Duckworth). Then there is that other comedian, Compton Mackenzie, whose *Vestal Fires* and *Extraordinary Women* are among the few modern novels that make the most of that wonderful subject, money, and which bring the Mediterranean lapping round our doors and the smell of cistus through the fog-bound windows. One day I want to do a dossier of the characters in those two books, and their mighty begetter, *South Wind*, with photographs of them all and pictures of their villas. And while still on satirists, there are *Cakes and Ale* and *The Moon and Sixpence* of Maugham. *Cakes and Ale* belongs to that group of satires on literary shop that form one of the most remarkable achievements of the English novel. Max Beerbohm's *Seven Men* belongs also, and Osbert Sitwell's *Dumb Animal* with that admirable short story *Alive, Alive-Oh!*

It would seem that I do not collect any women writers, but that is not the case. I have the books of Miss Compton-Burnett, though I cannot read them, and Mrs. Woolf complete to *The Waves*, which holds one of the key positions of modern novels, inferior only to *Ulysses* (no first edition, alas!), and all Miss Elizabeth Bowen's ironical and delicate studies, and all Rosamund Lehmann, another natural writer, and *Frost in May* by Antonia White, *Orphan Island*, the best novel of Miss Macaulay, *Voyage in the Dark* (Constable) by Jean Rhys, a short and tragic book—and even shorter, *My Mortal Enemy* and *A Lost Lady*, the two best books of Willa Cather, and *Winter Sonata* by Dorothy Edwards. Gay but less haunting are *Country Places*, Christine Longford, and Julia Strachey's *Cheerful Weather for the Wedding*. This leads one on to those novels that one feels are little known or underrated, that are never followed by a successor, or whose effect on people is unpredictable and subversive. Such are Clifford Kitchin's two books, *Mr. Balcony* and *The Sensitive One*. Nathaniel West's *Miss Lonelihearts* (a defiant masterpiece of futility), George Beaton's *Jack Robinson* and his *Almanack*. Or *How Like a God* by Rex Stout (Kennerley); *Blindness and Living* by Henry Green (who *is* he?), published by Dent; and *Murder, Murder* by Laurence Vail (Peter Davies), which begins so well and ends so badly. And *Arm's Length* by John Metcalfe, *Futility* by Gerhardi, *Some People* by Harold Nicolson (great period interest), and *Café Bar* by Scott Moncrieff (gloomy!). The *Four Just Men* by Edgar Wallace, and that strange sadistic highbrow thriller, and analysis of the Paris Commune, *The Werewolf of Paris* (John Long) by Guy Endore. And *Extra Passenger* by Oswald Blakeston, and *Tropic of Cancer* (Obelisk Press), a gay, fierce, shocking, profound, sometimes brilliant, sometimes madly irritating first novel, by Henry Miller, the American Céline. Anyone interested in the problem of American genius, whether it can ripen or ever achieve real freedom and honesty in its home surroundings, should try to get this book which would appear completely to justify expectation. Apart from the narrative power, the undulating swell of a style perfectly at ease with its creator, it has a maturity which is quite unlike the bravado, the spiritual ungrownupness of most American fiction. Miller's writing is more in the nature of a Whitmanesque philosophic optimism which has been deepened and disciplined but never destroyed by his lean years in a city where even to starve is an education. And there are books for the *sottisier*, such as the *Berry* volumes of Dornford Yates. Sometimes, at great garden parties, literary luncheons, or in the quiet of an exclusive gunroom, a laugh rings out. The sad, formal faces for a moment relax and a smaller group is formed within the larger. They are admirers of Dornford Yates who have found out each other. We are badly organized, we know little about ourselves and next to nothing about our hero, but we appreciate fine writing when we come across it, and a wit that is ageless united to a courtesy that is extinct. Or books for collectors which remind one of all the glass cases full of boring limited editions of Coppard, Collier, Hanley, Hampson, Powys, and Potocki de Montalk. And there are parodies like *The Oxford Circus* (Miles and Mortimer) and more American books, Dreiser, Glenway Westcott, Faulkner, O'Hara, Saroyan—and I see I have the complete works of Wyndham Lewis. But that should be enough.

January 1936.

FELICITY ENTERTAINS

GOOD MORNING, MY DIARY. I WONDER IF YOU REMEMBER ME. It's been a neglected little diary all the summer! Well, this is Felicity. "Fellow" to you! And she's going to take you out once a week and fill you up with interesting things. Happy now?

This is the Try-out Season. A Try-out is when someone you meet abroad who seems awfully sweet is asked to the house for the first time and the family don the winter warpaint. It's not much good looking nice in lederhosen now, and the wretched youth has to prove he's got guts. I decided to start with the most eligible. Wilfrid Wendover. He's terrifically important in the Wine and Food Society. I've explained all about it to the family, and told them they must ask H. K. Boot to meet him, and have everything just so.

Dads tries his hen-pecked line. "And so my offspring considers our modest social accomplishments may pall on Mr. Wendover? The formidable H. K. Boot has to be called in to provide an intellectual equal? And what of the unfortunate host whose duty it is to feed Mr. Wendover in the manner to which he is accustomed and minister simultaneously to the more ethereal—I hope—necessities of old H. K.?"

"Rubbish, Dads, you know you adore H. K.!"

"Of course—but I prefer to worship from afar."

"Nonsense—we all know you were lovers."

"How can you talk like that in front of Mums!"

"Oh, don't mind me," said Mums; "if I was to be jealous of H. K. I'd have no peace."

"She's a dam' sight too long in the tooth for you anyhow, isn't she, Dads?" said Baby, who'd been out on the Heath "Observing."

"See anything, Baby?" said Dads.

"Well, I'm pretty sure I spotted a schizophrenic fur-cap. The real thing, congenital idiot I should think, absolute bin-fodder! But we're not observing special cases at present.

119

Simply what everybody in England does at 3.57 for the 'Twixt Lunch and Tea' report."

"Talking of lunch and tea," I said (being one whom Psycho-analysis, Mass Observation, and the conversation of one's younger sister affect like a bad smell), "what are you going to give the English Brillat-Savarin for dinner?"

"I think we can leave that safely to Mums," he sliced back.

"Well, don't forget Miss Boot is the authoress of *With Gourd and Gherkin* and *A Weeny Tour in France*," said Baby.

"I don't suppose gherkins are in season," mused Mums.

Uncle Pat tried a bit of escapist stuff with the *Evening Standard*, but Dads was too quick for him.

"Ah—anything in the paper? Let's have a look at it. I wonder if you can give us any idea of a menu that will satisfy the exacting Mr. Wendover—and our old friend H. K.?"

"Roast mutton and caper sauce," suggested Mums, "and cheese-straws, with a fish pie or something for a start and some soup, I suppose."

"Come, come—we must do better than that for Mr. Wine and Foodover." (Family laughter.) "Turtle soup, turbot, guinea fowl, salad and spatchcock," amended Dads. "Your real gourmet likes a simple dinner—something that won't remove the emphasis from its proper place. The wine—he'll want something with a nose to it! I think that part of the commissariat had better be left to me!" The cellar is in the cupboard under the stairs and Dads is the only person who's allowed there. "You, Felicity, after your expensive lucubrations at the Finishing School, will justify the experiment by putting the menu into French. And what about Baby?"

"I will observe."

"Well, it keeps her quiet," said Mums—but Uncle Pat had got away with the *Evening Standard*, and Dads went after him. Uncle Pat is N.P.G., which doesn't mean what you think, but stands for Non-Paying Guest or Nobly Permanent, as Dads calls him.

*   *   *

The Fatal Night. Mums crunches a bit of paper with our names set out in order. Dads is busy between the cellar and the fireplace. He looks wonderful in his dinner-jacket. Fawcett is lighting the candles, the perfect parlourmaid. Uncle Pat's shirt-front crackles when he moves, and there's a black mark where he's tried to get the stud to do up again. Baby looks inoffensive, and Mums is absolutely regal in her brocade. I'm jittery myself. I can't help wondering if Will Wendover's going to seem different after that time on the raft. Still, I've got my green on! I finger my French menu:

Soupe à la Tortue

Suprême de Turbot
Pochaise

Poule de la Côte d'Ivoire
[Oiseau Dahomey]

Salade Arquebus

Spatchcock   [I know when I'm beaten!]
Café—chocs.

The bell rings. Gosh, I'm frightened! Dads takes a step forward. "Now remember, Family. Be Bright! Mr. Wendover may put us all into one of his *Memorable Meals*, and we'll all like that. So F. H. B. (Family Hold Back) and we want a nice genial evening—NO POLITICS."

Fawcett opens the door. Dads beams. But in walks my. brother Chris!

"Good God, what are you doing here? Why aren't you at Cambridge?"

"Thanks for the reception, Father. Well, if you must know, I've been sent down."

"Oh, Chris, how *could* you?"

"Sorry, Mums."

"Nothing dishonest, I hope?"

"No, Dads. For canvassing for the C.P. and making Communist speeches."

"You little rat!"

"Yes. I suppose you would say that. Who's coming to supper?"

"*Dinner*, Chris."

"If forty-five million comrades call it supper, I don't see why I should call it dinner."

"Oh, Chris!" cried Mums. "But here they are. Mr. Wendover, the Wine and Food expert, and Miss Boot. There's no time for you to change, you'll have to sit between Fellow and Babs."

"Right you are, Mums."

Will isn't as tall as I thought, and he didn't wear glasses on the raft. He's quite old really—over forty, and stoops a bit. Miss Boot is in a purple velvet suit with a purple ribbon to her eyeglass to match. She's done her hair in a short grey fringe.

"Sherry or cocktail?" says Dads, after the introductions.

"Manhattan," says the Boot.

"Sherry," says Wilfrid, giving her a dirty look.

"I wonder what you'll think of this?" says Dads, but not giving him any clue.

"Dinner is served, madam," whispers Fawcett, and the game is on.

"Ah," cries Dad. "What about a 'soup's on' of fish! Bring your sherry in with you—and we'll discuss it there."

With the usual knocking of knees we get our feet under the mahogany.

Wendy sloshes his sherry about, brings it up to his nose, sips it, throws his head back as if he's going to gargle—and pours it into the soup. We all do the same. Dads tries the turtle soup, catches Mums' eyes, and turns on the full current. One expects a fizzle of smoke to come from the top of her head. She's certainly in the Hot Seat. "Too Expensive," she lip-reads back. I get the idea, reach forward to the menu, grab my eyebrow pencil and alter it to *Soupe à la Tortue Fausse.* That's the first hurdle. There's still a terrific silence when Baby puts on her "observer's" voice and leans across: "Tell me, Mr. Wendover—do you do anything besides eat?"

Mums stops the rot. "Excuse my terrible daughter—she's been so impressed by hearing of Miss Boot's activities—*With Gourd and Gherkin* and *A Weeny Tour in France.*"

"What—*the* Miss Boot? But I can't talk to you—you're a frightful heretic!" cries Wendy. "Do you realize, Mrs. Arquebus, that Miss Boot believes in decanting wine without standing the bottle up for forty-eight hours? And then she leaves the stopper in! Why, she's a regular Trotskyite—a Hotsy Trotskyite certainly"—and he bowed. "But definitely beyond the Party line."

"Oh, don't be a cabbage," guffawed old Boot. "One can't always agree with André and A. J. A. The trouble with the Committee is that they consider any criticism to be treason. But I think you're quite wrong. After all, Saintsbury himself said—"

"Anyone can quote Saintsbury and twist his meaning around," hissed Wilfrid; "and besides, we do not oppose criticism, we welcome it—only we make the very natural reservation that it must be informed—in fact, that it must come from a member of the Committee. If we permitted any pre-judiced littérateur to air his or her view we should never get anything done. It's not a question of being loyal to Saintsbury. It's a question of 'Are you loyal to Simon? to Symons? to Wyndham?' If you insist on pretentious literary independence, Miss Boot, you will be instituting a parallel centre and be considered an enemy of the feeding classes. I warn you and I repeat—" he thundered.

"But do tell us how *you* decant wine, Mr. Wendover," implored Mums, and Fawcett whisked away the turbot, which had got quite cold by now.

"Certainly, Mrs. Arquebus. Thirty-six hours before serving I stand the bottle upright. Twelve hours before serving I place it in the decanting machine after the cork has been electrically drawn, then I leave the decanter standing in the room in which it is to be used—thank you, some guinea hen—and I remove the stopper one minute for every year the vintage is old. The older the wine the longer it requires to come to life—or, as we say, 'to breathe.'"

"Then your wine will certainly catch cold," roared La Boot. "Take out its little stopper—yes, some guinea hen, please— I never heard of such a thing—and Barry Neame—"

"Well now, here's a test," said Dads. "Here's a wine from my own modest *caves*—oh, nothing remarkable—just a well-fendered little wine—one that's honest and obliging enough to engage in a symplegma or amorous wrestling match with this charming bird we're debating—I won't tell you what it cost or where it came from, but I'm going to ask our two experts here to guess. By the way, how do you like our feathered friend?"

"It's most interesting," answered Wendy. "A veritable Phoenix."

"The phoenix and the turtle." Miss Boot giggled—and suddenly they both began to quote:

> The claw, the jowl of the flying fowl,
> Are with the glorious anguish gilt.

"Yes, that's it," they laughed, and I heard Wendover whisper: "The only difficulty is who's got the claw?"

"Glorious anguish," answered Bootsy, "that's the sauce all right."

Dads doesn't like his guests to get on too well together. It makes him feel empty. "Now—what about the wine judging?" he said. "I'll offer a prize—whoever guesses it can have anything he likes in the room—you can see I don't think it's going to be very easy."

The wine was brought in in two decanters which Fawcett handled somewhat gingerly. They were rather clouded and you couldn't tell much about the stuff from its colour. There was one stopper in, and one out, to satisfy both the experts, and a delicious winey smell steamed from the open one.

"Let me help you first, H. K.," said Dads, and then "God damn it! I've burned my fingers." The two tasters exchanged glances. "Mind you—it will take a lot of guessing," said Dads, and Wendy answered:

"I've never been wrong before. I think I know all the vintage clarets—though my period is pre-phylloxera."

"And I've never made a mistake," roared the Boot, "over a burgundy."

Dads filled both their glasses and they began to slosh the

stuff about as before. When it was going round and round in
the glasses they had to put them down and pick them up again
with their napkins. As far as one could see, it was a kind of
Virginia creeper colour. Then they sloshed it round again.
Slosh—slosh—once more—now up with it—sniff—gargle—
glug—glug-glug—and down. Wendy did it once and frowned.
Miss Boot had to do it all over again. The suspense was
colossal. Uncle Pat looked less fuddled. Mums was fascinated,
Babs was observing like Malinowski himself, and even Chris
stopped running his fingers through his hair and making
bread pellets.

Boot spoke first. "It's extraordinary. Quite unique. I've
only tasted something like it once. And that was in France—
on my 'Weeny Tour.' In that delicious debatable region
between Bédarieux and Agde that some call Languedoc—
and some call Roussillon—we had walked eleven kilometres
after drinking three bottles of Frontignan—my friend and
I—and had spent a pleasant day in arguing over the virtues
of the unicorn, and its deadly enemies—the basilisk and
amphisbaena—"

"Herkherm." Dads cleared his throat.

"Well, it's like a wine we had at a wayside inn," she finished,
"so old, the cobwebs even were returned to dust, and the
blushing cork dissolved around the penetrating screw. In
fact, to come to the point—a Château Neuf du Pape—château
bottled by his Holiness at Avignon!"

"Very warm," said Dads. "Now you, Wendover."

Wendy was still removing bits of stuff from his glass, but he
looked up and said: "As far as I can judge, I should say
Algerian, one-and-six a bottle. Sidi Bel Abbès to be exact—
1937. Ah, I can see I'm right, and now, since I may choose
anything in the room, I'll have a whisky-and-soda."

"Cook couldn't find no spatchcock, mum, she's turning out
some cheese-straws," whispered Fawcett, and Chris jumped up
and said he must be off to his meeting.

"Good heavens, it's nine o'clock!" cried Miss Boot; "I think
we can drop you."

I heard Wendy talking to her as they went out: "*Oxford*

Poetry 1910—but I edited it; and you wrote that thing about the amphisbaena?"

"It's sweet of you to remember it after all these years."

"Not at all. It *formed* me."

Dads went into his study and slammed the door, and the rest of us started on the chocs. What's so maddening is that the *Memorable Meals* don't come out till Christmas. It's a quarterly.

December 1937.

TOLD IN GATH [1]

(With apologies to Mr. A*d*us H*xl*y)

" Vulgarity is the garlic in the salad of charm."

St. Bumpus.

IT WAS TO BE A LONG WEEK-END, THOUGHT GILES PENTATEUCH apprehensively, as the menial staggered up the turret stairs with his luggage—staggered all the more consciously for the knowledge that he was under observation, just as, back in Lexham Gardens, his own tyrannical Amy would snort and groan outside the door to show how steep the back-stairs were, before entering with his simple vegetarian breakfast of stink-wort and boiled pond-weed. A long week-end; but a week-end at Groyne! And he realized, with his instinct for merciless analysis that amounted almost to torture, that in spite, yes, above all, in spite of the apprehension, because of it even, he would enjoy all the more saying afterwards, to his friend Luke Snarthes perhaps, or to little Reggie Ringworm, "Yes, I was at Groyne last week-end," or "Yes, I was there when the whole thing started, down at Groyne."

The menial had paused and was regarding him. To tip or not to tip? How many times had he not been paralysed by that problem? To tip was to give in, yes, selfishly to give in to his hatred of human contacts, to contribute half a crown as hush-money, to obtain "protection," protection from other people, so that for a little he could go on with the luxury of being Giles Pentateuch, "scatologist and eschatologist," as he dubbed himself. Whereas not to tip . . .

For a moment he hesitated. What would Luke Snarthes have done? Stayed at home, with that splayed ascetic face of his, or consulted his guru, Chandra Nandra? No—no tip! The menial slunk away. He looked round the room. It was comfortable, he had to admit; a few small Longhis round the walls, a Lupanar by Guido Guidi, and over the bed an outsize

---

[1] Reprinted from *Parody Party*, edited by Leonard Russell and published by Hutchinson's.

Stuprum Sabinarum, by Rubens—civilized people, his hosts, evidently.

He glanced at the books on the little table—the *Odes of Horace, Rome* 23 B.C., apparently a first edition, the *Elegancies of Meursius* (Rochester's copy), *The Piccadilly Ambulator*, *The Sufferings of Saint Rose of Lima*, *Nostradamus* (the Lérins Press), *Swedenborg*, *The Old Man's Gita*. "And cultivated," he murmured, "too." The bathroom, with its sun-lamp and Plombières apparatus, was such as might be found in any sensible therapeutic home. He went down to tea considerably refreshed by his lavage.

The butler announced that Lady Rhomboid was "serving" on the small west lawn, and he made his way over the secular turf with genuine pleasure. For Minnie Rhomboid was a remarkable woman.

"How splendid of you to come," she croaked, for she had lost her voice in the old suffragette days. "You know my daughter, Ursula Groyne."

"Only too well," laughed Giles, for they had been what his set at Balliol used to call "lovers."

"And Mrs. Amp, of course?"

"Of course!"

"And Mary Pippin?"

"Decidedly," he grimaced.

"And the men," she went on. "Giles Pentateuch—this is Luke Snarthes and Reggie Ringworm and Mr. Encolpius and Roland Narthex. Pentateuch writes—let me see?—like a boot, isn't it?" (Her voice was a husky roar.) "Yes, a boot with a mission! Oh, but I forgot"—and she laughed delightedly —"you're all writers!"

"Encantado, I'm sure!" responded Giles. "But we've all met before. I see you have the whole Almanach de Golgotha in fact," he added.

Mary Pippin, whose arm had been eaten away by termites in Tehuantepec, was pouring out with her free hand. "Orange Pekoe or *Chandu*, Giles?" she burbled in her delicious little voice. "Like a carrier pigeon's," he thought.

"*Chandu*, please." And she filled him a pipe of the consoling poppy, so that in a short while he was smoking away like all the others.

"Yes, yes," continued Mr. Encolpius, in his oily voice which rose and fell beneath the gently moving tip of his nose, "Man axalotl here below but I ask very little. Some fragments of Pamphylides, a Choctaw blood-mask, the prose of Scaliger the Elder, a painting by Fuseli, an occasional visit to the all-in wrestling, or to my meretrix; a cook who can produce a passable 'poulet à la Khmer,' a Pong vase. Simple tastes, you will agree, and it is my simple habit to indulge them!"

Giles regarded him with fascination. That nose, it was, yes, it was definitely a proboscis. . . .

"But how can you, how can you?" It was Ursula Groyne. "How *can* you when there are two million unemployed, when Russia has reintroduced anti-abortionary legislation, when Iceland has banned *Time and Tide*, when the Sedition Bill hangs over us all like a rubber truncheon?"

Mary Pippin cooed delightedly; this was intellectual life with a vengeance—definitely haybrow—only it was so difficult to know who was right. Giles, at that moment, found her infinitely desirable.

"Yes, and worse than that." It was Luke Snarthes, whose strained voice emerged from his tortured face like a cobra from the snake-charmer's basket. "Oh, decidedly, appallingly worse. The natives of Ceylon take the slender Loris and hold it over the fire till its eyes pop, to release the magic juices. Indicible things are done to geese that you may eat your runions with a sauce of *foie gras*. Caviare is ripped from the living sturgeon, karakul fur torn from the baby lamb inside its mother. The creaking plates of the live dismembered lobster scream to you from the *Homard Newburg*, the oyster winces under the lemon. How would *you* like, Mr. Encolpius, to be torn from your bed, embarrelled, prised open with a knife, seasoned with a few drips of vitriol, shall we say, and sprayed with a tabasco as strong as mustard-gas to give you flavour; then to be swallowed alive and handed over to a giant's digestive juices?"

"I shouldn't like it at all!" said Mr. Encolpius, "just as I shouldn't, for that matter, like living at the bottom of the sea and changing my sex every three years. Not that it might not"—and he twitched his nose at Mary Pippin—"have its compensations."

"S-s-s-s-s-s-s-s-s-s-s-s-s-s-s-s-s-s-s-s-s-s-s-s-suppose," said Reggie Ringworm, who stammered, etc., "vat ve thilly oythter is weally weady and villing to be ab-s-s-s-s-orbed, I mean ab-th-th-th-th-th-thorbed, by our fwend, vat vat is in f-f-f-fact exactly ve end for which it has been cweated. Vat th-then?"

"What are we to think then," snarled Snarthes savagely, "of the Person or Purpose who created creatures for such an end? Awful!" And he took out his notebook and wrote rapidly, "The end justifies the means! But the end *is* the means! And how rarely, how confoundedly rarely, can we even say the end justifies the end! Like Oxenstierna, like Ximenes, like Waldorf, we must be men of means"—he closed the book with a snap—"men of golden means."

"I know what you mean," cried Mary Pippin from her dovecot. "That if Cleopatra's nose had been half an inch longer Menelaus would never have run away with her!"

Luke's face softened, and he spread out his splayed fingers almost tenderly. "And I don't mind wagering, if we can believe Diodorus Siculus, that, the nose unaltered, she bore a remarkable likeness, Mary, to you!"

"Ah, but can we believe old Siculus?" The other nose quested speculative. "Any more than we can believe old Paterculus, old Appian, Arrian, Ossian, and Orrian? Now a Bolivar Corona or a nicely chambered glass of sparkling Douro— even a pretty tea-gown by Madame Groult, I opine"—and he bowed to Mary—"these convince me. They have a way with one. Oh, yes, a way, decidedly! And just because they have that way it is necessary for me to combine them, how often, how distressingly often, with my lamentable visits to the Ring at Blackfriars, or to my meretrix in Holland Park. Why is it that we needs must see the highest though we loathe it? That happy in my mud—my hedonistic, radio-active, but never-the-less quite genuine nostalgic *boue*, I should be reminded of the stars, of you, Miss Pippin, and of Cleopatra?"

And he snuffled serio-comically, "Why can't you let Hell alone?"

A gong rang discreetly. The butler removed the pipes and Mrs. Amp and Roland Narthex, who were still in a state of kif, while the others went away to dress. Giles, who found something stimulating in Mr. Encolpius' nose, took out his notebook and wrote:

"Platitudes are eternally fresh, and even the most paradoxical are true; even when we say the days draw in we are literally right—for science has now come largely to the rescue of folk-lore; after the summer and still more after the equinoctial solstice the hours do definitely get shorter. It is this shortness of our northern day that has occasioned the luxuriance of our literature. Retractile weather—erectile poetry. No one has idealized, in our cold climate, more typically than Shakespeare and Dryden the subtropical conditioning. But we can consider Antony and Cleopatra to have been very different from their counterparts in the Elizabethan imagination, for on the Mediterranean they understand summer better and, with summer, sex.

"What were they really like, those prototypes of Aryan passion, of brachycephalic amour? Were Cleopatra's breasts such as 'bore through men's eyes' and tormented those early sensualists, Milton, Dante, Coventry Patmore, and St. John of the Cross? We shall never know.

"Professor Pavlov has shown that when salivation has been artificially induced in dogs by the ringing of a dinner bell, if you fire simultaneously into them a few rounds of small shot they exhibit an almost comical bewilderment. Human beings have developed very little. Like dogs we are not capable of absorbing conflicting stimuli; we cannot continue to love Cleopatra after communism and the electro-magnetic field have played Old Harry with our romantic mythology. That characteristic modern thinker, Drage Everyman, remarks, 'Destroy the illusion of love and you destroy love itself,' and that is exactly what the machine age, through attempting to foster it through cinemas and gin-palaces, deodorants and depilatories, has succeeded in doing. Glory, glory halitosis!

No wonder we are happier in the present! If we think of the 'Eastern Star,' in fact, it is as advertising something. And when we would reconstruct those breasts of hers, again we are faced with the diversity of modern knowledge. What were they like? To a poet twin roes, delectable mountains; to a philanderer like Malthus festering cancers; to a pneumatogogue simply a compound of lacticity and heterogeneous pyrites; to a biologist a sump and a pump. Oh, sweet are the uses, or rather the abuses, of splanchnology! No, for details of the pathological appeal of these forgotten beauties we must consult the poets. The ancients were aware of a good thing when they saw it, and Horace knew, for instance, with almost scatological percipience, exactly what was what.

"There are altitudes, as well as climates, of the mind. Many prefer the water-meadows, but some of us, like Kant and Beethoven, are at home on the heights. There we thermostatically control the rarefied atmosphere and breathe, perforce, the appropriate mental air."

In another room Luke Snarthes was doing his exercises. Seated in the lotus position, he exhaled deeply till his stomach came against his backbone with a smart crack. After a little he relaxed and breathed carefully up one nostril and down the other and then reversed the process. He took a nail out of the calf of his leg, and after he had reinserted it, it was time to put the studs into his evening shirt. "I was there," he murmured, "when it started, down at Groyne."

When he had dressed he unlocked his despatch-case and took out a sealed tube. It was marked, "Anthrax—non-filterable virus, only to be opened by a qualified literary scientist." "Jolly little beggars," he thought, and the hard lines on his face softened. "I'll take them down to amuse Miss Pippin. She looked the kind of person who'd *understand*."

"Snuff, peotl buds, hashish, or Indian hemp, sir?" said the butler. Dinner was drawing to an end. It had been an interesting meal. For Giles and Luke (on the "regime"), grass soup and groundsel omelette, washed down with a bottle of "pulque"; for Mrs. Amp, whose huge wen, like Saint-

Evremond's, made her look more than ever like some heavily wattled turkey, a chicken gumbo; for the rest Risi-bisi Mabel Dodge, bêche de mer, bear steak, and Capri pie.

"There's some *bhang* on the mantelpiece," said Minnie Rhomboid, "in poor Rhomboid's college tobacco jar."

"Delicious." It was Mr. Encolpius. "Common are to either sex artifex and opifex," he continued. "But, golly, how rare to find them contained in the same person—qualis opifex, Lady Rhomboid! I congratulate you—and this *barask*— perfection!" And he poured himself some more, while the snout wiggled delightedly.

"And you can drink that when Hungary is deliberately making a propaganda war for the recovery and re-enslavement of a hundred-thousand at last sophisticated Slovakians!" It was Ursula Groyne.

Poor Ursula, thought Giles, she carries her separate hell about with her like a snail its carapace! Not all the lost causes, all the lame dogs in the world could console her for the loss of her three husbands, and now she was condemned to the hades of promiscuity—every three or four years a new lover. Poor Ursula!

"And if you knew how the stuff was made!" The phrase was wrung from Luke Snarthes on his tortured calvary. "The apricots are trodden by the naked feet of bromidrosis-ridden Kutzo-Vlachs who have for centuries lived in conditions far below the poverty line! The very glass-blowers who spun that Venetian balloon for you are condemned to the agonies of alembic poisoning."

"Doubtless," answered Mr. Encolpius urbanely, "that is why it tastes so good. It all boils down to a question of proteins. You, my dear Ursula, are allergic to human misery; the sufferings of Slovaks and Slovenes affect you as pollen the hay-fever victim, or me (no offence, Minnie) a cat in the room. To ethics, mere questions of good and evil, I am happily immune, like my cara doncella here—am I right, Mary? Let Austin have his swink to him reserved, especially when it is a swink of the Rhomboid order. Go to the slug, thou ant-herd! If you could make up to kings (you remember what Aristippus said to Diogenes, Snarthes), you would not have to live on grass!"

"B-b-b-b-b-b-b-b-b-b-b-b-b-b-b-b-b-but all flesh is gwath, so
ve pwoblem is only sh-shelved." It was Reggie Ringworm!

"Sit down, everybody, it's time for the séance," commanded
Lady Rhomboid. "We have persuaded Madame Yoni."

In darkness they took their seats, Mr. Encolpius and Giles
on each side of Mary Pippin, while Snarthes elevated himself
to a position of trans-Khyber ecstasy suspended between the
table and the laquearia. The *bhang*-sodden bodies of Mrs. Amp
and Roland Narthex they left where they were.

The darkness was abysmal, pre-lapsarian. Time flowed
stanchlessly, remorselessly, from a wound inenarrable, as with
catenary purpose. Madame Yoni moved restlessly, like
Bethesda.

In her private dovecot Mary Pippin abandoned herself to
the eery. What a thrill, to be here at Groyne, and for a séance!
There had been nothing like it since she had joined the Anglican
Church, to the consternation of her governess, Miss Heard,
because of the deep mystical significance (as of some splendid
sinner repenting on the ashes of lust) of the words, "for Ember
Days." All the same, she was not quite sure if she liked Mr.
Encolpius. But what was this?—another thrill, but positive,
physical. With moth-like caresses something was running up
and down her arm—1, 2, 3, 4, 5,—spirit fingers, perhaps:
the tremulous titivation continued, the moths were relentless,
inexorable, 86, 87, 88. Then on her other side, along her
cheek, she felt a new set of moth antennae playing. From the
chandelier above came the faintest ghostly anticipatory tinkle—
someone was on the move as well, up there! 98, 99 . . .
Suddenly Madame Yoni screamed—there was a crash, as of
three heads bumping together, and the lights went up to reveal
Pentateuch and Mr. Encolpius momentarily stunned by the
Ixionic impact of the fallen Snarthes. His power had failed
him.

"W-w-w-w-w-w-w—" stammered Reggie Ringworm, but
he was interrupted by a shout from Luke. "My God—the
anthrax!" He took from his pocket the fragments of the
broken tube. "At the rate of multiplication of these bacilli"—
he made a rapid calculation—"we shall all be by morning,

Lady Rhomboid, dead souls." His splayed face had at last found its justification.

"Death!" said Mr. Encolpius, "the distinguished visitor! One bids good-bye, one hopes gracefully, to one's hostess, and then, why then I think one degusts the Cannabis Indica. Well, cheerio, kif-kif!" And he picked up the Brasenose jar.

Imperturbable, schizophrene, the portraits of Groynes and Rhomboids by Laurencin and the excise-man Rousseau looked down from the walls. So Miss Heard had been right, thought Mary. The wicked *do* perish. Than this there could have been no other conceivable termination to a week-end of pleasure!

> They say of old in Babylon
> That Harlequin and Pantalon
> Seized that old topiary, Truth,
> And held him by Time's Azimuth. . . .

Why had the nursery jingle recurred to her?

Luke removed a nail or two disconsolately. They would be of little use now. He tried to reassure Minnie Rhomboid. "After all, what is anthrax? What, for that matter, are yaws, beri-beri, dengue or the Bagdad Boil, but fascinating bio-chemical changes in the cellular constitution of our bodies, a re-casting of their components to play their new cadaverous roles? Believe me, Lady Rhomboid," he concluded, "there are more things in heaven and earth than are dreamt of in the British Pharmacopoeia!"

Giles took out his notebook. "La Muerte, Der Tod, Thanatos," he wrote.

"Your C-c-c-Collins perhaps?" stammered Reggie.

Giles began again: "It was at Groyne, during one of Minnie Rhomboid's most succulent week-ends, that it all happened, happened because it had to happen, because it was in the very nature of Luke Snarthes and Mary Pippin that exactly such things should happen, just as it was character not destiny, character that *was* destiny, that caused Napoleon . . ." He paused and looked up. The menial was regarding him reproachfully.

1936.

WHERE ENGELS FEARS TO TREAD

From Oscar to Stalin. A Progress. By Christian de Clavering.
(The Clay Press, 12s. 6d.)

Reviewed by CYRIL CONNOLLY

AT LAST THE AUTHENTIC VOICE OF A GENERATION! "YOU ARE
all a lost generation," remarked Gertrude Stein of us post-war
age-groups, and now, thanks to Mr. Christian de Clavering,
we know who lost us. Let me try and tell you all about this
book while I am still full of it. First thing you know you
have opened it, and there is the dedication:

"TO THE BALD YOUNG PEOPLE"

Then comes a page of fashionable quotations all in German.
The middle part by Kafka, the fringes by Rilke and Hölderlin.
The rest by Marx. Impeccable! And the introduction.

"Why am I doing this, my dears? Because I happen to be
the one person who can do it. My dears, I'm on your side!
I've come to get you out of the wretched tangle of individualism
that you've made for yourselves and show you just how you
can be of some use in the world. Stop worrying whether he
loves you or not; stop wondering how you will ever make any
money. Never mind whether the trousers of your new suit
turn up at the bottom; leave off trying to annoy Pa. We're
on to something rather big. The Workers' Revolution for the
Classless Society through the Dictatorship of the Proletariat!
Yes! It's a bit of a mouthful, isn't it! We're used to words
of one syllable, words like Freud, Death, War, Peace, Love,
Sex, Glands, and, above all, to Damn, Damn, Damn! Well,
all that's going to be changed. Morning's at seven, and you've
got a new matron.

"I'm told Mr. Isherwood is writing a book about the 'twenties.
Mr. Isherwood is a Cambridge man, and we who made the
'twenties do not wish them looked at through the wrong end

of a cocoa-tin. Through either end. My precious 'twenties! He shan't have them! Avaunt. Avanti!"

(And so the autobiography starts. I will quote a few of the dazzling vignettes. For the reasons with which the author concludes, I have refrained from comment.)

Home. Background. Mother.

"Mother, who is that horrible old obesity with the black chin? I believe he's following us."

"Hush, that's Daddy."

And so dawned my second birthday.

Home.

"Mother, where is home this time. Heliopolis? Hammamet? Ragusa? Yalta?"

"Guess again."

"I know. Prinkipo."

"Warm."

"Monte Carlo."

"Very warm."

"Has it got a clever coastline? I know! Cannes!"

And home for the next two months it was.

"Mother—what does Father do?"

"He has his business, boy o' mine."

"And what is that?"

"He's a sort of accountant."

"On 'Change?"

"On the Turf!"

"Poor Mother, poor darling Mother—but we needn't see him, need we?"

"Of course not, precious, but I thought you were old enough to know."

I pulled the hood down and for a moment it was very stuffy inside the pram. . . .

Children's Party.

"What is your father, Christian?"

"He's interested in racing—my mother is the Honourable. What is *your* father, Edelweiss?"

"A mediatized prince. What sort of racing?"

"Oh, never mind now—let's ask Mother to play some *Rimsky*."

But I realized I couldn't stay on in Montreux Territet.

My mother an angel. My father a bookie!

"And don't forget, my boy, a tenner for every little nob you bring home with a handle to his name."

Eton. Henry's holy shade. An impression, above all, of arches, my dears, each with its handsome couple, and study fireplaces always full of stubs of Balkan Sobranie. And the naughtiest elms! While the battle of Waterloo was being fought all round me, I just sat still and watched my eyelashes grow. There were books, of course. Pater, Alma Pater, with his worried paragraphs. His prose reminded me of stale privet—and Petronius, who made me long to know more Latin. (I only learned two words, *curculio* and *vespertilio*, a bat and a weevil, but they got me everywhere, afterwards, on Mount Athos.) And Compton Mackenzie as he then was, and Huxley, before he had acquired his Pope and Bradley manner, and Verlaine of course; Rimbaud, Mallarmé, Baudelaire.

"What is that book, de Clavering?"

"*Les Chansons de Bilitis*, sir."

"And what is this lesson?"

"You have the advantage, sir."

"What do you mean, boy?"

"Ah, sir, fair's fair. I told you what my book was. You must tell me what's your lesson."

"Elementary geometry."

"But it sounds fascinating! Then this delicious piece of celluloid nonsense is—I know, sir, don't tell me—a set-square?"

"I have been teaching it for twenty years, and never met with such impertinence."

"Twenty years, and still at Elementary! Oh, sir, what a confession." And it was a very purple face one glimpsed behind the blackboard. Ah, those Eton masters! I wish I could remember any of their names, for I was really sorry for them. What tragedies went on under their mortar-boards! Some of them were quite young, and one often got the impression that they were trying, inarticulately, to communicate; would have liked, in fact, to share in the rich creative life that already was centring round me. They used to teeter round my Baksts, and once I caught my housemaster sniffing at a very special bottle made up for me by Max of Delhez, and gingerly rubbing some on his poor old pate. Worldlings, yet deprived of all worldly grace, of our rich sex-life how pathetically inquisitive! They are all there still, I suppose, and I often wonder, when I motor through Switzerland in summer, if one will not find a bunch of them spawning round some mouldy *arête*, in their Norfolk jackets, like eels in the Sargasso Sea.

The boys of course took up most of my time. I soon found that it was easy to get on with them by giving them presents, and making them laugh. A dozen of claret here, a humidor of Coronas there, a well-timed repartee, and persecution was made impossible. It was easy to find the butts and make rather more skilful fun of them than anybody else. In fact, I give this advice to those of my readers who are still at school. In every group there are boys whom it is the fashion to tease and bully; if you quickly spot them and join in, it will never occur to anyone to tease and bully you. Foxes do not hunt stoats. But always defer to the original teasers, and hand your prey over to them for the *coup de grâce*. And boys like expensive presents, though they are genuinely embarrassed by them. All the same, they were a provincial lot. I never felt very safe unless I had several of them round me, in coloured caps and gaudy blazers, puffing away at my cigarettes and looking for dirty jokes in the *Vie Parisienne*. By cultivating all the Captains of Games in this way I found my afternoons were left free. I would watch them troop away with their shinpads to some mysterious district on the way to Slough, then saunter up to Windsor with a book—on the bridge I would wave to any who seemed to be pushing a particularly big boat underneath it. Happy river of Eton-Windsor! I have always been very vague about its name, but I often pictured it winding away past Reading Gaol and into the great world somewhere— the world of the Ballet and the Sitwells, of Cocteau and the Café Royal.

"Hello, Faun, what a way to spend your *Après-midi*."

It was Harold, my most uneasy disciple.

"I was just thinking that summer made a noise like the. rubbing together of biscuits."

"Yes, it is hot," he replied. "If it goes on like this I shall have to buy some FLANNELS."

"And be mistaken for Peter Fleming?"

"Oh, you're cruel. But seriously, what *shall* we do?"

"Well, there's Tull's, and I haven't eaten a lobster patty since this morning—or one might buy a gramophone record— or a very cool Braque of half a dozen ash-blonde oysters—then there's that place one goes to London from."

"You mean the G.W.R.?"

"Thank you—and by now the school library will probably have heard of William Morris—or one might try the arches and see what one could pick up."

"Or the Castle."

"I'm bored with bearskins—but, my dear, that man—he's touched his cap—so familiar."

"You mean the headmaster?"

It seemed an evil omen.

Then there was the Corps. I quickly joined the signal section. You didn't have to carry rifles. It was there that I first met intellectuals, dowdy fellows mostly, who went in for Medici prints and had never heard of Picasso. I realized for the first time what a gap separated cultured and cosmopolitan art lovers like myself, people who cared equally for music, painting, and literature, from those whose one idea was to pass examinations; literature is a very different thing to a poet and to someone who has to make a living out of it. "What do you think of Apollinaire?" I asked one of them. "Good God, we won't get a question on that—he's well outside the period." "On the contrary, he's very much of it. His book on Sade is vital." "I thought you meant Sidonius Apollinaris." I could make no contact with them. But signalling was delightful. One sat for hours beside a field-telephone while little figures receded into the distance with the wire. "Can you hear me?" "No." "Can you hear me now?" "No." "Well, try this." "This" was the morse-code machine, and nimbler fingers than mine would fill the air with

a drowsy song. Iddy iddy umpty umpty iddy umpty iddy . . .
However, all things come to an end, and there were tiresome
scenes—long waits in red-brick classrooms looking at huge
sheets of paper—"write only on one side of the paper."ʻ But
which side? and the precious minutes were wasted. Suddenly
a lot of people I had always been willing to avoid seemed to
have no object in life but to want to meet one. They would
cluster round some old cannon outside New Schools, gowns
fluttering and tassels wagging. One afternoon, when the place
was looking more Raphael Tuck than ever, I went upstairs,
and unforgivable things were said. It seemed one was suspected of all the alluvial vices, in fact one was not getting the
best out of the curriculum. For the last time I crossed the
bridge over the mysterious river, past Tom Browne's, where
rather a good pair of "sponge bags" were being created for me
for Ascot, past Hills and Saunders, who had turned out some
passable groups of my tea-parties. "These people are my
friends," I would implore the photographer, "I want them to
look fresh and good-looking and aristocratic and rich." "But,
sir." "Remember, they are not the Shooting Eight, or
Mr. Crace's Old Boys, and I don't want to sit in the middle
with folded arms and a football. I shall stand rather over to
the side and at the back, and the only way you will know I am
the host is by this enormous cocktail shaker."

*   *   *

"Oh, my boy, my boy, 'ere am I sweating away on the Turf
to edicate you, and just when I 'ope you'll bring the nobs in
you go and get sacked. Sacked from Eton!"

"Not sacked, Pater,—supered."

But my father could never appreciate an academic distinction.

*   *   *

Before one can understand Oxford one must have lived in
Capri, and it was there that I spent the next few months,
cramming. Mother had taken a quiet villa with a view of the
funicular. At seventeen it was rather odd to figure fairly
recognizably in five novels in three languages. But Monty

and Norman were insatiable. "No one would think it absurd if you sat to five painters," they remonstrated, and I retorted that I had a jolly good mind to—but I was too busy at that time, sitting for Fersen.[1] It was my first introduction to *les paradis artificiels* (not counting Tidworth), and with all a boy's healthy craving for novelty I flung myself down on the Count's couches and sampled poppy after poppy through his amusing collection of Chinese pipes. When the time came for my Oxford vivâ, I was older than the rocks and my eyelids were definitely a little weary. I could not decide. Magdalen and *Sinister Street*, Merton and Max, Balliol and Gumbril? or the House—Peers and Peckwater? Max had praised my eyelashes. Harold said Balliol was perfect for case-histories like mine, but I realized I should find it madly ungay. That Buttery! Finally it was the House I chose, two vast eighteenth-century rooms which I did up in pewter and cinnamon. Harold supplied wax fruit, and antimacassars for the Chinese Chippendale chairs, I added incense, brass trays and Buddhas, and Robert a carpet from the Victoria and Albert (the Yacht, not the Museum).

My father had become reconciled to me. "'Appiest days of your life, my boy, and don't forget, a pony for every youngster you bring 'ome with a 'andle to his name. Good for the business." I was worried about my father. "Mother," I said, "don't you think Daddy is looking definitely *blafard*?" "Is he?" she replied. "You're sitting on the Continental Bradshaw."

Most of my Eton friends had also come up to the House, and, as my father had taken a flat in Bicester, "ponies" and "monkeys" came rolling in. I spent them on clothes and parties, on entertaining and on looking entertaining. Parties! "Are you going to de Clavering's to-night?" and woe betide the wretch who had to say no. Nothing much happened at the time, but he soon felt he was living on an icefloe, drifting farther and farther from land, and every moment watching it melt away. De Clavering's to-night! The candles burn in their sconces. The incense glows. Yquem and Avocado pears— a simple meal—but lots and lots of both, with whisky for the

[1] The Marsac of *Vestal Fires*.

hearties and champagne for the dons. "Have a brick of caviare, Alvanley? More birds' nest, Gleneagles? There's nothing coming, I'm afraid, only Avocado pear and hot-pot." "Hot-pot!" "Christian, you're magnificent!" "Caviare and hot-pot—Prendy will be blue with envy!" And then dancing, while canons go home across the quad, and David stomps at the piano. I took care at these parties to have a word and piece of advice for everyone.

There was an alert young man in a corner, looking rather shy. "I know—don't tell me," I said to him, "it's your first party." "Yes." I pinched his cheek. "Si jeunesse savait!" I laughed. It was Evelyn Waugh.

Another merry little fellow asked me if I could suggest a hobby. "Architecture," I gave in a flash. "Thank you." It was John Betjeman.

"And for me?"

"Afghanistan."

It was Robert Byron.

"And me?"

"Byron," I laughed back—it was Peter Quennell.[1]

And Alvanley, Gleneagles, Prince Harmatviz, Graf Slivovitz, the Ballygalley of Ballygalley, Sarsaparilla, the Duc de Dingy, the Conde de Coca y Cola—for them, my peers, I kept my serious warnings.

"These bedroom slippers, Dingy? I flew them over from my *bottier*."

"You ought to look a little more like a public school prefect, Alvanley. The front cover of *The Captain*, it's rather more your *genre*. There! Wash out the 'honey and flowers,' and try a fringe effect. I want to see a pillar of the second eleven."

"Good jazz, Gleneagles, is meant to be played just a little bit too slow."

"Graf Slivovitz, this isn't the *Herrenclub* in Carpathian Ruthenia, you must take off your hat. Yes—that green growth with the feudal feathers."

"Sarsaparilla, only the King rouges his knees when he wears a kilt, and then only at a Court ball."

[1] All of whom, I am told (autumn 1937), still keep afloat.

"Harmatviz, I can smell that Harris a mile away. What on earth is that terrifying harpoon in the lapel?"

"That, de Clavering, is a *Fogas* fly." [1]

"More Yquem, Ballygalley?"

"What's that?"

"That—if you mean the thing under your elbow—is how I look to Brancusi; the other is a kind of wine. Stand him up, will you, Ava?"

"Before the war we heard very little of the Sarsaparillas— he would not dare wear that tartan in Madrid."

"Before the war I hadn't heard of you, Coca y Cola, either; Count, this is a democratic country."

"I am democrats, we are all democrats. *Vive le roi.*"

"Thank you, Dingy, you must have been reading *Some People*. Now I want all the Guinnesses and Astors to go into the next room and get a charade ready. Alvanley, Gleneagles, Harmatviz, and Slivovitz—you will drive quickly over with me for a few minutes to Bicester to say good-night to father."

"No I don't think."—"My price is ten guineas."—"Jolly well not unless we go halves."—"Where is my hat and gotha?" —and madcap youth was served.

My crowning moment. The Summerville Grind. Peers and their mothers and sisters in mackintoshes and shooting-sticks. My mount. A huge animal whose teeth need cleaning. For the first time in my life I wear a bowler hat. And my racing colours. White silk shirt with a broad blue stripe— but zigzag! Alvanley and Gleneagles on each side of me—off! I was petrified, my dears; the first fence was enormous and my animal seemed hours getting over it. There was time for me to get down, and I rolled over. On it thundered, its great ugly stirrups banging together. A man leant over me. "Not hurt, are you?" he said. And then, *plus fort que lui*, "Where *did* you get that shirt?" It was on a sigh that I answered, as I lost consciousness, "Sire, at Charvet's." It was the Prince.

And there was talk—all kinds—the banter of my friends.

"Ah, de Clavering, if you were only of the nobility. I would

[1] An amusing fish from the Balaton.

ask you to stay at Dingy. What a pity you are not a real goodfellow."

"Apfelstrüdel! He is coming to Schloss Slivovitz with Pryce-Jones, is not that good enough for you?"

"Slivovitz—how picturesque it must be. But at Dingy we have to consider the *convenances*, my aunt Doudeauville, my Uncle Sagan. . . ."

"She 'appens to be *my* aunt Doudeauville too.[1] Her mother was of the German branch."

"I can find no Harmatviz on Madame Sacher's tablecloth."

"Rosa Lewis says the Claverings are an old Scotch family."

"Sarsaparilla would know that."

"Before the war we heard very little of the Sarsaparillas, now it appears . . ."

"Ah, bonjour, Coca y Cola, how is the Alvis?"

"Very well, would you like to look under the bonnet?"

"Haw, haw, haw, what a suggestion."

"But seriously, de Clavering—you are rich, you are intelligent, why have you no titles? Have you spoken to the King?"

"He may have no title, but I would trust him with my waistcoats."

"And I shake him by the hand—and say—'Well, what the hell, who cares?'"

"Bravo, Harmatviz, it's a democratic country. *Vive le roi!*"

Then there was brilliant conversation at Balliol, where the food makes long journeys to the dowdy sitting-rooms, under tins.

"We were discussing, de Clavering, whether it was more correct to say Theophylactus Simocattes or Simocatta—"

"You should consider yourself very lucky, Sparrow, to be able to say either."

"And what the collective noun is for a group of pelicans; there is a gaggle of geese, of course, and a pride of lions."

"A piety of pelicans, I suggest."

"Thank you—how delightfully Thomas Browne. I shall repeat that."

---

[1] By the marriage of Graf Hubertus Mary von and zu Slivovitz-Slivovitz with Katarina Auburn-Cord.

"I don't know which I dislike most, people who repeat my epigrams or people who copy my ties—and, by the way, I hope you don't mind. I've brought Raymond Radiguet."

"Where's he up?"

"He's not up. He lives in Paris."

"Paris! If I get an All Sogger I am determined to go there. It's right on the way to the British School."

"I know a very nice little hotel near the *Bibliothèque Mazarine*."

"I can't see why they don't build an arcade from Brick Top's [1] to the Ritz." Nobody laughs. As usual, one can find no contact with them.

My twenty-firster. Fifty people in fancy dress. The orchestra from the *Grand Ecart*. A large silver waste-paper basket. "To Christian de Clavering, the Great Commoner— Alvanley, Alba, Ava, Abercorn, Andrassy, Aberconway, Argyll, Auersperg"—you can imagine the signatures. As the college barge, which I had taken for the occasion, glided up the Cher, life's goblet seemed full to brimming. But Nemesis pursued me. The dons descended. I suppose they hadn't had enough invitations. It appears that those afternoons which I spent under some hot towels in Germers were full of goings-on, lectures, tutorials, Heaven knows what. Divinity seemed a prominent element in the City of Lost Causes. I went down. Oxford, like Eton, had never really "given."

London at last.[2] The 'twenties. Parties. Parties. Parties. And behind them all an aching feeling.—Was it worth it? What is it all for? Futility. . . .

"Christian—you must dine with me to-night!"

"Gawain—I can't—I've engaged myself to the '*Derries*."

*   *   *

"Are you the manager?"

"Yes, sir."

"My name is de Clavering. I should like to say I have

[1] Always my favourite nightbox.

[2] A London then where everybody knew everybody and we all squeezed into one telephone book !

never eaten such a disgusting meal. *Même à la Cour*. But haven't I seen you before?"

"Oui, monsieur, je vous connais depuis l'Eldorado."

* * *

"Es usted el cuadro flamenco?"
"Si."
"Si."
"Si."
"Si."

* * *

"Beverley, my dear, such a gaffe! I've just gone up to the old Dowager of Buck-and-Chan and mistaken her for the old Dowager of Ham-and-Bran!"

"*Christian!*"

* * *

"She's got what the Americans call 'that.'"
"What?"
"What the Americans call 'that.'"
"What's that?"
"'That'—that's what she's got."
"But what the Americans call what? I don't even know that."
"Oh, my dear Duchess!"

For it was sometimes my privilege to give instruction to a very great lady.

* * *

"M. Picasso—Mr. Hemingway. M. Hemingway—Señor Belmonte. Mr. Nicolson—Mr. Firbank—and now shall we begin without Miss Stein? I'm starving."

* * *

"I can't decide whether to stay with Lorenzo in Taos or Crowley in Cefalu—where *does* one go in August?"

* * *

"Dear Evelyn, *of course*, put me into it!"

* * *

"Voulez-vous téléphoner à Mr. Proust de venir me trouver dans les bains de la rue de Lappe?"

*   *   *

"Herr Reinhardt ist zuschloss?"

*   *   *

"You know Diaghilev, of course, Dingy?"

*   *   *

"I've found the title for you, Breton—*Surréalisme*."

*   *   *

"And for this rather brusque poem, Osbert, I shall need the 'meg.'" [1]

*   *   *

Parties. Futility. You can read of most of them in old gossip columns. I still remember my tropical party, when a punkah was heard for the first time in Egerton Crescent. Palms and bananas decorated the rooms. The central heating (it was in July) provided the atmosphere. Some stewards from the P. & O. worked away at the punkahs, or at distributing *reistafel* and planters' punch. The guests wore shorts, sarongs, stingah shifters, or nothing at all.

"But this is *me*," I remember saying, holding up a slim volume. "Why haven't I been told about this before, Dadie? Who is this T. S. Eliot?"

"He works in a bank, I believe."

"Works in a bank—and writes *The Waste Land*! But he should be here, at my Tropical Party! Go and fetch him."

But there is a new disturbance, and Bolitho, our butler, is at my elbow.

"Some young people, sir."

"Their names?"

"The *Blackbirds*."

"Ask them to come up. We shall want some more room.

---

[1] A megaphone, and such small ability as I may have acquired with it, now constitute my " platform manner."

Patrick, help me spread Elizabeth somewhere else. Ronald, come out from under that sofa, you're hunching the springs.[1] Fallen out of the window, you say, with Brenda? Never mind, for the moment. I want to be alone. I want to read this book."

And then the blow fell. A summons, next day, to the Royal Automobile Club. "I'm ruined, my boy. I'm ruined. 'Aven't got a penny left. Those pals of yours, Alvanley and Gleneagles. They've skinned me. You'll 'ave to earn your own living from now on. Oh, your poor mother!" "It's poor me, you old banana. I've no intention of earning my own living, thank you."—"Ow, wot a boy, wot a boy." And I flung out. Tears. Consultations.

"I can always sell my Gris." "But what will you do then?" "Oh, write—paint—don't fluster me."

"And we were to have gone to the Londonderry del Vals!" "Poor mother."

One thing stood out with terrible clarity in those dark days. The old life was over. I could never associate any longer with those friends who had been used to look to me for advice, loans, old clothes, and entertainment. They would see to that. The Ritz, the Blue Lantern, must know me no more.

Exile. A few months in Paris—but Montparnasse, now, my dears, *Montparnasse*; a few offers for my memoirs; then Berlin, Munich—and finally, Greece. There, "in the worst inn's worst room," I existed, miserably, on fried goat and raki. To write or to paint—to work—but how? Write only on one side of the paper. But which side? It was the old dilemma. A wandering exile, the quays of the Piraeus knew me, the noisy bars of Terreno, the Dôme and the Deux Magots, Bohême and Silhouette, and that place in the Marokaner Gasse. I ate rose-leaf jam with the good monks of Holy Luke, and fried locusts with the dervishes of Moulay Idris. And one crazy 4th of June, lobster salad with my housemaster! My slim figure lingered, winterbound, in dim cathedrals, and there were beaches where summer licked me with its great rough tongue. Ah, summer! There's a crypto-fascist for you! The spring I never cared for. It held nothing but a promise, and I, too,

---

[1] Firbank's shyness was proverbial.

was promising. The autumns I adored; they smelt of cassia.
But poverty was crippling. To whom life once had been a bed
of roses—no, of *Strawberry-leaves*, there remained only the
"Welcome" at Villefranche, the old Bœuf in the Boissy
D'Anglas, the Pangion. It was not good enough. I came back
to live with my mother.

It was then that I saw the light. One day I wandered into
a little book-shop near Red Lion Square. It was full of slim
volumes by unfamiliar names—who were Stephen, Wystan,
Cecil, and Christopher? Madge? Bates? Dutt? These blunt
monosyllables spoke a new kind of language to me. I looked
at the books. Not at all bad, and some of these young poets,
I realized, had even attended my university! One quatrain in
particular haunted me.

> M is for Marx
> and Movement of Masses
> and Massing of Arses
> and Clashing of Classes.

It was new. It was vigorous. It was real. It was chic!

> Come on Percy, my pillion-proud, be
> camber-conscious
> Cleave to the crown of the road

and

> It was late last night when my lord came home
> enquiring for his lady O
> The servants cried on every side
> She's gone with the Left Book
> Study Circle O !

And everyone was called by their Christian names! So cosy!
From that moment I've never looked back. It's been pylons
all the way. Of course they didn't want me, at first. The
meetings behind the Geisha Café—they suspected me of all
sorts of things, I'm afraid—I said quite frankly: "I realize I
shall never understand eclectic materialism but I'm terribly
terribly Left!" And I showed them one or two things I'd
written for the weekly reviews, all among the waffle-receipts
and the guest-house advertisements.[1] And I called myself

[1] Soon to be published under the title of *I Told You So*.

Cris Clay. Then—on a drizzling February morning—came my first Procession! It was for me a veritable *Via Crucis*, for we had to march up St. James's Street—past Locks, and Lobbs, and Briggs, and Boodles. All my past was spread out before me. There weren't very many of us, and it was difficult to cheer and shout our slogans

> One, two, three, four
> Pacifism means War.

I raised my eyes to White's bow-window.

Yes, there they were—Alvanley and Gleneagles, with their soiled city faces and little moustaches, their bowlers and rolled umbrellas—and, good heavens, there were Peter, and Robert, and Evelyn! I never felt more ridiculous. When suddenly something made me look round. "De Clavering, old horse!" "Well, I'm spifflicated." "You old *finocchio!*" "*Spinaten!*" It was too good to be true.

"But, Harmatviz—I see you don't know the first thing about the cut of a corduroy."

"Not a red shirt, Slivovitz—a red tie if you must."

"And you, Coca y Cola—you look like a scarecrow."

"These are good workmen's pants, de Clavering, real dungaree!"

We gave a boo to the bow-window that made the *Tatlers* rattle in their holders.

"But how did you get here?"

"I was expelled for plotting against the Regent in favour of the traitor Otto."

"I was turned out for lack of enthusiasm for the present regime and communicating with the traitor Wilhelm."

"I wanted to annoy Sarsaparilla."

"Anyhow, we're all good anti-Fascists," cried Comrade Graf Slivovitz.

I wanted to say something more—that I had even been told by the Party that I should be more useful outside it, but I couldn't speak. Old friends had met, travelling a stony road, coming to the same hard conclusions, and together.

* * *

And that's about all. There are one or two things I've left out, the war, the slump, the general strike, and my conversion to Catholicism, because I'm so vague about dates. But I think this will remain—A Modern Pilgrimage. And now for the reviewers. I think they'd better be careful. They'd better be very careful indeed. A line is being drawn. I'm going to say it again, and very slowly. A line is being drawn. Quite quietly at present—just a few names jotted down in a notebook —one or two with a question mark after them. They have another chance. And the rest don't. Those lines mean something. Tatatat! Yes, my dears, bullets—real bullets, the kind of bullets they keep for reviewers who step across the party line. One day you're going to see something rather hostile. It will make you feel, perhaps, a little uneasy. It's heavy—and stubby—and rather pointed. Guess? Yes. A machine-gun. POINTED AT YOU. And behind it, with his hand on the trigger, Comrade—no, COMMISSAR—Cris Clay. Did you write such and such an article? Yes (No). It doesn't matter which. Tatatat. It's no good then bleating about how you voted in the last election, or where your sympathies have always been. We don't want your sympathy. We don't want you at all.

You subscribed to the *News-Chronicle*, did you? I am afraid you will be under no necessity to renew that subscription.

You wrote for the *New Statesman*? What did you write about? "Gramophone records."

"To sit on the fence is to be on the wrong side of it—line him up, Gollancz."

"Yes, Commissar."

"And you—what were you?"

"Turf-Accountant."

"Your face seems vaguely familiar—but that doesn't make it more pleasant—line him up, Stephen."

"It was no accident, Pryce-Jones, that you have lived near three royal palaces."

"But—"

But I am anticipating. There are two ways to review a book like mine, a right and a wrong. The wrong way is to find fault with it, for then you find fault with the book clubs behind it, in fact, with your advertisers. And if I seem too clever it's because you're too stupid. Think it over. The right way is to praise it, and to quote from it in such a way that you can all learn my lesson. I stand no nonsense. Remember, my dears, a line is being drawn. Tatatat. See you at the Mass Observatory.

> Something is going to go, baby,
> And it won't be your stamp-collection.
> Boom !

And that I think could particularly be meditated by the Fascist Connolly.

CRIS CLAY.

PARIS—BUDAPEST—PARTON ST.
1936-1937.

[Reprinted from *Press Gang*, edited by Leonard Russell and published by Hutchinson's.]

YEAR NINE

AUGUR'S PRISON—YEAR IX. I HAVE BEEN TREATED WITH great kindness, with a consideration utterly out of keeping with the gravity of my offence, yet typical of the high conception of justice implicit in our state. Justice in sentence, celerity in execution in the words of Our Leader. Excuse my fatal impediment. I call attention to it, as eagerly as in Tintoretto's plague hospital they point to bleeding bubos on the legs and shoulders. Let me tell you how it all happened. With a friend, a young woman, I arranged to spend last Leaderday evening. We met under the clock outside the Youngleader-boys building. Having some minutes to spare before the Commonmeal and because it was raining slightly, we took shelter in the glorious Artshouse. There were the ineffable misterpasses of our glorious culture, the pastermieces of titalitorian tra, the magnificent Leadersequence, the super-statues of Comradeship, Blatherhood, and Botherly Love, the 73 Martyrs of the Defence of the Bourse, the Leader as a simple special constable. There they were, so familiar that my sinful feet were doubly to be blamed for straying—for they strayed not only beyond the radius of divine beauty but beyond the sphere of ever-loving Authority, creeping with their putrid freight down the stairs to the forgotten basement. There, breeding filth in the filth that gravitates around it, glows the stagnant rottenness called Degenerate Art, though only perfect Leadercourtesy could bestow the term Art on such Degeneration! There are the vile pustules of the rotting Demos, on canvases his sores have hideously excoriated. Still Lives—as if life could be ever still! Plates of food, bowls of fruit; under the old regime the last deplorable nightdreams and imaginations of starving millions, the prurient lucubrations of the unsterilized—bathing coves of womblike obscenity, phallic church towers and monoliths, lighthouses and pyramids, trees even painted singly in their stark suggestiveness, instead of in the official groups; all hideous and perverted symbols of an age of private love,

154

ignorant of the harmony of our Commonmeals, and the State administration of Sheepthinkers Groupbegettingday. There were illicit couples, depicted in *articulo amoris*, women who had never heard of the three K's, whose so-called clothes were gaudy dishrags, whose mouths were painted offal. Engrossed in disgust and mental anguish I thoughtlessly began to mark on my official catalogue the names of the most detestable fartists. This was partly to hold them up to ridicule at Commonmeals, partly to use in articles which would refute the pseudocriticism of our enemies, but above all unconsciously—a tic expressive of my odious habit, for *I only chose names that were easily or interestingly reversible*. That is my only justification. Nacnud Tnarg; Sutsugua Nhoj; Ossacip. Repip. The filthy anti-Fascists who dared to oppose our glorious fishynazists! Hurriedly we made for the clean outdoors, the welcoming statues of the great upstairs, and outside where the supreme spectacle streams on the filament—the neon Leaderface. In my haste I dropped my catalogue by the turnstile. The rest of the evening passed as usual. We attended Commonmeal in seats 7111037 and 7111038 respectively, and after the digestive drill and the documentaries went to our dormitories. The young woman on departing blew me a kiss and I called out merrily yet admonishingly: "None of that stuff, 7111038, otherwise we shall never be allowed to produce a little 7111037-8. ♂ on Groupbegettingday."

During the next week nothing happened. But some four days after that, having occasion to telephone the young woman, and while speaking to her in a spirit of party badinage, I was astounded to hear a playful repartee of mine answered by a male eructation. "Was that you?" I said—but no answer came. On picking up the receiver again to ask the janitor for ten minutes' extra light, I heard—above the ringing noise—for he had not yet answered—an impatient yawn. These two noises made an enormous impression, for I realized that I was an object of attention (though unwelcome attention) to a member of a class far above my own, a superior with the broad chest and masculine virility of a Stoop Trauma!

The next morning my paper bore the dreaded headline,

"Who are the Censors Looking for?" At the office we were lined up at 10.10 and some officials from the censor's department, in their camouflaged uniforms, carrying the white-hot Tongs, symbol of Truth, the Thumbcaps of Enquiry, and the Head on the Dish, emblem of Justice, passed down the line. As the hot breath of the tongs approached, many of us confessed involuntarily to grave peccadilloes. A man on my left screamed that he had stayed too long in the lavatory. But the glorious department disdained force. We were each given three photographs to consider, and told to arrange them in order of aesthetic merit. The first was a reproduction of a steel helmet, the second of a sack of potatoes, the third of some couples with their arms round their necks in an attitude of illicit sexual group-activity. I arranged them in that order. One of the inspectors looked for a long time at me. We were then asked to write down the names of any infamous poets or painters we could remember from the old regime. "Badshaw, Deadwells, Staleworthy, Baldpole," I wrote. Then, in an emotion, a veritable paroxysm stronger than me, with the eyes of the examiner upon me, my hands bearing the pen downwards as ineluctably as the State diviner bears down on his twig, I added: "Toilet, Red Neps." And once more: "Nacnud Tnarg, Sutsugua Nhoj, Ossacip. *Jewlysses. Winagains Fake.*" The censors this time did not look at me, but passing down the line made an ever more and more perfunctory examination, towards the end simply gathering the papers from the willing outstretched hands of the workers and carelessly tearing them up. They then swept out of the room, escorted by the foreman, the political and industrial commissars of our office, and Mr. Abject, the Ownerslave. We were instructed to continue our duties. As the envelopes came by on the belt I seized them with trembling hand, and vainly tried to perform my task as if nothing had happened. It was my business to lick the top flap of the envelope, whose bottom flap would then be licked by my neighbour, the one beyond him sticking the flaps together—for all sponges and rollers were needed for munitions. At the same time I used my free hand to inscribe on the corner of the envelope my contribution to the address (for all envelopes were addressed to the censor's headquarters) the letters S.W.3. Alas how many illegible S.W.3's that morning betrayed my trepidation, and when I came to licking the outer flap my tongue was either so parched by terror as to be unable to wet the corner at all, or so drowned in nervous salivation as to spread small bubbles of spittle over the whole surface, causing the flap to curl upwards and producing in my near neighbours many a sign of their indignant impatience and true party horror of bad work. Shortly before leaderbreak the commissars, followed by Mr. Abject, returned down the line. My companions on the belt, now feeling that I manifested emotional abnormality, were doing everything to attract attention to me by causing me to fail in my work, kicking me on the ankles as they received my envelopes, and one of them, seizing a ruler, made a vicious jab upwards with it as I was adding S.W.3, causing acute agony to my public parts. As the commissars came near me they began to joke, smiling across at my neighbours and grunting: "As long as you can spit, man, the State will have a use for you," and "Don't try and find out where the gum you lick comes from, my boyo." Friendly condescensions which seemed designed to render more pregnant and miserable the silence with which they came to me. At last, with a terrible downward look, the commissar paused before me. The smile had faded from his face, his eyes flashed lightning, his mouth was thin as a backsight, his nose was a hairtrigger. Mr. Abject looked at me with profound commiseration till he received a nudge from the other commissar, and said in a loud voice: "This is your man." I was marched out between them while the serried ranks of my old beltmates sang the Leaderchorus and cried: "Show mercy to us by showing no mercy to him, the dog and the traitor." Outside the newsboys were screaming: "Long live the Censor. Gumlicking wrecker discovered."

Our justice is swift: our trials are fair: hardly was the preliminary bone-breaking over than my case came up. I was tried by the secret censor's tribunal in a pitchdark circular room. My silly old legs were no use to me now and I was allowed the privilege of wheeling myself in on a kind of invalid's chair. In the darkness I could just see the aperture high up in the wall from whence I should be cross-examined, for it is part of our new justice that no prejudicial view is obtained of the personal forces at work between accused and accuser. The charge was read out and I was asked if I had anything to say. I explained the circumstances as I have related them to you, and made my defence. Since an early initiation accident I have never been considered sound of mind, hence my trick of reversing words—quite automatically and without the intention of seeking hidden and antinomian meanings, hence my subordinate position in the Spitshop. My action, I repeated, was purely involuntary. The voice of my chief witness-accuser-judge replied from the orifice:

"Involuntary! But don't you see, that makes it so much worse! For what we voluntarily do, voluntarily we may undo, but what we do not of our own free will, we lack the will to revoke. What sort of a person are you, whose feet carry you helplessly to the forbidden basement? Yet not forbidden, for that basement is an open trap. Poor flies walk down it as down the gummy sides of a pitcher plant; a metronome marks the time they spend there, a radioactive plate interprets the pulsations which those works inspire, a pulsemeter projects them on a luminous screen which is perpetually under observation in the censor's office. It was at once known that you were there and what you felt there. But instead of being followed to your Blokery in the normal way you eluded your pursuers by dropping your catalogue. They decided it was their duty to carry it immediately to the cipher department and thus allowed you to escape. Your crime is fivefold:

"'That you of your own impulse visited the basement of degenerate art and were aesthetically stimulated thereby.'

"'That you attempted to convince a young woman, 7111038, of the merit of the daubs you found there, thereby being guilty of treason—for Our Leader is a painter too, and thereby being guilty of the far worse sin of inciting to treason a member of the non-rational (and therefore not responsible for her actions) sex.'

"'That you made notes on the daubs in question with a view to perverting your fellow-workers.'

"'That you caused deliberate inconvenience to the board of censors, attempting to throw them off your trail, thus making improper use of them.'

"'That you did not confess before your offence was notified, or even at the time of your examination.'

"The penalty, as you know, for all these crimes is death. But there has interceded on your behalf the young woman whose denunciation helped us to find you. To reward her we have commuted your crime to that of coprophagy—for that is what your bestial appreciation of the faeces of so-called democratic art amounts to. Your plea of involuntary compulsion forces me to proclaim the full sentence. For with such a subconscious libido there must surely be a cancerous ego! I therefore proclaim that you will be cut open by a qualified surgeon in the presence of the State Augur. You will be able to observe the operation, and if the Augur decides the entrails are favourable they will be put back. If not, not. You may congratulate yourself on being of more use to your leader in your end than your beginning. For on this augury an important decision on foreign policy will be taken. Annexation or Annihilation? Be worthy of your responsibility. Should the worst befall, you will be sent to the gumfactory, and part of you may even form the flap of an envelope which your successor on the belt, Miss 7111038, may lick! You lucky dog."

Yes, I have been treated with great kindness.

January 1938.

WHAT WILL *HE* DO NEXT?

By Rear-Colonel Connolly

AS FAR BACK AS 1873 I WAS ADVOCATING A SMALL HIGHLY
mechanized striking force to be employed in "expanding
torrent" tactics, i.e. "deep infiltration." The War Office paid
no attention. Clausewitz did. "Dear Captain Connolly," he
wrote, "I have read *The Lesson of Omdurman* with interest,
and was most impressed by your definition of Peace." [Peace,
I had written, is a morbid condition, due to a surplus of
civilians, which war seeks to remedy.] In my *Lesson of Norway*
(April 1940), *Lesson of the Bulge* (May 1940), and *Lesson of
Britain* (in preparation), as well as in this series of fifteen
articles, I have consistently advocated the same principles. "A
defensive force," I wrote in 1884, "should be in a certain ratio
to an offensive force, depending on (*a*) the size of the offensive
force, (*b*) its striking power." For that force to become an
offensive-defensive force the ratio will have to be considerably
higher. How can I explain this to the non-military mind?
I think it can best be expressed by a formula. Invasion=The
incidence of men and material on hostile or unfriendly territory
where that incidence is of sufficient impact to do permanent
or semi-permanent damage to military objectives. Thus
incidence of material without man-power (air-raids) or of man-
power without material (parachutists) do not in themselves
constitute invasion. Will, in this sense, an invasion be forth-
coming? Certain it is that some such step has been contem-
plated. We can, in fact, state the problem as follows:

(1) Will Hitler invade us?

(2) Will that invasion be successful?

(3) If not, will some counter-move be made in the Mediterranean or the Far East?

(4) Or will both (1) and (3) or some variation of them be
attempted?

To all these questions we may answer, categorically, yes and no. What we can be certain of is that the attack, when it does come, will attempt to take us by surprise, either in the time chosen, or the place, or the means, and that in any eventuality I shall be ready with my article. A study of the map will reveal that the situation, if not grave, is at least critical. Nevertheless it must constantly be pointed out to the lay mind that (1) for every tactical danger there is a strategical *quid pro quo*. (2) 'Retreat is an advance in a reverse direction.'[1] As I understand the position, and taking into account what we know of Hitler's previous moves and what may be termed his psycho-strategical make-up, there will be an element of bluff. Thus either the main attack is on these islands (England, Ireland, Iceland, etc.) or else-where—it is no good, if it is elsewhere, keeping all our forces at home, it is no good sending them elsewhere if it is here.

Which of these alternatives will be adopted? Which will be, if adopted, feints? The answer is that, since a feint will hardly follow the main attack, *the first offensive* in point of time will be a feint and destined, if here, to prevent our troops being sent elsewhere; if elsewhere, to get them away from here. Should the offensives open simultaneously, a further elucidation, in a new series of articles, will be necessary. What can be told now by those of us whose training enables us to dominate military events is that, should Hitler invade us at a moment when thick fog, high tides, and bright moonlight are in conjunction (and these moments only occur once in three weeks), he would meet with very serious difficulties, which only the possession of new "secret weapons" would enable him to surmount. Such weapons as he is known to possess, an undetectable new gas which puts us all to sleep for a fortnight, after which we wake up raving mad, an artificial fog of enormous dimensions, a channel tunnel, a fleet of *stationary* planes, and a key to the Great Pyramid, are sufficient to produce total annihilation, but that would hardly amount to annexation in a military sense. As a fellow strategist remarks in his book, printed as long ago as 1939:

[1] Fabius Cunctator, *Manual*.

"The war was born under strange stars . . . it will end suddenly: and the manner of its ending will prove for all time the vanity of human anticipations. . . . It will be a very short war or last for longer than the three years visualized by politicians. . . . It started with the invasion of Poland, and it will finish with the invasion of some other country after a decisive sea-action. The frontier of no country in Europe can be regarded as safe." (R. H. Naylor, *What the Stars Foretell for 1940*, Hutchinson, 3s. 6d.)

Meanwhile there are three questions, arising out of invasion, which I am constantly asked, and which I will now reply to:

1. *How to stop a tank.*

Most of you who have had no experience of stopping tanks will have had some of shooting elephants. A tank is simply an armoured elephant. In every group of tanks there is a leading tank, whose signals are obeyed by the others; if the leading tank is trapped, the others will "come quietly." The best elephant trap was a large pit over which branches were laid. For a tank trap it is only necessary to remove the paving stones outside your house (borrow a wheelbarrow from the man next door) and dig a pit some forty feet wide by twenty deep. Place a sheet of wire netting over the road, cover it with cardboard or brown paper, and a top dressing of asphalt. Your trap is made. If you are lucky enough to live near a blast-furnace, borrow some sheets of eleven-inch steel, solder them with a blower's lamp, and lean them up supported by a prop over the water-hole; when the tank comes down to drink, pull the prop away, or, if you are very close, insert a knitting-needle into the tank's most vulnerable spot, the back-ratchet. But remember, nothing will really stop a tank except another tank going in the opposite direction, and these should be left to the competent military authority.

2. *What further safety measures do you advise?*

The greatest danger to the military in war-time is the civilian, because he is not subject to military discipline; a moving civilian is even more dangerous—he is anarchy in two places at once. I therefore advocate a permanent day-time curfew and night-time lock-up for civilians, with an internal passport system for those whose deployment is essential. The internal passport would include reports on the civilian from his school, university, employer, and bank manager, and the visa to move about would be granted, if at all, by a military policeman.

3. What will He do next? For that I must refer you to my subsequent article: *Pros and Cons of Invasion.*

August 1940.

AN UNFORTUNATE VISIT

IN A WORLD WHICH EVERY DAY GROWS LAMENTABLY MORE LIKE Candide's, how many ideas for which we are fighting can be traced back to their source in the sparkling mind of Voltaire? It is just over two hundred years since he lived in London and for the first time presented us to Europe in modern dress.

Of all his writings, those which bear most upon the present day are to be found in the *Dictionnaire Philosophique*, and one of our publishers would be doing a service if they would reprint the two-volume Garnier edition with the admirable introduction by Julien Benda. Writing years before the war, he says:

"A question often arises when we read the Dictionary— Whom is the author getting at? When we see him cripple with blows the religion of force, the poetry of blood, the hero cult, the contempt for the universal, the superstition of the Past, we are compelled to ask ourselves which of his contemporaries he has it in for. Nobody, not even the poets, sang in 1760 of the holiness of war, of nationalist differences, of the abasement of reason, of the mystique of force, of the worship of the land and of the dead. These things date from Hegel, Nietzsche, Barrès, and Sorel. On many a page we feel that above all the cannon balls of Voltaire fall on the men of our time . . . Goethe says somewhere that the true sign of genius is a posthumous productivity. Voltaire has, by the natural expansion of his work, produced the adversaries who were not to appear till a century and a half later, and whom he has answered."

* * *

Dipping about in the Dictionary, where all is lucidity, gaiety, intelligence, and courage, I came on the article "Liberté de Penser," a short dialogue on the Inquisition between two wounded officers, Lord Boldmind and Count Médroso, who are taking the waters in the Pyrenees. Here is the conclusion:

164

"*Boldmind.* Anybody can educate himself.

Médroso. They say that if everyone thought for themselves there would reign complete confusion.

Boldmind. Quite the opposite. When we go to the theatre we all say what we like and the peace is kept; but if some insolent protector of a bad poet wished to make all people of taste find good what seemed to them bad, then the whistling would start, and the two sides would throw apples at each other, as happened once in London. It is the tyrants over the intelligence who have caused part of the misfortunes of the world. We have been happy in England only since everyone freely enjoyed the right to say what he thinks.

Médroso. We are also very peaceful in Lisbon, where no one can enjoy that.

Boldmind. You are peaceful, but you are not happy; it is the calm of galley-slaves, who row in rhythmical silence.

Médroso. You think then that my soul is in the galleys?

Boldmind. Yes; and I wish to set it free.

Médroso. And if I'm quite comfortable in my galley?

Boldmind. In that case you deserve to stay there."

* * *

These last few lines are like a neat chess-ending, but it is not their crispness which has been haunting me. Voltaire set his dialogue for 1707. What would he find if he came here to-day? Innumerable Mr. and Mrs. Stouthearts, of whom he would be justly proud. But what has happened to Milord Boldmind? One can imagine the headlines:

"Famous Swiss journalist arrives in England. Guest of Lord Coalmine. Worth three divisions."

"François Voltaire, the famous Swiss journalist who occupies a position there somewhat similar to Hannen Swaffer's, has arrived in this country, and will be the guest of Lord Coalmine, the regional commissioner, at Goslow. 'I have no plans,' said M. Voltaire, 'I want to see my old friends and revisit my home at Wandsworth, which I hear has been blitzed.'"

"Voltaire to broadcast! To-night's postscript will be by Mr. Frank Voltaire. . . . Owing to an indisposition to-night's postscript by Mr. Voltaire has been postponed, and instead there will be a recording of a talk by Lord Elton."

"Voltaire on Brains Trust. The Spanish Ambassador, the Papal Nuncio, the *Catholic Herald*, and the Irish Representative have protested against the inclusion of Mr. Voltaire in the Brains Trust. Statement in Parliament. 'While nothing personal is intended it is felt that the inclusion of a non-British subject on the Brains Trust might set an unfortunate precedent.'"

"Voltaire leaves Lord Coalmine. No statement to make. M. Voltaire, 'For once, I have nothing to say.' Says Lord Coalmine, 'A purely private affair.'"

"Voltaire to preach. The Rev. M. T. Pew, rector of a large church, has invited M. Voltaire to deliver a lay sermon. 'In these days when the church has a mission to perform and it is absolutely essential to obtain a congregation, I have taken the unusual step of asking M. Voltaire to speak and to tell us quite frankly what he thinks is lacking in the Church of England.'"

"Outbreak in church. Home Guard called out. Swiss journalist claims extra-territorial rights. Aspersions on Abraham. Rector's indignation. 'Remove this Trotskyite spy.'— *Daily Worker*. 'M. Voltaire's place is in the Pioneer Corps.'— *Truth*."

"Voltaire to join the Free French. 'We, Charles de Gaulle, are delighted to welcome to our ranks the Sieur de Voltaire to serve in the capacity which shall be dictated by us.' Voltaire leaves Free French."

"Voltaire for America. M. de Voltaire, whose arrival here caused such a stir some weeks ago, is to go on a lecture tour to the United States, where he will be the guest of Mr. Bertrand Russell. 'I am looking forward to finding among the free Iroquois a better welcome than in Carlton Gardens,' said M. de Voltaire, at the Ritz."

"Stop Press.—Peer's home raided. Acting on anonymous information Ministry of Food officials raided the mansion of Lord Coalmine, regional commissioner, and found part of a ham, a bottle of Oxo, and two tins of birds' nest soup. An apology was made."

"M. de Voltaire, whose American visa has been unexpectedly

cancelled, arrived to-day in Switzerland. 'I was growing anxious about my garden,' he said."

*   *   *

This may be an exaggeration, yet we cannot but agree with Frederick the Great, who prayed in later years, "Je lui dis, Divin Voltaire, ora pro nobis." For although England has become again the heroic country which Voltaire knew in his youth, it is lacking in the quality of bold-mindedness which he attributed to it. The Liberal Party, the heirs of the great Whig tradition which did so much to form the youthful Voltaire (and so to precipitate the French Revolution), still maintains the principles for which he fought, but lacks the courage of them. The Labour Party does not think boldly for itself, and there is no party in which the love of truth for its own sake is not now vitiated by political tactics. We forget that the great truths of liberty, tolerance, and justice for which our ancestors fought were not casual themes of the day but bitter lessons painfully learnt from centuries of fierce struggle and oppression. They represent the only way out from the permanent vendetta which life becomes when governed by racial instincts and mass-phobias. If in our long struggle with totalitarianism we lose the intellectual courage of Renaissance man, we lose the primary emotion—the fuse train—which fires all the discoveries of art and science and morals by which we can improve our lot. All the physical bravery and technical skill of our country are useless without the political wisdom and invention of our forefathers. What would have shocked Voltaire most, disillusioned though he was, would have been the apathy and the timidity with which we accept our role as the saviours of Europe and the masters of our own destiny. The partial rejection of the Beveridge Report might have seemed to him a natural compromise of party politics. The complete resignation with which such a rejection is accepted by 90 per cent. of those who would most benefit from it—that he would not understand.

Something, despite all our achievements in this war, is weighing down on us, is keeping us from thinking clearly, acting promptly and wisely. "Too long a sacrifice can make a stone of the heart . . ." When all Europe looks to us for liberation, when we should have ideas to export as dangerous, as delightful, as irresistible as those which Voltaire drank in, we are sinking back into the past, relying only on patriotism, cut off from those in other countries who think as we do, distrusting our intellectuals (Voltaire praised England as the country where Addison, Gay, Congreve, Newton, and Prior all achieved high offices of state), letting "I dare not wait upon I would" on a rubber stamp, and—*O divin Voltaire*—allowing our allies to conduct their private gestapos on the soil where our law once made every runaway slave on his arrival automatically free.

Our two greatest inventions have been our political system and our national literature, and they were created out of the wisdom and richness and imagination and variety by which we were once characterized, and of which it is time we were reminded. And the two inventions are connected: liberalism is the air which most writers breathe, even those who have never heard of it, it is the flowering of security and the fruit of liberty; its tolerance, humanity, dignity and hopefulness forms the only virtues worth learning from the intolerance, inhumanity, indignity and despair of tyranny and war. It is a philosophy, a state of mind in which Montaigne was confirmed by the wars of religion and Voltaire by Bourbon despotism— the calm broad reach which awaits the few who successfully navigate the rapids of passion.

March 1943.

ACKERMANN'S ENGLAND

THE GREAT DICTATOR WAS GROWING OLD: FOR THIRTY YEARS
he had enforced his will on England, welding his people into
as many shapes as a ship's steward can fold napkins. They
had bled in wars, they had perished from overwork, they had
performed like a well-drilled guard of honour, but in spite of
their inexhaustible servility, their boundless capacity for
suffering, they were not really happy; the birth-rate went
steadily down. Boredom suffused the mind of the great
Dictator like a galloping dermatitis. On such days there was
only one man whom he could bear to see, Lord Cavalcade, his
maître des plaisirs.

The vizir entered in the uniform of an Admiral of the Blue.
"Noel, I gottem again." "Oh, bad luck, sir!" "It's the
British people. — them! What can I do with 'em now?"
Sir Noel also was a prey at times to ennui. I'll risk it, he
thought. "There is one experiment you have never made, sir.
War, pestilence, famine, the eighty-hour week—all that's old
stuff. Have you ever thought of Beauty?" "Wodgermean?"
"This island once had a reputation for being beautiful—
unspoilt scenery, eighteenth-century towns, lovely villages,
Elizabethan manors—the clean fresh England of the Georgian
aquatints." "Aquatints?" Sir Noel showed him one.
"Righto," said the Dictator. "I'll try anything once. Go
ahead. What'll you need?" "A handful of artists and absolute
power for a year." "You have it—Karblonsh." The Dictator
reflected. "Arfamo, what about the International aspic?
Will the Empire mind?" "The Empire now consists of Libya,
Abyssinia, the Beach-head, and, somewhere in the Indian
Ocean, Rodd Island; I think we can take their consent for
granted." "And the Big Two?" "They won't interfere.
Too busy with the Tunnel." The Tunnel, begun simultaneously from Duluth (Iowa) and Krasnoyarsk, was to provide
a rocket route from North America to Siberia, through the
centre of the earth itself, and so lessen the congestion in the air.

"A triumph of global engineering which will put the Tundra in direct communication with the Dust-Bowl," said Sir Noel with his famous dead pan. But the Dictator was already napping.

Cavalcade at once got to work. He combed the mines and labour camps for a few surviving artists and men of taste; advisers and civil servants in the ill-starred governments of Butlin and Beveridge. With great secrecy, in spite of cynical comment from the envious Chief of Police, some Betjemanites were let out; long-haired, red-eyed intractable prisoners who remembered Grigson and who had marched with Piper. When the conditions of their release were explained to them a look of incredulous fanaticism filled their eyes. "Betch" would be revenged at last!

That night the wireless gave out the terrible announcement: "Are guilty: every house built since 1840, and all those who live in them. Commissioners will examine as from to-day any doubtful cases and all such houses will be destroyed within one calendar month. This order applies as well to all towns built since 1840, and only houses with proven aesthetic qualities, airports, and factories connected with essential services are exempt." The television screen threw up the picture of a wild-eyed screaming announcer which the listeners, though it was a breach of regulations, were quick to eliminate. That week the Regional Commissioners began their work. Scarborough was spared because of its associations with the Sitwells, Wigan with Orwell, but the Commissioner for Southern England was an extreme Betjemanite who remembered the Master's curse on Slough, the closing down of the Barnstaple-Lynmouth light railway, and other sacrileges. He refused to spare Reading for the sake of Wilde and Rimbaud, Bournemouth for Verlaine, or even Westward Ho for the sake of Kipling and Tarka the Otter. Middle-aged veterans of the Fourth Great War were called up from their second-hand businesses and preparatory schools; joyfully they saw their "kites" again and briefing officers for the Southern Zone showed them their "piece of cake," "Bournemouth! What a target!" Swindon—Woking—Southampton—Brighton—"Except for the Front"—

and that slab of grimy South Wales smeared on the edge of Exmoor—sunny Ilfracombe! "Wizard," they shouted, "for England, Home and Beauty."

In spite of such threats the British were unexpectedly stubborn and only a few obeyed the order to leave their homes and take up temporary quarters in luxury liners, mystery cruisers, and pre-1840 gaols and mental institutions in "safe" areas like Bath, Clovelly, Burford, and King's Lynn. The Corporation of Bournemouth made a pathetic appeal for their city "so fond of music—so careful of the Chines." Macaulay's praises saved a large part of Torquay, and London received the special privilege of keeping its buildings up to 1860. In the Tudor hotels, pubs and road-houses, half-timbered resorts for the half-plastered, false optimism reigned. "They won't do anything to us—besides, the warming-pans are genuine." A month later the Commissioners acted. Bombs fell day and night on Bournemouth and Brighton, Southampton and Slough, Reading and Woking, Ilfracombe, Paignton, Weston-super-Mare; avenue by avenue, terrace by terrace, grove by grove. The Dictator panted into the microphone: "If you bastards ain't beautiful we're going to bomb you until you bloody well are." The American papers almost forgot the Tunnel. "Merry England gets a facial," they screamed, and then fell to speculating, as before, on how the immense energy below the earth's crust should best be employed.

After a year's hard bombing all the post-1840 towns had disappeared from the map. Aldershot and Camberley were open heath, Southampton a small winter resort; the New Forest ponies grazed over Bournemouth; Slough was a haunt of the great crested grebe, Woking a sandy birch-forest, and our sea coast an unspoilt wilderness. The red deer roamed over Ilfracombe and the scholar-gipsy was seen again in Oxford. Country houses had now been deprived of their Victorian additions, and the landscape of England was revealed in all its planned untidiness as if it were an eighteenth-century noble-man's deer-park. "I wonder if we shouldn't have gone back to Rufus," said the Dictator. "Why?" asked Lord Cavalcade. "This is authentic enough. Except for the 'planes, the telegraph poles, the war memorials, the pylons, the arterial roads, the airports and the essential factories, we are back in Ackermann's England: this is our country as it was meant to be." He was circling slowly round in the Dictator's helicopter. "Look at that wide curving street with the pale green and cream Georgian houses and the fields beyond—that is a country town— it used to be 'town country' a year ago. And that village there with its warm church tower, and its golden manor—breath-taking! and those downs without a house on them—what a skyline!—and over there where those two old mussel-gatherers are walking—that used to be the Palace Pier! This is the country that Blake and Jane Austen loved, where Constable and Samuel Palmer painted, where Cobbett rode and Dr. Syntax ambled, an agricultural island with a few local industries —there is the lace factory at Tiverton. It's as lovely in this long May sunset as it has ever been." "All the same," grumbled the Dictator, "there's something wrong. It's the people. — them." "Yes, you're right": the Chief of Police, the third occupant of the plane, was speaking. "It's the people. You forgot about them. What made Regency England, 1840 England, so beautiful? I will tell you. Its architecture represented its beliefs. It believed in itself and in its harmonious relation to Nature: the population was neither large nor small, the ecology was correct. Our Georgian architecture, so graceful, so classical, so airy, was the last vision of humanism. And the nation was young: its beauty was in its power, in its hope, in its prospects, in its magnificent role as arbiter of the nineteenth century which lay ahead. What prospects have these people got? More than half of them are over fifty: in the casualties (though reduced of course to a minimum by precision bombing) another three million have perished. Those who survive believe in nothing except nicotine and alcohol. Of what use to them are town halls and churches? The architecture of a culture is the outward expression of its spiritual health." "You talk like a Betje-manite," said the Dictator. "Come down a little lower then." The helicopter descended over the blistered ruins of Brighton. Crowds were bustling about like ants. Tiny posters could be seen: "Acacia Avenue." "Ready soon." "Desirable residence." "Old Tudor Teas." "Nell Gwynne's cottage." "Balmoral." "Kosy Kar-wash Kafé." "Madame Desdemona, clairvoyante." Mysterious bubbling noises came from the centre of the crowd. "My God," cried Cavalcade. "They've got hold of a concrete-mixer." A new hoarding faced them: "Buy now." "Site for Bungalow Town."

The Dictator was speechless. The helicopter returned to Downing Street. "Blast the whole bloody lot." Cavalcade felt for certain that his last moment had come. "Still, it was fun while it lasted," he ventured. "— you," replied his master. "Three million lives—we can ill afford them," remarked the Police Chief. "Eddication—that's what them bastards need. Why in hell didn't you think of it, Admiral?" roared the Dictator, his face mottled with anger. "You'd better go back to jug with the Betjemanites." But a message was handed in. "Terrible explosion of natural gas. Tunnel wrecked. Twelve million workers buried." The Dictator smiled again. "Never mind, Noel," he grunted. "It seems we all make mistakes."

Lord Cavalcade backed out. Once safely in the passage he put on his cocked hat, took a quick look at himself in the glass, straightened up to his reflection, and saluted. His sword clattered as he marched briskly down the ceremonial stairs.

May 1944.

SPRING REVOLUTION

THE BOREDOM OF TRAVEL! THERE IS AN ACUTE CONDITION which develops in enforced lulls before the wholesome drudgery of getting from place to place makes a brute of one again. If you knew how bored we were in Athens! Stagnation and self-disgust engender a low fever that lays waste the curiosity and resolution which might have cured them. The weather was too bad to go anywhere, and the nearest sun was in Egypt. Sleeping late to shorten the day, one went to the window and found the Acropolis and the Parthenon blocking the horizon. A thing of beauty, that is a joy once or twice, and afterwards a standing reproach. Downstairs it would be nearly lunch-time. In the bar, which was an embottled corridor smelling of gin and Gold Flake, the Greek business men jollied each other up in cinema American and Trocadero English. The sombre dining-room was like the Dickensian coffee-room of a Midland hotel. The French dishes all tasted the same, like food on a liner; the Greek joints seemed made of sweetened gelatine. Coffee was served in the lounge amid the engineering papers, and snatches of conversations.

"I hope you are never troubled by the green-eyed monster."

"Pliss, Mr. Insull?"

"Why, you know what the green-eyed monster is! Jealousy!"

"O yais, Mr. Insull, Pliss?"

A walk in the afternoon. Tram-lines, blocks of yellow houses, demolition, everywhere the metamorphosis of a tenth-rate Turkish market town into a tenth-rate Californian suburb. A pause in the book-shop where one must choose between expensive art-books on the Acropolis and diseases of the stomach, or sixpenny editions of Edgar Wallace and Wilhelm Meister. There were also the newspapers, and glancing at them phrases would enter with a little stab and begin to fester. "Ruskin, one felt, would have disapproved," "wherein promise and achievement touch hands very agreeably," and "Bébé is painting a portrait of Baba." Before the gossip-writer's ingenious vulgarities I would gape like a mesmerized chicken.

In the hotel *thé dansant* will have begun. A hundred bearded ladies have brought their black little daughters. The ballroom reeks with stale flowers and cheap scent. All the tables are taken. The fathers in spats and clean collars try to eradicate from their faces the expression which forty years of Levantine practices have implanted. The mothers employ the vocabulary of the underworld of elegance. "Très réussi . . . convenable . . . on aura dit . . . ça se remarque." The daughters fidget. The young men attempt polish. All move in the psychologist's wonderland which is revealed to us when we watch charmless people trying to be charming.

At dinner a piano and a violin play evening music, with *Peer Gynt*, *Rosamund*, *Chansons sans Paroles*, *Toselli*, wistful and gallant compositions that empty over one all the slops of capitalist sentiment. Afterwards, there are the cinemas with wooden seats and German films unknown to the Academy, and a few places for supper. In Greek cabarets one is not allowed to sit with a woman unless one has champagne. The sexes are therefore divided on opposite sides of the floor. If a young man dances with a "hostess" he scurries back at the finish like a male spider trying to escape from the nuptial embrace before he is eaten. The girls are sulky, the whisky tastes of sawdust. Back in the hotel there are mosquitoes in February, and, four days old, the Continental *Daily Mail*. This day, repeated ten times, was typical of Athens. As boredom gathered momentum one felt all the ingredients of personality gurgling away like the last inch of bathwater. One became a carcase of nonentity and indecision, a reflection to be avoided in mirrors. Why go abroad? Why travel? Why exchange the regard of a clique for the stare of a concierge?

On the day of the elections the sun was shining. It was one of those Sundays in early spring when there is an air of displacement. A sensation of keels lifting from the mud, of new skin, and of new acquaintances. We motored to Kephissia for lunch. The butter was good. Refugees paraded about in their hideous best, and gramophones were playing in Tatoi.

At Hagios Mercurios we looked down over the plain to the blue lake of the Aegean, Chalcis, Eretria, and the snows and forests of Euboea. In the wet weather we could not conceive a reason for being here, in this moment it became impossible to imagine being anywhere else.

When we got back to Athens everybody had voted. The bars and cinemas were closed, and in the restaurant wine was served from teapots and drunk in cups as in an old-fashioned speakeasy. Crowds cheered. Venizelos was sweeping the polls. "The best thing for the country." As in all companies where politics are discussed, to compensate the dullness of the subject one began to feel an illusion of far-sightedness and worldly wisdom.

Next morning the town was quiet. I was particularly annoyed to find an antique shop closed, and tried to get the concierge to rout up the missing proprietor. Down the empty street moved a kind of grey Noah's Ark on wheels. At the English tailor's we heard the news. Venizelos had lost the election. Tsaldaris, the head of the Royalist-Popular party, was in, but he and all his colleagues had been put in prison. There had been a revolution in Macedonia. The shops were closing and the proprietors of travel agencies stood in the doors with the keys in their hands. Lorries of mud-coloured soldiers passed down the street distributing handbills. Martial law was proclaimed, newspapers suppressed, groups of people shot at sight, by order of the Chief of the revolution, Plastiras. By lunch-time it was accepted that we were under a dictatorship. All the *plats du jour* were "off," and we bawled out the head waiter. An aeroplane flew over, dropping pamphlets in which Plastiras described the collapse of parliamentary government. Rumours collected. "Plastiras was a Venizelist." "He was going to cancel the elections and keep Venizelos in office." "He was not a Venizelist and was going to govern by himself." I walked down the University boulevard. It was warm and sunny. A straggling crowd that was moving about suddenly thickened and made way for two archaic fire-engines, whose hoses were playing over it. The smell of wet earth followed their path through the sunshine. Everybody laughed and teased the soldiers on the engines, who laughed back at them. The crowd began to cheer a motor-car from which a very ugly man waved his arms, and to follow it up the avenue clapping; with them went the police and the fire-engines. One could not tell if they were shouting Tsaldaris or Plastiras. In the hotel we received more explanations. "Plastiras was in prison. It had all been done very quietly. Venizelos and Tsaldaris had arranged it with the President of the Republic. The soldiers had fraternized. The dictatorship was a wash-out. General Condylis had flown last night to Athens from Salonica. Plastiras had taken him prisoner, but he had escaped and was marching with his army from Thebes on Athens. To-night there would be a big battle as Condylis wished to avenge Plastiras' execution of the Cabinet in 1922."

We went out again. "Tsaldaris" was being shouted everywhere. There were still crowds in the boulevard, but suddenly down a side street we saw a ragged collection of men marching with staves in their hands, on many of which the olive leaves still remained. Some carried only small untrimmed branches. They looked like a woodcut of Jack Cade's rebellion from a child's history-book. It was at this moment that we heard the rattle of machine-guns. Everyone ran giggling into doorways. "They're only blank, of course," was said knowingly. Turning into Stadium Street some soldiers rushed up to us pointing down and crying, "Katô, Katô." The machine-guns began again.

The street, in normal times so straight and dull, became an enormous affair of shadows and relief, of embrasures and exposed spaces. The kiosk at the corner seemed as far away as it would to a baby who could just walk, or to a very lame old man. As we ran round the corner volleys seemed to come from every direction. People threw themselves flat on the ground and hid behind trees. The Noah's Ark passed down the end of the street with the snouts of machine-guns thrusting from the wooden windows. We came to a little restaurant where we had dined the day before. The crowd surged on the steps and the doors were barricaded, but when they recognized us we were let in. In the falling night more men with staves could be seen from the balcony. A small cannon boomed at intervals and shook the windows. A man was helped along with a bleeding arm. While one-half of my brain dealt in realities—"revolution, street fighting, baptism of fire"—the other continued to function as if nothing had happened, and remembering that a friend was coming for a cocktail, I insisted on trying to telephone to the hotel that we should be a little late. The wires were cut, but if we went back directly we should still be in time for him. From the balcony we saw a crowd collecting at the foot of the University. A man ran up the steps waving something. A machine-gun rattled, the crowd fell apart, and he was revealed lying in a growing pool of blood and brains. An ambulance bell sounded and a man with a woman in a mink coat walked down the middle of the street from the other side. Slipping out, we made our way round by narrow alleys and crossed the Place de la Constitution in the yellow dusk. We reached the side entrance to the Grande Bretagne. It was heavily barricaded. We knocked and rang, when another crowd of people surged round the corner and up the steps. There was a sudden feeling of complete hopelessness and panic. After the crowd, turning elaborately, glided the armoured car. What had once seemed comic and antediluvian was now implacable and fatal. The machine-guns pointed straight at us; a fat woman tried to turn us out from behind a pillar where we were, but we quickly shoved her away. The car passed without firing and we got round to the other entrance. Inside the hotel all was cheerfulness and commotion; everyone felt important and with a reason for living. We dined in a large party which included several people whom we had avoided for weeks, and retired upstairs with a gramophone and a bottle of whisky. The inevitable business man explained everything. "Plastiras was master of the situation. He was a patriot. He would force a coalition between Venizelos and Tsaldaris. The latter's victory was illegal because he had promised the refugees bonuses which he hadn't got." "Plasiras does not play," he said with admiration. "He knows his head is at stake. If he fails he will shoot himself. He had eight officers shot who tried to arrest him. General Condylis was locked up. He sent him a telegram signed 'Tsaldaris' telling him to fly to Athens. When he landed he took him prisoner. There would be no battle. The army was with him. It was the best thing that could happen for Greece." Outside, the night was dark and cold; a few small tanks patrolled the streets. From the balcony of the palace machine-guns looked down. In previous volleys the armoured car had chipped bits off the masonry along the front of the hotel. All was quiet, and with the cessation of firing people began to experience the anti-climax and grow irritable. One wondered why one was cooped up with the tiresome business man; · with the young Frenchman and his crisp platitudes; with the "clergyman's daughter" chorus-girl of dubious status, who was explaining why she would 'never have a lady-dog in the house.' Everyone separated, secretly hoping for the roar of Condylis' artillery.

Next morning we were woken by the noise of trams. There were no guns trained from the palace. Newspapers arrived. The shops were open, and of the day before nothing remained but the pool of wet blood by the University, surrounded by gaping students. At a time when Plastiras was supposed to be master of the situation, he had surrendered to the eight generals who commanded the rest of the army for Venizelos under Zaimis and Tsaldaris.

The dictatorship was over, and had been over since eight o'clock the night before. Plastiras had seized the government with only one regiment; his party had repudiated him. Whether a patriot or a power-grabber, he was ridiculous. He had wounded thirty-three people, killed one, and cured two or three discontented pleasure-seekers of a curious stoppage of the sensibility to which they had fallen victim. They, while secretly admitting the futility of the eye-witness, the meaninglessness and stupidity of all that had happened, knew also that they had. tasted the intoxication and the prestige of action, and were soon rearranging the events of the day on a scale, and in an order, more worthy of the emotions which had been generated by them.

March 1933.

BARCELONA

I

THE FIRST THING ONE NOTICES ABOUT GOING TO BARCELONA IS the peculiar meaningful handshakes of one's friends. Accompanied though they are by some such phrase as "I wish I were going too," one cannot avoid detecting in the farewell a moment of undertaker heartiness, of mortuary appraisal. In the early morning among the lagoons, the brown landscape and rainy sky of Languedoc, one begins to share it, only at the Spanish frontier does it completely disappear. As a rule, the change from Cerbère to Port Bou is one from gaiety and comfort to gloom and emptiness; to-day it is the Spanish end which is alive. The first thing one notices is the posters, extremely competent propaganda, of which that of a peasant's rope-soled foot descending on a cracked swastika in a cobbled street is the most dramatic. The frontier is guarded by cultivated German and Italian anti-Fascists, and one begins at once those discussions on political ideology which are such a feature of present-day republican Spain. "You journalists are the worst enemies of a revolution," explained the Italian, "you all come here with letters like yours; then you go back and write Right-wing propaganda about us." "Why can't you admit that England is not prepared to help any democracy until its rearmament is carried out, when it will be too late?" said the other. Down in the little harbour the militiamen, in their blue uniforms and forage caps, were fishing with bits of starfish. The sombre Spanish train had been painted all along the carriages with crude pictures of troops departing and with harvests being gathered. As it drew out into the autumn sunshine one first became conscious of the extraordinary mixture of patriotic war-fever and revolutionary faith, and of that absolutely new and all-pervading sense of moral elevation which since the revolution is the most dominating note in Catalonia. For here one never says "since the military rebellion," "since the Fascist revolt," but simply "since the Revolution" or "since the 19th of July." At the end of the train were two carriages of Anarchist troops, mostly under twenty, who waved their black and red banners, pointed their rifles at one, and in return for some cigarettes burst into a shout which was taken up all down the train of "Viva la Revolucion."

It is in Barcelona that the full force of the Anarchist revolution becomes apparent. Their initials, C.N.T. and F.A.I., are everywhere. They have taken over all the hotels, restaurants, cafés, trains, taxis, and means of communication, as well as all theatres, cinemas, and places of amusement. Their first act was to abolish the tip as being incompatible with the dignity of those who receive it, and to attempt to give one is the only act, short of making the Fascist salute, for which a foreigner can be disliked.

Spanish Anarchism is a doctrine which has gone through three stages. The first was the conception of pure anarchy which grew out of the writings of Rousseau, Proudhon, Godwin, and to a lesser extent of Diderot and Tolstoy. The essence of this Anarchist faith is that there exists in mankind a natural trend towards nobility and dignity; human relations based on a love of liberty combined with a desire to help each other (as shown, for instance, in the mutual generosity of the poor in slum districts in cases of sickness and distress) should in themselves be enough, given education and the right economic conditions, to provide a working basis for people to live on; State interference, armies, property, would be superfluous as they were to the early Christians. The Anarchist paradise would be one in which the instincts towards freedom, justice, intelligence, and *bondad* in the human race develop gradually to the exclusion of all thoughts of personal gain, envy, and malice. But there exist two stumbling-blocks to this ideal— the desire to make money and the desire to acquire power. Everybody who makes money or acquires power, according to the Anarchists, does so to the detriment of himself and at the expense of other people, and as long as these instincts are allowed a free run there will always be war, tyranny, and exploitation. Power and money must therefore be abolished altogether. At this point the second stage of Anarchism begins, that which arises from the thought of Bakunin, the contemporary of Marx. He added the rider that the only way to abolish power and money was by direct action on the bourgeoisie in whom these instincts were incurably ingrained, and who took advantage of all liberal legislation, all concessions from the workers, to get more power and more money for themselves. "The rich will do everything for the poor but get off their backs," Tolstoy has said. "Then they must be blown off," might have been Bakunin's corollary. From this time (the 'eighties) dates militant Anarchism with its crimes of violence and assassination. In most of its strongholds, Italy, Germany, Russia, it was either destroyed by Fascism or absorbed by Communism, which has usually seemed more practical, realizable, and adaptable to industrial countries; but in Spain the innate love of individual freedom, a personal dignity of the people, made them prefer it to Russian Communism, and the persecution which it underwent was never sufficient to blot it out. Finally, in the last few years it has gone through a third transformation; in spite of its mystical appeal to the heart, Anarchism has always been an elastic and adaptable faith, and looking round for a suitable machinery to replace State centralization it found syndicalism, to which it is now united. Syndicalism is a system of vertical rather than horizontal Trade Unions, by which, for instance, all the workers on a newspaper, editors, reviewers, printers, and distributors, would delegate members to a syndicate which would negotiate with other syndicates for the housing, feeding, amusements, etc., of the whole body. This anarcho-syndicalism through its organ, the C.N.T., has been able to get control of all the industries and agriculture of Catalonia and of most of those in Andalusia, Valencia, and Murcia, forming a more or less solid block from Malaga to the French frontier, with considerable power also in the Asturias and Madrid. The executive militant spearhead of the body is the Federacion Anarquistica Iberica, usually pronounced as one word, *FAI*, which, partly owing to acts of terrorism, partly to its former illegality, to-day is clothed in mystery. It is almost impossible to find out who and how many belong to it.

The ideal of the C.N.T. and the F.A.I. is libertarian Communism, a Spain in which both work and wealth are shared by all, about three hours' work a day being enough to entitle anyone to sufficient food, clothing, education, amusement, transport, and medical attention. It differs from Communism because there must be no centralization, no bureaucracy, and no leaders; if somebody does not want to do something, the Anarchists argue, no good will come of making him. They often point to Stalin's dictatorship as an example of the evils inherent in Communism. The danger of Anarchism, one might argue, is that it has become such a revolutionary weapon that it may never know what to do with the golden age when it has it, and may exhaust itself in a perpetual series of counter-revolutions. Yet it should be an ideal not unsympathetic to the English, who have always honoured freedom and individual eccentricity and whose liberalism and whiggery might well have turned to something very similar had they been harassed for centuries, like the Spanish proletariat, by absolute monarchs, militant clergy, army dictatorships, and absentee landlords.

Life in Barcelona begins very early—that is to say in the small hours, when the cocks begin crowing, as in the tropics, and batches of the sixteen thousand reinforcements start leaving for Madrid. Later, after breakfast, it is good to walk down the Ramblas while the sun beats warmly through the wet planes and shines on the long rows of flower-stalls, covered with roses, lilies, violets, and tuberoses, till one reaches the harbour. Most of the houses bear banners and initials; "We have too many banderas" is a common saying. There is the red and black of the F.A.I. and C.N.T., the red with joined hands of the U.G.T. (Caballero Socialists), the hammer and sickle of the Catalan Communists, the separatist flag of Catalonia, and that of the Trotskyist P.O.U.M. Gradually one learns to differentiate between the faces; where there used to be the inevitable couple of priests mumbling about pesetas, or the business men in their wicker armchairs, one learns to recognize the U.G.T. type of pleasant and intelligent young Socialist, the restaurant-manager or head-waiter face (Right-wing, Besteiro or Prieto Socialist), and the types of the C.N.T. and F.A.I. The C.N.T., since it contains a great many Murcians and also appeals to all the thorough-going have-nots, includes the most alarming of the faces met with in Barcelona and also most of the young militia-women. Among the F.A.I. is to be found the pure Anarchist type, the long head with high brow and thin nose, enlivened by the mixture of mysticism with revolutionary energy which is so characteristic. These are the men who saved Barcelona, who destroyed a whole military division within twelve hours and rushed a battery planted in the Paseo de Gracias in open cars armed only with kitchen knives. Along the Ramblas are booths selling the local newspapers (no others are obtainable) together with photographs of Marx, Lenin, Kropotkin, and the chiefs of Anarchist columns, Santillan, Ascaso, Durruti.

An English journalist, chiefly on account of our non-intervention policy and the Fascist propaganda of our newspapers (headed by the ghoulish *Daily Mail*), is not a popular figure. The Spaniards do not understand non-intervention, nor why it should be harder for Madrid and Barcelona to get arms than for Burgos and Seville. They consider that the battle between the democracies and the tyrannies of the world is being fought out by them on their soil, and are inclined to ask if we think they would refuse an English Labour Government arms, supposing the English Fascists to be attacking London with Indian troops.

In the afternoons one can wander about the old town or the harbour or the crowded patios and the Generalidad or the park with its zoo, or up in the gardens of the Montjuich where the Exhibition used to be. The churches are mostly locked and blackened, like our city churches; the Sagrada Familia has been destroyed except for its extraordinary front, whose two vast towers now stand up like a radio-station. I was five days in Barcelona and only once was stopped for my papers, and that was on the way up to the military post on the Tibidabo. When I told the Anarchist guards I wanted to look at the view they let me proceed. One could walk about the patios of the Generalidad or into the actual rooms of the Anarchist building quite freely, nor did I ever come across any kind of rowdiness or even hear a shot fired. Yet the American residents have to report three times a day to their consul to show they are

still alive, and there are rumours of some English living in a
kind of compound down by the sea. At night the Ramblas
become a huge milling crowd of people, radios blare out, cafés
fill up. The streets are very badly lit and acquire a rather
sinister war-time aspect. Small things bring home the civil war,
like the restaurant menus, where all dishes including food
from enemy parts of the country (sea food from the Atlantic,
butter and mutton from the West) are struck off, and the notices
in every room about air raids. The cinemas are all open,
showing *Top-Hat* and a gruesome Anarchist film of the storming
of Sietamo. Afterwards there is the café of the Oriente. It is
huge and badly lit; three enormous coffee-machines glitter
in the darkness and there is a counter which sells cakes and
sausages. It is used almost entirely by men and women of
the militia, who clank their rifles up against the bar. It is sitting
there at night that one gets the completest picture of the world's
youngest nation, Anarchist Catalonia, fighting its first war.
A man will begin to talk about the siege of Madrid, show one
his Anarchist permit, explain how he drives a lorry there every
week, hand one an enormous revolver to look at, and suddenly
pay for any drinks one has had before his appearance. "Look
here. You can't pay for that whisky, I had it before you came."
"But I feel like it; besides, what's money anyhow? We shall
soon have abolished all that." "Very well then, you must have
one with me." "But I don't want to have one with you, why
should I have to have a drink with you because I give you one?
It is not dignified or logical—next year, perhaps, you will give
me a drink; you do not understand our Anarchist principles,"
and he goes out to his lorry. After one o'clock the streets are
deserted and silent except for the screech of the brakes of the
vigilant patrols as they tear down the Ramblas or face each
other suddenly at corners.

One thing that is perfectly clear, after seeing Barcelona, is
that, in any ultimate sense, it cannot be conquered. Catalonia,
unlike the rest of Republican Spain, is a compact country; its
language frontiers are now its class frontiers, and the whole
population of the Eastern coast, so rich in industry and man-
power, are now racially and politically solid. These provinces

could also much more easily attain unity of command. President Companys is a figure of enormous power and prestige who works in co-ordination with the now combined forces of the C.N.T. and U.G.T. There are six hundred thousand Anarchists in Catalonia, and they have already, without outside help, the organization and determination necessary. A Spanish Fascist in Paris has declared: "There are two million people in Spain we have to get rid of, and we have already accounted for five hundred thousand." He will find he has miscounted. It is much more interesting to speculate what will happen afterwards, when the victorious Anarchists wish to abolish the State, and the victorious Socialists to preserve it. While everybody, including the Anarchists, prophesied another civil war, it now seems possible that it can be avoided. The Coalition between the two parties is working well and they may be able to divide up Spain in such a way that the Anarchists recognize a highly decentralized government as a necessary *étape* on the road to its complete disappearance, or they may themselves become corrupted.

I fear I have written all this and still not explained the feeling one gets in this city. The pervading sense of freedom, of intelligence, justice, and companionship, the enormous upthrust in backward and penniless people of the desire for liberty and education, are things that have to be seen to be understood. It is as if the masses, the mob in fact, credited usually only with instincts of stupidity and persecution, should blossom into what is really a kind of flowering of humanity. We are used to processions in London, either State or dismal affairs of policemen and mackintoshes, but round the procession in Barcelona on Sunday there were no police. Two hundred thousand people marched by in the sunshine—Anarchists, Socialists, Communists, Federalists in their brown and green with their bands playing nostalgic sardanas, foresters with their axes, peasants with their hoes, nurses, children, regiments of militia-girls, all singing and watched over by a few stewards with badges. They took five hours to pass. Anyone who could see this could see that here was something which it would be an unimaginable piece of human malignity to destroy, which it would, indeed, be impossible to destroy; for such a movement can only go underground, as it has gone in Seville and Saragossa, to reappear in some Sicilian Vespers with a bitterness that is now lacking. Meanwhile we must learn to sit quiet and practise non-intervention, an arrangement by which every democracy is allowed to remain in the privacy of its own burrow, awaiting the visit of the stoats.

*   *   *

II

Coming back to Spain, with the papers full of the threatened bombardment of Barcelona, the rain falling all day, the passengers thinning out after Perpignan, one had a certain apprehension. Everything about the country had assumed a war-time aspect. "Militians! Not a word to your brother, not a word to your sweetheart about your positions!" read one notice, and the familiar "les oreilles ennemies vous écoutent" had made its appearance. Other slogans warned people against wasting time in the café or the brothel. "Are you doing your bit?" one felt, was near at hand. The vast influx of refugees from Madrid had made an appreciable dent in the food supply. Sunday was a day of impressive gloom marked by the funeral of Durruti.

Why did half a million people turn out in the rain on this occasion, marching in silence twenty-five abreast, climbing up trees, crowding the windows to see this man's coffin carried on its six-hour journey by the pall-bearers? Why did the car bringing his body from Madrid have to speed through the villages in the small hours to avoid the lorry-loads of waiting flowers which there would be no time to fetch? It seemed that if one could get the answer, penetrating beneath the verbose eulogies, one would understand something of the Spanish revolution.

Durruti was born in 1896 in Leon. He came to Barcelona in his teens, and was already a metal-worker and a militant Anarchist. There he met his two lifelong friends, Ascaso and García Oliver. Ascaso had been a baker and a café waiter in Saragossa. Both had been in sufficient strikes and other activities to have had to leave Spain by 1917. They wênt to the Argentine, where they started an Anarchist organization and were accused of holding up a bank. They wandered through Chile, Peru, Brazil, and found their way to Paris, where Durruti went back to his steel-work after having had to live in the woods of the Dordogne on mushrooms. In Paris, after the Argentine had made an unsuccessful attempt to extradite them and enforce the death-sentence, they founded a book-shop called the Librairie Internationale, and, with García Oliver, an anti-monarchist newspaper which was smuggled into Spain. They were accused of an attempt on Alfonso and imprisoned in the Conciergerie (Durruti had Marie Antoinette's cell). They were released and went to Belgium, whence they were expelled into Germany and back again, at one moment having to camp out on the International bridge. Finally they returned to Spain, where they were imprisoned, released, and imprisoned again for their activities in the general strike in Saragossa. Their friends broke into the Archives and destroyed the dossier of the case.

When the 6th of October revolution collapsed in Barcelona they were imprisoned for nearly a year in Valencia. When the Fascists, who had left their garrisons in the small hours of July 19th, were defeated in the Plaza de Cataluña, the Anarchists, led by Durruti and Ascaso, went down the Ramblas to the Plaza de Colon. On the top platform of the column, sheltered by Columbus himself, two machine-gunners were firing on the crowd, and the whole of one side of the square was occupied by the barracks of the Atarazanas. While they were storming these, Ascaso was shot through the heart. He was small, consumptive, with a pale, intelligent face and large dark eyes. To-day there is a monument on the site where he fell, a few yards from the barred windows and gaping walls of the shattered barracks.

Durruti was one of the first to realize the importance of attacking, and led a column up to Aragon. He proved a natural organizer, and his column, on the front of Bujaraloz, became famous as the perfect example of "organized indis-

cipline," that is to say, of a kind of "honour system" by which
the Anarchists, who detest militarism and disapprove of all
orders and words of command, were able to establish a sort
of natural obedience to his wishes. He lived the same life as
his men, accessible to all, going barefoot till all had received
boots, and differentiated only from them by the possession of
a pair of field-glasses. He was put in command of the Catalan
reinforcements sent to Madrid, and was killed while returning
by car from the front by a bullet in the spine, fired from behind,
from the upper window of a deserted villa. His last words
were "se me para el corazon," though he had previously said
that he could never regret dying now, for he had lived, in the
last three months, through what had been the dream of every
revolutionary for centuries. He was a rugged, lion-like man,
possessed of natural intelligence and reckless courage, capable
of complete devotion to his ideals of "madre anarquia" and
to the people who shared them, and of equally untiring energy
in using direct action against the capitalists who didn't. His
gift of leadership made him an extreme danger to the Fascists
(who had already shot his mother), and his death made him a
revolutionary martyr, a symbol to all the parties of the Left
of the sacrifices they would have to make and the privations
they would have to undergo. His mammoth funeral ("no
king could have a better," said an Anarchist to me) was not only
a tribute to him but an act of defiance to the enemy.

A week later I went to see the coffin moved from a vault to
its ultimate grave. The cemetery of Barcelona is one of the
most beautiful in the world. It lies on the western slope of the
Montjuich, and to get there one has to skirt the gloomy fortress
whose cells were so often full of Durruti's comrades and in
whose trenches they were shot. The cemetery is laid out in
rocky terraces planted with groves of cypress, pepper, and
eucalyptus. On the extreme edge, overlooking the *huerta*
and the sea, they had made a grave for Durruti and another
for Ascaso, beside a third, that of the unfortunate Ferrer y
Guardia, the old gentleman who was shot in 1909 for attempting
to introduce secular education into Catalonia. This time it
was a very small crowd; the sextons were incompetent at

getting the huge coffin into the grave; they talked and asked advice, the others stood about smoking or watching the winter sunset. When it was lowered, a soldier laid the black and red Anarchist flag over it and said, "We, the German soldiers serving in your column, will not forget you. Salud! Kamerad."

*   *   *

"Yes. I like New York best—ever been to Rockaway Beach? That's where I like in summer; my girl and I go out there with a bottle of whisky or we go to the movies, Ginger Rogers, Laurel and Hardy. Look at the orange groves—we must be getting into Castellon. I wish this full moon would be over. Marlene Dietrich in *Desire*—there was a good film now. They turn all the lights out in the train here and we must go on in the dark. They'll give us candles in the restaurant car. Well, I dunno. I dunno. Of course, I think we're right, but maybe you ought to go in on the other side and see what they're thinking. I only know I got seven bullets in this gun and the last one's for myself. Jus' now the planes come two or three times a week to Cartagena; where I live is about 5 kilometres out when I'm not on the ship. I hear them come over in the night. Brrrr. Zoooom! Then they drop them. There's nothing you can do but stay in bed. Then if they get you, well, bad luck! The only safe place is in a field. You see, these bombs don't explode when they strike; they have a time-fuse in the end that rotates, and when they fall in a field the earth stops it rotating. That's why they go through eight stories of a house and don't explode till they get to the bottom, and the *refugios* are not much good. We have no Metro in Valencia or Cartagena. If you go out you get hit by glass or by anti-aircraft bullets or by a Fascist from a window. That's why I carry this. You see, the anti-aircraft is not much good. They can light up all over Cartagena with searchlights and when the planes are in the lights they can fire, but when the planes fly high above the lights it is no good. And when they fly very low they lose their heads and it is no good either. And often they send over one plane with lights and the gunners all fire at that while the bombers are somewhere else. I dunno.

They do terrible things. We all do terrible things. Since we had the Prison Ship nobody eats fish any more in Cartagena."

The candles gutter in the restaurant car. The sailor looks out of the window at the laden orange trees, the sea breaking on nameless coves in the moonlight. He has a small, brittle face and a sensual mouth, like a lemur. All the other tables are taken by Anarchist militia on their way from the front at Barbastro to Madrid; they have black and red scarves tied round their heads, and their appearance, by candlelight, is terrifying. They give one cigars which they light from lengths of dynamite fuse. When the ticket-collector appears, the first one asked cries, "I am a Valencian going to Valencia. That is my ticket," and the others applaud him.

Valencia at night is perturbing. Up till ten o'clock lights are allowed. The street lights are painted dark blue and the white houses under them look like something on the moon. At ten o'clock they are all turned out, the town is in darkness; outside many houses and windows are piles of sandbags. By day it rains. The town is noisy and political; it is the seat of the Government, so one sees and hears much more of the official democratic point of view in it and less of the revolutionary one than in Barcelona. This point of view is naturally more pessimistic, for while the workers are fighting to create a new world for themselves, the liberal bourgeoisie whom the original Azaña Government represented are fighting only to preserve something of what they had before. Consequently they are more able to see the extent of the destruction which the Civil War has brought, the ruined towns, the scattered harvests, the decimated population, the acts of violence, the appalling spectacle of a brave race splitting itself into two and by its very bravery (as with the miners outside and the rebels inside Oviedo) prolonging the agony of the internal conflict. There is no defeatism—it is the difference between August 1914 and January 1915, that is all. In the evening, sitting with the sailor and his doctor friend in a music-hall, one is conscious of the gravity of the Civil War for those to whom it is not the dawning of a new day, but the eclipse of an old one. They sit on chairs in a box with their backs to the stage, across which passes, from time to time, an enormous undressed woman singing the same words to the same tune. The doctor is talking of his wife and children whom he has not heard of since July, when they were holidaying in the mountains in what has become rebel territory. "Is there any organization in England for finding out if such people are alive?" The sailor says good-bye. "We are going on to Cartagena now by car. I do not think there will be very much of it left—the planes came last night, while we were on the train, and they were there five hours. Well, I dunno. Maybe I will see you in England or you will come on my ship to New York and I shall be the purser again—but I dunno. If not, it will be bad luck."

*　　　*　　　*

In fact, it would be hard to find an atmosphere more full of envy, intrigue, rumour, and muddle than that which exists at the moment in the capitals of Republican Spain. While Malaga falls and Madrid struggles heroically, the farther one gets from the front, the dimmer grows the memory of the 19th of July, the louder the mutual accusations and reproaches of the parties. They are now even jealous of their one hope, the International Brigade, and it seems useless to clamour for unity of command when there is no one worthy of it. Here are some notes on people's conversations. They will show how many different points of view are permitted.

*　　　*　　　*

A German : "They ask why don't we attack on the Aragon front. I will tell you. I am in the International Column. There are twelve of us alive out of my company, and a hundred out of my battalion. If we do decide to attack it is known to the other side almost before we know ourselves. The Spaniards will not attack at night in any case. We have no artillery, few machine-guns, and obsolete 1870 rifles, old German ones bought from Mexico."

A Hungarian of the P.O.U.M. : "Look at those crowds. Look at those women. It's disgraceful. All bourgeois, bargain-basement people, prampushers. Is this what I'm **fighting** for?

I tell you we are only at the beginning—yes. There will come a day when father will be killed by son and sister by brother, not just at the front, but here in the streets of Barcelona! At least I hope so. But the Spanish people are like this." He lights a match and holds it upwards till it goes out.

A High Official (Catalan Left): "We are all sick of the war in Barcelona. The front is just for people who like fighting, I think. Most people on this side don't know what Communism means, most people on the other don't know what Fascism means. The priests were not Fascist, most of them didn't know about the large sums of money hidden in their churches—only the bishops did—and we got the archbishop out all right. I don't even think Franco is a Fascist."

Another (Catalan Left) : "This is a very interesting revolution, because it is the only Western revolution since 1789—only do not exaggerate it. We have taken over a few large factories and estates, but we have only socialized transport, hotels, cafés, theatres, cinemas, barbers, and boot cleaners—not very much, really. You see, we are a nation of *petits bourgeois* and we have naturally left them exactly as they are —no, I should rather describe our present regime as a 'capitalism without capitalists.'"

English Communist: "But how can one co-operate with these people? The P.O.U.M., of course, are simply Fascists: as for the Anarchists—one can't go bumping people off in 1937! And besides, they're inefficient, anti-militarist, they won't accept officers, they can't keep step. You know Durruti was killed by an Anarchist, they were jealous of his friendship with the Russians: his views were very unpopular. And look at the Aragon front—if the enemy attack they will get to Lerida, and a very good thing too, it will bring people to their senses. That and a stiff bombardment of Barcelona is what we've all been hoping for for two months."

Spanish Communist: "I see no reason why the Anarchists and Communists shouldn't be united. The Anarchists are very simple people, they do not realize how long their ideas must take to put into practice. Their Ministers do—and they often turn into Communists when they realize this."

Anarchist at the "Shanghai": "Anarchism with us is very old, very old indeed, and very international—look at me, I drove a tram at the time of the strike in 1933. I arranged some sabotage, I was an idealist—so I escaped to England, and then Belgium. I knew García Oliver, I drove him eight hours unconscious in my lorry once, after the police had knocked him out. You found him friendly? We of the revolution are like that—besides, who cares about death? A tile might fall on my head at this moment; in any case, to die for an ideal is not death." "But what about being blinded or lamed for an ideal?" "Spain would never forget her sons!" "Would you say there was still a revolution here?" "Don't you worry about the revolution, the F.A.I. will take care of that—nor about Russia—Oliver sleeps in the Russian Embassy, that is the terms we are on. You worry about England and France; it is they who are deceived about where their interests lie. England and Spain, what couldn't we do together, two rich democracies like ours!"

*   *   *

I was able to interview the two men of to-morrow, if there is a to-morrow, in the Spanish Cabinet, Juan García Oliver, the Minister of Justice, and Indalecio Prieto, the Minister of Munitions, Marine, and Air.

*   *   *

Oliver is a man in his thirties, sturdy, good-looking, with one of those stoical, open Iberian faces which reflect the Anarchist blend of idealism and militancy. He was indeed one of the three heroes of the street-fighting in Barcelona. I asked him if the idea of violence was really part of Anarchism or not.

"Certainly not; our ideal is the brotherhood of man. Man first is a beast on four legs, then the family make an agreement to tolerate each other, then that is extended to the tribe, then to the nation, so that it is murder to kill in one's own country and war to kill in another, and ultimately that must apply to all nations. Anarchism has been violent in Spain because oppression has been violent; in England it has not. But Anarchist justice will not be violent; we will consider ignorance of the law as a real excuse. The law has been made by the rich and strong, as in feudal times, and crime can never be suppressed till the economic and cultural level of everybody has been raised. Revolutions fail because they do not raise the country, only the towns. They do not even acknowledge the problem—all culture and education is centred in the towns, in the museums and universities, while people in the country who do not even know their own name are punished for ignorance of the law. I would abolish military service and substitute instead service by which everyone who is well educated has to spend a year passing on his education to the peasants; the capitalists and the professors are guilty of hoarding culture which must be digested by the whole country in a solid block. People who say 'après moi le déluge,' they are the real criminals. I would like to re-educate Fascist prisoners after the war in reformatories—if a guard used violence on them he would go to prison himself. I have been fourteen years in prison, and I know. There are not many books about Anarchism, because the Spaniards prefer to talk in meetings and act. It was theorizing that caused the failure of the Austrian and German democracies. If I had to sum up Anarchism in a phrase I would say it was the ideal of eliminating the beast in man."

November 1936.

ENGLAND NOT MY ENGLAND

THE LOVE-AFFAIR OF WHICH THESE EXTRACTS FORM A RECORD is in a closing stage, even at the moment where they begin. Indeed, it had already lasted twenty-three years, and for the seven before this diary opens been dangerously articulate. Actually we have selected only the lover's vows and recriminations to his country from a batch of other declarations he made during the same period to literature, autumn, and even life itself. Only in autumn, in fact, does he seem happy, and for the rest of the year his country, unwilling to be desired merely for its climatic accidents, takes a cruel revenge. "The course of true love" is more than applicable to this *passion malheureuse* whose every phase seems to echo the complaint of Martial: "non tecum possum vivere, nec sine te." Finally, Paris seduces him; with all his passion turned to hate he runs away, and the affair ends on a note of benign disillusion that is perhaps more cynical than any wrath could ever be. Like most lovers, the author appears fractious, embittered, egotistical, and not always inclined to be sincere. Well, there it is, and we cannot help feeling that if things had been different, if there had been a little more patience and understanding on both sides, if he had been more industrious with his pen, and his country more generous with her money, we might still see them billing and cooing together. Alas for him and his Lesbia, it seems that this was not to be; now Mr. Punch, a few Georgian poets, gossip-writers, and lady novelists woo the cool green Motherland—who yields herself, however, only to Mr. Galsworthy. Does she ever regret—we try sometimes to imagine—her odd-eared lover? Is the wound incurable? The breach—we wonder muzzily—the whole thing over? And somehow we cannot help feeling that it isn't; but then, in this country, we usually feel that.

30th June 1927

Dined alone and caught boat to Caen. Leaving England felt like losing a limb.

22nd July 1927

I have no ambition, but will a horror of being stationary, a panic fear of keeping still, make up for it?

27th July 1927

Bad lunch on Dover boat and dreary crossing. Oh, the superb wretchedness of English food, how many foreigners has it daunted, and what a subtle glow of nationality one feels in ordering a dish that one knows will be bad and being able to eat it! The French do not understand cooking, only good cooking—this is where we score. Pleasant journey up to London reading newspapers; a grey and windy day. Arrive at Victoria and feel like Rip van Winkle, but with a vague sense of home-coming and security at being back again. All foreigners are frightful, and Europe is crawling with them.

29th July 1927

Asked Desmond about himself, and he spoke of his life at twenty-three, he told me he was as idle as I was and eventually it made him ill. I said I knew the feeling.

2nd to 4th August 1927

I ought in fairness to announce that these two days by the sea I have been distinctly happy.

3rd August 1927

Perfect summer's day, which seems the flower of all the summer days in history and makes England incomparably richer than Greece. Went out after dinner and walked down to the shore, where the cat followed me. There were some men cutting up a log of driftwood. The sky was rose and the sea pale green, and though the hills of the Island and the lights of Fawley were clear, there was a thick mist on the shore, through which the men at the timber loomed large as I walked along with the cat over the pebbles. Came back and called up an owl. Bonfires on the air, horses in the mist, the boy scouts singing and their tents glowing in the dark. The black cat very lively on the garden wall, and the light in a bed-

room window shining out over the fields. It seemed terrible
to be going to London, even in a month, on such a day.

3rd September 1927

Depressed, unhappy, and apprehensive. This fag-end
London.

8th September 1927

My thoughts run to depression as a child to its mother.
Not to be born is best, or being born, to live at Cadiz.

17th September 1927

Lovely, unexpected, hopeless summer's evening. Resolve:
to live more and more in the present, cultivating especially
intensity and inconstancy in personal relations, to break free,
so far as loyalty permits, from all unions that chain one to the
past, while retaining them in so far as they provide a commentary, otherwise to fall in love as impermanently as possible
with whoever is nearest, to study life not death, the present
not the past, the actual not the literary. Only by giving the
whole of myself to the moment can I make it give its best to
me. A rapid series of unbearable partings is the best proof
that one is living—to live in the present is the most provident
of all ways of life, for by that alone can one create a valuable
past. "Pas de recherche sans temps perdu"—no chronicles
without wasted time.

20th September 1927

Depression over. Here and now I recant like Stesichorus:
life is thrilling, valuable, wholly adequate and enough. This
spurt of the senses; this welling up of the mind; the magnificent power of expenditure and recovery; the accumulation
of richness and depth like a symphony whose orchestra grows
always fuller, whose melodies begin to develop and repeat
themselves always with a greater promise and a new implication, are finer than anything that can be deduced about them;
are not adorned by any tale. Life has no moral, and the moral
of art is that life is worth while without one.

I am just twenty-four and dangerously happy. For once I feel ambitious and desire and believe in my chances of fame. I want to give lavishly to everyone, to enrich life as it is enriching me—granted but the vitality to enjoy life, I will give it everything that has made it enjoyed. Till then, spare me ὦ τὸ φθόνερον.

As I wrote this I found the pages of Logan's diary in the 'nineties, left in at the end of a blank notebook: "Venice. Church at twilight. Candles. Singing, Per i poveri morti. People die. I shall lose them, no more hear their voices. Let us cling to the best, forgive, not notice. I too shall die: this colour and this warmth will pass from me. Let me treasure the right things, see this world brighter for the frame of death." The same pleading, the same appeal as mine. The rhetorical cry of all youth to all life, to be allowed merely to love it, to love the sphinx that breaks her lovers, to feed the hand that bites them, the indifferent hour.

27th September 1927

Converted to Paris through finding a Spanish cabaret where flamenco is sung, and by the lovely spacious autumn light and the contented people. A living crowd, while in London all the faces are dead.

To be obtained before I am twenty-five: £1000 a year, a book published, a Spanish mistress, some fame, more friends, a knowledge of German, and a visit to Cadiz.

When I was going through a bullying phase at Eton I made Buckley write a weekly essay for me on Wayne, Milligan, Eastwood, and other boys. At first he disliked these essays as much as the subjects, but soon he grew conceited over them and resented any criticism. I can't attach any moral to this or discover why it cropped up in my mind.

London, 10th October 1927

I get happier and happier—autumn intoxicates me. So does London. Richer, deeper, and more delicate, what can life hold in store? I find it gets harder and harder to read or write: I tremble on the verge of plain material hedonism though still

retaining the capacity to moralize about it; the senses continue
to feed the mind though nothing else does. The sun shines
through my window, the air is fresh and cold, and the bell
rings to take me down, to lunch alone off beer and a cold
partridge, before going for a walk in the park. Life alone is
worthy of being worshipped, and with the highest blend one
can bring to it of scholarship and vitality.

15th October 1927

Long quiet evening alone, dining off tea, and digestion very
bad. I must go to Cadiz in the spring and live and write
there: London is too dangerous.

1st November 1927

Depression, literary and physical. Literature is a dead form.
Avoid literary people, they go round and round like water
running out of a bath, dregs that never can forgive each other.
Avoid tea-tables; envy and affectation are within you, but
you can at least avoid tea-tables. Sulk through life and in
sulky places, Russia or the untidiest parts of South America.
Possess nothing but lumber, store everything in houses, but
do not live in them. Find the most confidently material
civilization and see how it behaves. Scheme of life, make
money, drop writing, go long voyages, hang round life: shadow
it, worry it, bore it, only come back to England when you have
learnt to miss it. Take notes and fix moments, but leave the
task of setting them in order to your old age—if you can die
young with nothing finished, you do well to do so.

On a base of profound and wary disillusioned indolence stands
all my hope of tolerating death.

17th November 1927

Damn life, damn love, damn literature! In other words,
damn journalism! Live out of London, drop journalism—yet
to quit one made impossible by loneliness, the other by finance.
Make £1000 a year, make pots of money out of a novel! Too
soft for journalism, too rough for literature, I should be wretched
abroad, bored in the country—what can one do? Trust to the

ultimate creative effort of my own impatience? O for Old
Buffer, I for ink-slinger, G for Jesus, A for Agag.
"What's the Latin name for parsley?
What's the Greek name for swine's snout?"

March 1928

General sense of depression and disgust, with usual horror
of literature. Last days in London characterized by financial
needs, desperate anxiety to get abroad, and deepening passion
for low life. Spent every evening exploring London; one
should be able to live at least three lives concurrently, and
heaven knows how many in rotation. In a complex age, why
not be complicated? Resolve: to associate with all the people
I am afraid of most.

June 1928

Back in England; feel nothing but an intense disgust at
its stupidity. Fatuous newspapers still fussing about the
Prayer Book. The wireless with its children's corner, reports
of tennis matches, lectures on the composition of the cricket
team, on the searchlight tattoo. Absurd music, jolly, idiotic,
or merely oodly. Miss Ivy St. Helier beginning: "Don't be
afraid, I'm not highbrow"—nor is she. All actors and actresses
with their frightful genteel Balliol and Tottenham accents.
Miss Gladys Cooper married to a gentleman at Dorking. She
drew a blank for her profession, dodged the crowd, and gave
some money to a charity. 'He's all right, he's a gugnunc.'
Really, the most deplorable country, Americanized without
America's vitality or variety of race. And this absurd fuss
about Shaw and Galsworthy. Assets of England: the climate,
the countryside, the children, the presence of a few kindred
spirits in rebellion, the country houses, the fact that I can speak
its language, that it is in easy reach of the Continent.

The problem is not how to attack the Jewish-American
gugnunc world, but whether there is any ideal of equal activity
that we can put in its place. At present it absorbs almost all
the vitality of the Western races, and no half-timbered
sanctuary, no pagan rockpool, can be substituted for it. Again,

since it is at its worst in America, it is from America that the
rebellion will come—we are all too soaked in tradition and
culture, and not sufficiently aware of this to create anything
outside of them.   Saving the countryside must make it a
museum.

Tatters of rain streak from a dishcloth sky.   Soon England
will be a slagheap city in a rubble field, stogged bottles in the
dingy grass, burdock and peeled hoardings stretching down to
a litter of boots and halves of empty grape-fruit cast up by a
bathwater ocean on an insanitary shore.

Why not let the countryside be finished, instead of propping
it up in this long agony, this imbecile position between death
and life?

October 1928

Back in London after five weeks in Spain.   General dissatisfaction and distress.   Unpleasant sense, not only of being
just where I was this time last year, but of being practically
just where I was the year before.   As homeless, futureless,
hopeless, and unestablished as ever.   Shall I live in Paris or
the country?   I am also less interested in literature, if anything,
and not really so interested in life, no sign either of the flow
of natural high spirits that I had last year.   I suppose my
happiness is a difficult crop that requires sun, rain, soil, manure,
and tending to make it flower at all.

10*th October* 1928

By some seasonable miracle I seem to be falling in love with
London and recapturing the same exaltation that I attributed
merely to youth last year.   To feel this jungle come to life
all round one in the evening, the same October mists, fires,
lights, wet streets, blown leaves, to plunge into its many zones,
not knowing what one will discover, and to return with a
growing sense of confidence and power as a new street or a
new district falls beneath one's rule, is to feel a true explorer,
or rather is to combine the intimacy of a wooer with the
excitement of an adventurer; to run my fingers through the
town's soft pelt, to caress the lax pulsating city as rashly, as

apprehensively, as a Greek might approach an Amazon, or a small spry leopard, male of some great cat.

1st *November* 1928

General disgust, especially with literature. Same as this time last year, only feebler.

2nd *November* 1928

Terrible *envie* for Paris. The cafés, the lights, the crowded warm interiors, the wasters, the artists, the drunks, the sense of liberty and rebellion, the cold transition, on the Boulevard, from afternoon to evening.

5th *November* 1928

Almost as depressed and dissatisfied as this time last year, my life seems in every way to have retrogressed. Poorer, older, idler, stuck in the same house, the same groove, with even fewer friends and considerably less curiosity. Resolve: to be more of an artist and a Bolshevik, to write a lot and go to Paris and live in Montparnasse, if not in love or otherwise adequately detained here by December 1st. *Envie* for Paris continues severe. "The slow gradations of decay."

November 1928

One cannot really love London. It is disappointing in every way. A foggy, dead-alive city, like a dying ant-heap. London was created for rich young men to shop in, dine in, ride in, get married in, go to theatres in, and die in as respected householders. It is a city for the unmarried upper class, not for the poor. Every writer and artist must feel a sense of inferiority in London unless he is (like Browning or Henry James) a romantic snob—or else fits into the Reynolds-Johnson tradition of Fleet Street, Garrick, good burgundy, and golf. Arnold Bennett is the English Bohemian. Of course, there are Bohemians, but they have to be smart ones, otherwise they are afraid to show themselves; without a quarter, without cafés, their only chance is to get rich and fashionable and give cocktail parties. In Paris they have a quarter assigned to them, and are lords of it. They aren't much better as artists, but they are freer, happier, and harder-working, and live in an atmosphere where great art is more likely to arise.

The more one sees of life the more one is aware how hopeless it is without art to give it meaning. "To love life in all its forms" is like loving pumice-stone in all its forms, or journalism. Life is only in exceptional cases worthy of being loved—to love life is to have the curiosity to search for the occasions when life is lovable—or rather the enterprise to create them.

And in London they are few.

Moment of happiness in Yeoman's Row. Yellow sunlight falling through the panes on golden cushions and a glass of wine; reading in the armchair, far cries of children playing.

Fear of life, hate of self, general misery and intermittent self-pity these last few days. "Quando ver veniet meum." "Sombra soy de quién murío." Culmination of misery on Saturday night, lost a five-pound note at a bad revue—the most unlovable mug in England. Feel ill unless I drink, and depressed when I do. Wild fits of mawkish gloom, "genteel canine pathos"—the world whips only those who look as if they've just been whipped.

> O douleur, O douleur, le temps mange la vie,
> et l'obscur ennemi qui nous ronge le cœur
> du sang que nous perdons croît et se fortifie.

December 1928

A wild month, intoxication of London as before.

1929

With a deepening sense of guilt, failure, loneliness, and insecurity, I greet the New Year.

General reflections.—Read and written far too little: increased confidence, however, and aptitude for life. Deterioration in general highmindedness; a year of social success, amorous enterprise, aesthetic Bolshevism and physical, moral, and emotional falling back.

January 1929

> "Thou hast led me like a heathen sacrifice
> with garlands and with sacred yokes of flowers
> to my eternal ruin."

Resolve: To be altogether more advanced and intelligent, to have more friendships and fewer affairs, to write and read more than I eat and drink, to revisit Paris and write a prize novel.

'We have no precedent for an English intelligentsia. The flower of our civilization is a certain splenetic enterprise, an instinctive dignity in living, an absolute grasp of the material splendour of life—a young buck tilting down St. James's Street, a clean old man in a club window, a great writer married to an earl's daughter, a country gentleman reading Keats—these are the fruits of our mind and upbringing, these are the images we should preserve. Writing is a lapse of taste rather than a crime: it is explicit and hence in opposition to our character and our climate.'

Back from Yorkshire appalled at my enjoyment of a week in the country. Enjoyed the countryside under snow, the warm house, the tobogganing, the shoot, the smell of cartridges, the heavy winging and thud of falling birds on the smoky evening air. Standing in the wet woods listening to the beaters tapping and whistling; watching the farm-cart full of birds bowling home over the park. Oh, the joy of lingering over port and brandy telling dirty stories with men in pink coats while it snows outside! The grim, rich, game-pie England of eighteenth-century squires, brown woods, and yellow waistcoats.

Abroad, I was at least interesting to myself—in London I can't be even that. I exist only to celebrate my sense of guilt.

1st February 1929

Back in London, miserably depressed. Persecution mania, sense of solitary confinement. Finally decided London unendurable and packed up in the middle of dinner and left. It was raining as I fled to St. Pancras. The train was a red Midland express; huge drays kept coming down the platform, I lit my cigar and played the gramophone. It was one of the most pleasant solitary journeys I have ever made. The train slid through Barking and the wet stations of the East End: I played slow foxtrots in my empty carriage and felt that at last I had become a real person again. It was very wet and windy at Tilbury. I stood on deck and watched the lights along the Thames. I had a perfect moment as the boat moved out. The wind was cold and the water choppy, all the passengers were below and I saw the pilot dropped. As the little tug shot away from the ship in an Ionic curve like the prong of a boathook I had an exquisite sense of the finality of leaving, of which that seemed a definite symbol. It was very rough and I reached Dunkirk in icy cold, pitch-dark and freezing. In the train this became a beautiful winter morning, and with no remorse I played a flamenco record to the rising sun.

July 1929

Landed at Newhaven. Depressed at being back in England. The countryside so dirty, sky and fields the colour of corrugated iron. Everybody so weak and knock-kneed, a race of little ferrets and blindworms. England is a problem: parts of it so beautiful, a few people in it so intelligent, yet never can I manage to fit in. The intelligent ones are so stranded, such detached and *défaitiste* observers; the extraordinarily nice people, of whom there are probably more than in any other country, are also extraordinarily stupid; the "amusing" ones so dull. I hate colonels, but I don't like the people who make fun of them. Those who conform become impossible, and those who rebel rebel only towards a continental snobbery instead of a 'county' one. A wave of retrograde and stupid conservatism seems to be sweeping the country. There is no place in England for a serious rebel; if you hate both diehards and bright young people you must, like Lawrence, Joyce, or Aldous Huxley, go and live abroad. It is better to be *depaysé* in someone else's country than in one's own.

Disgusted by the crowd at Brighton. "So dull, so dead, so woebegone," hardly a soul in holiday clothes: they might be waiting on a tube platform. Women all dowdy, men undersized and weedy. Pathetic voices and gestures, newspaper-fed ignorance, wistful cannon-fodder larvae that trail around whining out their day's ration of bromides as if at any moment somebody was going to hit them. No trace even of char-woman Cockney or Dickensian vulgarity either—just little ferrety robots squeaking round an empty bandstand. Oh, the stupidity of the old regime and the silliness of its detractors! Yet for this Mr. T. S. Eliot changes his brown passport for true blue!

16th July 1929

Went for a long walk to Lulworth Cove. For an instant, on the lonely crest of the downs, above an old house that sloped down through a semicircle of beechwoods to the sea, I had a moment of love for my country, just as we may suddenly prepare to forgive someone who has deceived us before the memory of their infidelities swarms in on us again. As we walked farther, however, I remembered not so much the beauty of the downs as the awfulness of the people who wrote about them: Kipling's thyme and dewponds, Belloc's beer, and Chesterton's chalk, all the people writing poems at this moment for the *London Mercury*, and two tiresome undergraduates who discuss culture at the inn. They gaze, between mouthfuls of tomato, at the Victorian lithographs round the parlour: "Caught Napping," "The Love-Letter," "Their First Quarrel," "The Story of a Brave End." "Pretty serious!" grunts one to the other. "Terrible," grunts the culture specialist. "Glubet magnanimos Remi nepotes," I thought, undeterred by a burst of exquisite woodland ride between the cliffs and the valley. Peter was more loyal to the Motherland, but talked exclusively of Villiers de l'Isle Adam all the way. We reached a cottage by the sea for lunch. Peter flattered the landlady and praised the bread and cheese rather professionally. For this, to my joy, we were charged two shillings each, and I maintained that one couldn't be robbed more if one was a foreigner. I asked if I could bathe from the rocks without a costume. "There be bobbies' eyes from here to Weymouth," she said. Eventually we got to Lulworth Cove through a maze of complacent military reminders that a fatal accident

had occurred in 1927 "through a pedestrian using the path
along the cliffs when the red flag was flying." From Arishmell
the sound of church bells was wafted down the petrol-scented
English lanes past the carefully thatched cottages.

> O God, to hear the parish bell
> in Arishmell, in Arishmell !

Lulworth Cove was like a fly-paper. People in every
direction, and twelve charabancs parked across a space for
building lots. "I wish I had a camera," I cried, and Peter
answered: "I wish I had a machine-gun." At that a miracle
happened, the helpless bitterness with which he vainly protested seemed to snap something in my head, and I felt the
relief with which one passes an old flame and feels "that face
can never trouble me again." The deformed and swarming
trippers, the motor-car park, the wooden bungalows and the
tin tea-sheds seemed a heavy joke at which I could look on
with ironic detachment. I felt suddenly quit of everything:
my sense of possession, in regard to England, had been finally
scotched. Besides, even if it is beautiful, I thought, from my
point of view (that of finding things to write about) this
countryside, except for a few still unchronicled phases of
winter, is virtually dead. "The country habit has me by the
heart," wrote someone trying to find a fresh approach to that
Grantchestered old trollop—this England—or, as the papers
archly call it, "This England of ours." I thought of all the
ardent bicyclists, the heroic coupleteers, the pipe-smoking, beer-
swilling young men on reading parties. The brass-rubbers,
the accomplished morris dancers, the Innisfreeites, the Buchan-
Baldwin-Masefield and Drinkwatermen, the Squires and
Shanks and grim Dartmoor realists, the advanced tramp lovers,
and, of course, Mary Webb. I thought of everyone who was
striding down the Wordsworthian primrose path to the glorious
goal of an O.M. "The country habit has me by the heart,"
I chanted to the Lulworth trippers, and in an usher's voice
of mincing horror "procul o procul este profani"—but it was
my friend, not they, who fled.

Went down to the cove for a bathe. Warm sunny evening.

Walking back (the grace of childhood still irradiates the "walk to the sea"), I met a man with a motor-caravan. Stayed and talked to him and his wife and daughter. Green beds spread in the open, a book lying on the grass, some pails, and his wife cooking porridge. He had spent his life in the East and had just retired. Walked up with them to the vicarage garden, where they were to do country dances. A few children, one or two village women and farmboys, and a couple of bustling ladies with muddy red faces and fringes of greying hair. They danced on the grass to a gramophone. "Now come along— if all the world were paper—siding, turn, slips, take your partner and swing!—if all the world were paper—too slow— too slow—too slow!" The village women pant seriously, the spinsters dance briskly, giving directions from a little book. I gingerly take part, put out to find myself also among the prophets; the Anglo-Indians skip with experience and the children stare. The girls are breathless and light-footed, yet heavy with a kind of rustic materialism, their faces and figures are gauche with adolescence, like unfinished statues left in the marble. They grin and call to the children in thick sweet Dorset voices. "Now Newcastle—now gathering peascods"— or is it "picking up sticks"? The plaintive music so naïvely vicious, so innocently sophisticated, floats out on the evening. "We want only the best for 'Clergyman's Farewell'—it's very difficult—single hey, turn, slip, siding, now be careful, double hey, grand chain!" I walk away up the road, the distressful notes of "Clergyman's Farewell," the young voices, sad slice of wan little England, pursue me over the fields. A sheep-dog is sleeping by the pond, and outside the inn some boys are playing cricket with a stone. The sun westers brightly over the folded plateau, and every flower and every weed, the air, the downs, the grey cottages, unite with the distant archaic music to cry "Saul, Saul, why persecutest thou Me?"

A mood of final emancipation came to me the next morning. I leant against a long wall underneath a window, when suddenly a voice began to thunder from inside. "Very important. Causal conjunctions. We went very deeply into this last week. Read it out." "Causal conjunctions," quavered a choir of young

voices. "Quippe, qui, and quoniam take the indicative."
"Quippe, qui, and quoniam," bellowed the usher, interrupting
them, "take the indicative." The rasping voice sounded like
the cry of a wild animal, as if one had passed on the top of a
bus by the Zoo, but the uncouth language blended perfectly
with the summer scene outside. "Take this down—take it
down, will you," the roar continued. "Conjectus est in
carcerem—he was thrown into prison—quod patrem occidisset
—on the grounds that he had killed his father—qui eo tempore
—who at that time was flying into Italy—in Italiam refugiebat.
RE-FU-GI-EBAT," he thundered, and the pedagogic rhythms
floated out into the sun and along the dusty hedgerows. "Conjectus est in carcerem," mumbled the scribbling pupils;
"quippe, qui, and quoniam," they chanted; "causal conjunctions," till the words were lost above the Isle of Purbeck,
a drone above the drone of bees.

October 1929.

CONVERSATIONS IN BERLIN

(H=host)

WE HAD SOME INTERESTING TALKS IN BERLIN. ONE NIG᾿᾿T WE discussed ourselves when young, at what age we should like most now to have met ourselves, and where. H described himself motor-cycling in Germany and held up two forlorn days in Dortmund. I would like to have come across myself at eighteen: droll, earnestly decadent, thin and hopping birdlike among the second-hand book-stalls of Cologne. Raymond deplored his shyness at that age, and we all admitted that at a time when we were longing for intelligent conversation with people older than ourselves we had been too gauche to begin them, and so had been reduced to getting stones from schoolmasters as our dry intellectual bread. I said this did not really matter. Youth was a period of misadventure, and should only be enjoyed as such. The long lines of missed opportunities were more rich and significant in their maladroitness than the competent never-miss-a-moment grasping philosophy of late youth and middle age. Later we walked in the Kurfurstendam, which was gay and exciting. Raymond said his father had taught him the importance of loafing in any big city, and he remarked how few people really appreciated the personality of towns at night, their danger, and great beauty. I said Sterne was one of these travellers with a true city sense. "So this is Paris. Crack! Crack! Crack!"

Last night I asked him if there was any book that could be laid down as a test of intelligence, something that would draw a definite line between Bloomsbury and Chelsea, a real *pons asinorum*. I suggested Proust, because to read it all through we must require more than culture—snobbery, and actually to have read it all through must remove most second-handedness from one's mind. Proust's real importance was that he taught one how best dramatically to interpret one's own life. R

211

suggested *Adolphe*, *Clarissa*, and the heavier French classics. H exclaimed that a whole set of smart and stupid people had religiously read every word of Proust and remained as stupid as before. Probably they had read Joyce as well. He disapproved so strongly of any kind of culture being made the test of any kind of intelligence that he hardly allowed us to go on talking at all. This was absurd, as both of us really agreed with him. We tried to analyse intelligence. I said all intelligence was really criticism of life; the first person to say life was short or boring was using his mind to stand apart from the atmosphere in which he moved, which no animal or fish could do. Intelligence went on from an ability to be detached from life to an ability to be detached from oneself, and finally to relate one's experience to other people's and so to generalize from the particular to truths about living. Our ability to discuss sex without feeling sexual emotion was the first proof of intelligence. R said he thought I was against intelligence, or rather, against the intellect. I said I was, for intellectual pride had always a dehumanizing effect. One appreciated one's knowledge of a subject rather than the subject itself, one lost the capacity for worship or for seeing a thing or a person apart from our sense of power over them. I preferred the imagination. R said, and H agreed, that the perfect intelligence was an absolutely free mind gifted with infinite curiosity, hence able and anxious to grasp and illuminate any non-technical subject. I said that was just what I had not got. Obscurity was my tonic, and I believed in and practised incuriosity. I hated well-informed people with fluent general knowledge and vivid curiosity about contemporary problems, they drove me to the Dark Ages. All the same, I respected R's passion for actualities. He came down to every day as to an examination paper, the hours lay before him like blank foolscap, and he was excited, wondering what the questions were going to be, while I was still writing idle scrolls over those of the week before. I was only interested in that part of the present relevant to my imagination; for instance, I seldom went to concerts, but when I found a tune I liked I made it last as long as possible. I treated all the arts as a Narcissus pool;

when I found no reflection I was absent-minded and bored. H said, flatteringly, that he thought, too, that there was a streak of scholar in me, both in my nature and in my admiration of scholarship. I said I hoped it was true. R went on about what insufferable bores great scholars were, or all great brains that only exercised themselves on one subject. Whitehead, the mathematician, was not intelligent at all. "It's not the scholar in me that is incurious," I said, "only the Celt." I happened to have a good intellect and a classical education, but underneath lay the Celtic dreaminess, incuriosity, and tendency to brood. I brooded and vegetated for hours over the past; going over conversations and characteristics of people. I could sit for two or three hours chewing the cud or indulging in day-dreams over the near future. R said he had no day-dreams, not even sexual; he supposed this was because he had no imagination, and because he had no imagination he was not really self-dependent and couldn't bear being left alone. We were surprised, and said we did not think it possible to have no day-dreams. H described a few of his, which were mostly simple visions of wealth or power and of being able to help his friends. "To find you crying, Cyril," he said, "is one of them." I added revenge as a subject for day-dreams, and R said he thought all day-dreams were unhealthy. "This doesn't apply," he added, "to sitting still and making use of your mind."

"Well, now, what I'm really curious about is life," said H, "and I don't expect you know what has thrilled me this evening most."

"Yes, I do," I said, "our landlord coming down from his own flat to answer a trunk call from Munich." I suggested we should all say how that struck us. R had hardly noticed it at all except to be glad when H took us out of the dining-room so that the bell didn't interfere with our conversation. I. had been excited by the call from Munich, but, the doctor having been in once already, I had been annoyed like Raymond, and only deduced a general reflection that it was just like a German landlord to let his house and yet to be continually popping into it with his own key, while an Englishman would scrupulously avoid going near it at all. H then came out with a string of observations: how he had wondered if one of the children were ill in Munich, known it was the doctor's wife that was ringing him up, wondered how the husband would take it, and thought, while the phone rang a second time, "now I shall be able to tell if his child is ill by the look on his face as he turns away." Then he had thought this was unpleasant, and had bundled us all out of the dining-room so that he wouldn't be tempted to watch the doctor at the telephone at all. Thus doing to spare the doctor and his own conscience what we thought he had done so as not to bother us. R said this observation was the true novelist's gift. I said it was being able to write down what one had observed. H said it was the capacity to keep the bones together and not smother them with digressions and irrelevant facts. I was sure one ought to write down everything that interested one and skimp, even if it affected the plot, all that it bored one to write, and then go over, taking out what was unnecessary. Revision should be a case of taking things out and not of putting them in. H agreed.

Another evening we dined by the water in Potsdam. A hot and beautiful night; we had a table by the trees on the edge of the lake. I thought of canoeing past the flowering chestnuts on the canal by Oxford castle; of the extraordinary spell of this time of the year. The talk was mostly of archaeology. I had a sore throat and could not join in, but the music, the warm night, the river crowd made it like some classical scene in fiction; I smelt the lilac, memorial of so many wasted summers, and tried to remember a Chinese poem about 'May in the waterside city.' Two brown youths glided by in a canoe, emerging like savages out of the night and disappearing into it again. At home happiness was discussed, and we agreed that H was the happiest and most fortunate person we knew. He had an interesting wife, fine children, good friends, position, enough money, an active mind and a settled future, a literary success, and a profession in which one was still young at fifty, with excellent scope at playing for ever at being an *enfant terrible*. H was very pleased, and said he could not, as a matter of fact, remember ever having been so happy as he was at that moment. We all touched wood and laughed at ourselves for doing so. The candles lit up the polished table, the dark glow of port, the lighter one of brandy in our glasses. The night air smelt of lake-water and of smoke from our cigars. R's dark head was thrown back in meditation; H was staring at the table. We were all going over our pasts to see if they contained moments as happy as this one. I thought of our security, our freedom from worries, our friendship and free play of ideas and intelligences, and what a good setting we were in for the end of the world. Yet a few hours before I had been restless with anxiety to be travelling, and had tried to make my mind a blank and write down what came into it: "Wet Sunday afternoon in summer. Timeless abyss of all the year. Four other people in the room, all reading. The wind worries the heavy sycamores; rustle of turned pages; crackle of the *Manchester Guardian*. In this stillness I wait for the first sound, in this blackness I wait for the first image—a cough, a motor-horn, the scratching of the dog's leash on the floor. Doors banging in another house, in another country. Sète. The dog fidgeting; the wind rising; the image forming. Sète at midnight on the way to Spain. The sleepy ride to a hotel near water; the seaside cemetery where Valéry wrote; the lagoons of Frontignan.

> Beau ciel, vrai ciel, regarde moi qui change
> Après tant d'orgueil, après tant d'étrange
> Oisiveté, mais pleine de pouvoir.

Remembering the afternoon, I felt that true happiness contained more distress than rapture; that this moment was not one of happiness so much as of perfect civilization, an example of the intricacy of Europe, the discrete and many-folded strata of the old world, of the strength of the north in this town where the texture of the day coarsened so slowly into dusk, and of the power of ideas. R's slight expression of melancholy and H's silence meant that they, too, were being forced to refer their greatest happiness to the past. "Yes, I don't think I have been so happy before," said H, concluding, "and I don't suppose, either, that I shall be so happy again."

March 1930.

THE FATE OF AN ELIZABETHAN [1]

THIS IS A REMARKABLE BOOK, EXTREMELY INTERESTING FROM three points of view—as a portrait of contemporary youth, as a study of the relations between parents and children, and as a picture of the governing class—not of the delightfully eccentric upper classes, but of a small knot of powerful aristocratic families. First we are presented with an adorable child, living in the world of the Homeric heroes, driving a pony-cart like a chariot, standing up in his Greek costume and galloping about the park at Knebworth with a spear in his hand. At his private school he is first introduced to the world where for fifteen years games and popularity are to matter more than anything else—and there are lectures on the last war. "He is talking all about bombing, glorious! We have got a God in the room, it is great fun. He is talking so well that he makes you think you are in the trenches. Good-bye." Already he wrote vigorous natural letters which he signed "someone," and already his father remarks: "He lost something of his originality, as all boys do at school." At fourteen he writes from Eton a brilliant description of an interview with his tutor about making friends with a boy from another house who cribs:

> "'He is a boy with a very bad past record and he is not the sort of boy I like my little children to be friends with. . . . He seems to me to be a boy with a great lack of honour. What sort of a boy do you think he is?'
>
> 'I think he is a very nice boy.'
>
> 'How can you think that a boy who cribs is a very nice boy?'
>
> 'I don't see that it makes any difference to a boy whether he has had the bad luck to be *caught* cribbing or not.' (I did not tell him that there wasn't a boy in his house, or for that

[1] *Antony*. By his Father the Earl of Lytton. Peter Davies, London.

216

matter in the school, who hadn't cribbed, and it was bad
luck on anyone who happened to be caught.)"

And so the battle rages.

The letters from Eton suffer because they are all written to
his parents and consequently dwell on triumphs rather than
disappointments, and on functions, which are the natural copy
of schoolboys' letters home, while their real life is a series of
friendships, conversations, intrigues, and awakenings in which
an event like the 4th of June is as unimportant as the Lord
Mayor's show. What matters is getting popular and winning
colours, tasting the joys of power for the first time, acquiring
knowledge and avoiding punishment; in fact, growing up.
I remember very well that Eton of fifteen years ago, it was still
almost entirely pre-war in feeling. After a pathetic year or so
of serfdom, when fear was the dominating emotion, one
emerged gradually into the full blaze of feudal sunlight. The
masters represented the Church, praising, cajoling, blaming,
pointing the way, with the headmaster as a kind of terrible
Pope; the boys, with their great hierarchy of colours and
distinctions, were the rest of the population, while the prefects
and athletes, the captains of houses and self-elected members
of "pop," were the feudal overlords who punished offences at
the request of the Church (and in return were tacitly allowed
to break the same rules themselves); in those days they could
beat almost anybody for almost anything at sight, and it seemed
to a droll, idle, timorous little beetle like myself that most of the
staff were deeply in awe of them. Work was generally deplored
as too drastic a remedy for our unemployment; games oddly
enough were not in themselves a sure passport to popularity; for
the last time in our lives money didn't matter, and if one had to
say what really counted one would have had to admit that it was
a curious blend of elegance and vitality to which the addition
was much appreciated of a certain mental alertness and the gift
of being amusing. The times when I am really transported
back to Eton are when I read the memoirs of Grammont, or
La Princesse de Clèves. But there were two serious influences
that stood out above the general gaiety and magnificence, Mr.

Headlam and Mr. Marten. Both taught history to the history specialists, from whom the feudal princes were recruited. Otherwise the atmosphere was eighteenth-century and political, much as in the days of Gray and Walpole. It was assumed that in after-life ravens would feed us; science and most contemporary knowledge was taught but discredited, and we continued to be happier than we could have conceived possible and to acquire a wide, but (for me) on the whole rather useless, knowledge of the way to govern an empire or a board.

Supreme among these thousand boys were a small group of powerful dandies, who were looked on with an awe that luckily in most of us atrophies, or we should be miserable still: Nico Davies and Edward Woodall (to whom the best letters in the book are written), Antony Knebworth, the exquisite Mr. Edward Jessel, the languid Lord Dunglass. Lord Knebworth was remarkable for his vitality, which was often boisterous, his fits of melancholy, his ability and his charm. He was a beautifully built and slightly stooping athlete, an incarnation of that adventurousness and courage which is so alluring to intellectuals and which usually ends in them breaking their legs. The group transplanted itself in a body to Oxford and was disappointed at first, as are all boys who are happy at Eton, by the dismal emptiness and ugliness of Oxford and the difficulty of starting life all over again.

"I dare say Oxford is a good interesting place for old men of forty, but for boys, why I'd rather be at a girls' school for knitting. It would be better exercise. . . . I want an incentive to do something. I have ambition, but no goal and therefore nothing to work for. Money? I want it, but it doesn't thrill me. God? I don't understand him and he doesn't fill me. Passion? Yes, but what does it mean? How do I get it? What do I do? Strength? Yes, but what good is physical strength? Power is perhaps the only light I can see clearly, but that is very dim and very far and the obstacles are incredible and the pleasures which distract one from getting it too good."

To this questioning his father replied with words of golden wisdom, recommending the pursuit of happiness and drawing a distinction between happiness and pleasure. But his son is already bitten with the idea of political realism.

"I think the most fatal thing of all is the general tendency everywhere to be good. It is such a mistake and so unnatural. I mean by 'being good' things like disarmament, upholding the integrity of smaller nationalities, prohibition, League of Nations. . . . It's these drivelling idealists like Woodrow Wilson and Bob Cecil (is that libel?) who want to try to make people do everything for the peace of the world at the expense of nationality. It is fundamentally communism and a fatal thing for everyone."

To which his father replies: "You may not agree with idealists like Bob Cecil, and you are fully entitled to disagree with them, but if you call them 'drivelling' you betray a want of confidence in your own case."

For the moment ski-ing solves the problem, for Lord Knebworth was one of the fastest and most enterprising ski-ers of his generation, but it only made him more dislike Oxford and the idea of an office to follow—but other places are worse; of the sailors at Dartmouth he says: "They are so concentrated on modesty, ignorance, and manhood as to be almost unnatural." Then *Don Juan* revives him with its appeal to the blend of cynical and romantic which shows in his own rather histrionic nature. At twenty-one the "career" seems to burden him more than ever.

"I have a dread of becoming just one of many young men living miserably in London and working hopelessly in the city. . . . But I suppose really the conventional life is the right one or it would not be the conventional one. . . . I hate the thought of Parliament, or the City, or of London, or of anything except something quite peculiar."

He is saved by going out as A.D.C. to his father in India, where he plays polo, climbs to Tibet, skis in the Himalayas ("Believe me, the plains of Tibet are horrid. They are all like a desert to look at; only the yak, who lives on rocks and sands and snow (poor sweet) can subsist there—they're so high you can't breathe, eat, or move without being sick, and you have headache all the time.") In India he is blissfully happy: "It is Eton. Play, sport, games are the thing; work the odious duty, the side-show!" He wishes to stay on there, but is not permitted to. The prison-house is now closing rapidly round him—he works first at Conservative Headquarters, then in the Army and Navy Stores, still hopelessly rebelling.

"This method of life persistently carried on for about forty years eventually produces wealth, dignity, power, position, and universal respect. It is called Christian civilization. . . . I see in these things only the same piece of green blotting-paper every morning."

He became a Conservative member of Parliament in 1931, but was already turning entirely against democratic government. He worked in the Army and Navy Stores, went to the House, and spent his spare time flying, finding in aviation that escape from daily routine (his description of flying to Milan reads like the Airman's journal in Auden's *Orators*) which for most of us becomes all we can hope for in the way of real self-expression. He more and more hates the liberty which he has had to abandon, and his last letters are devoted to Fascism, Roman Catholicism, and a crusade against the decadent influence on English debutantes of the works of Mr. Noel Coward.

"They are going to make us promise not to use bombs in the next war. It is all too fantastic and futile for words. . . . My political and philosophical and social war is a revolt from Liberty and Liberalism. . . . That is why I admire the Catholic Church."

In his last letter to him he quotes a saying of his friend Windham Baldwin, whom he had known at Eton:

"'Only gods can stand freedom; we turn bad on it.' . . . I have been lucky and rich and happy and prosperous and have felt, as a boy, like a god. Then I have had no hemp, himp, homp [work in steel mill] like you, no clutch of circumstance, and I have gone bad, that's all."

Three months later he was killed, flying, obeying an officer in an impossible manœuvre. He was then twenty-nine.

Well, there is the picture, the picture of a young Elizabethan, gifted with a good deal of brain, a strong character, and a wonderful body, and aided by every advantage of birth and education, and every help that a devoted family life, and the wisdom of one of the few obviously perfect fathers in literature, could give. One should think of him as a terrible loss to his country, as an example to other young people of the scope for physical adventure and moral energy that exists in the world— and yet one can't, one can see him only as the victim of a system, as a young man crowned with too early success and afterwards struggling hopelessly to disentangle himself from it, noting down in his letters with the amazing alertness and self-criticism that were so typical of him the alternative lives that, always presenting themselves, are yet always forbidden. We hear a lot of criticism of public school education from those who were failures at school—but is there anything in reality more dangerous than early success? I was myself a success at school, and it seems to me that only recently have I recovered my balance. Early laurels weigh like lead, and looking back at Antony Knebworth's schooldays, I see now, not only all the envy and irritation which his successes must have caused his rivals, but the effect of the competitive system on him; always to be going in for something and always having to win it, and then to find that there are no more competitions, just a slight dazzle from the conflagration of his early successes to remind him of the small school-universe where he had been most fully alive. If competition is carried into after-life with similar violence it becomes a kind of piracy, and a kind at which Antony Knebworth was too high-spirited and romantic to succeed. Hence his discontent, his regret at not having fought in the last war—for temperamentally he was Edwardian; intolerant, egotistic, and bred to consider the world his oyster and politics his game. He lacked the idealism which alone could dominate the fatal inherited family facility, and without which all natural gifts must spoil. But any system of education derives from the class which bring it into being, and it is this governing class, I feel, which is really to blame for the transition of Elizabethan into Fascist that we have watched take place. For, although there are exceptions, of which Lord Lytton is obviously one, it is a class which has persistently underestimated the intellect, which regards it as a source of evil and not a source of pleasure; where ability, self-interest, and shrewdness, heavily coated with good-fellowship and charm, are what matter, and from which an intellectual or artistic member must often drag himself out with ignominy or without success, distrusted by his old friends, and discontented with the new. "Power makes men stupid," it has been said, and the power of the governing classes is cumulative and hereditary. Had Lord Knebworth belonged to another class, had he been like Lawrence a miner's son, he would have risen by his intellect rather than been kept down by his athletic accomplishments. He would have met his intellectual equals instead of remaining all his life with his intellectual inferiors, and might have become what he wanted to become, a writer. "I know I could write a great book," he says, "that I could make my living with my pen, that I could be really great in that line, and then I should be happy. But I know, too, that I never shall." As is to be expected, his writing has great ability but no standards. The writers who were at Oxford with him, Evelyn Waugh and Peter Quennell, for instance, were impossible—they were aesthetes—and so instead we see someone whose intellect (as opposed to his intelligence) remains the same as at his private school, who never looks at a picture or a building, who mentions no music but Gilbert and Sullivan, who mentions no living writers but Belloc, Chesterton, Philip Guedalla, and Maurice Baring, and who enjoyed Mark Antony and *Wuthering Heights* at school, but afterwards read and re-read *The Constant Nymph*. What did he gain by cutting himself off from the life of the mind, from all genuine aesthetic experience? He did not write better or ski better or box or fly better; he only missed entirely the two great conceptions of our day: that of artistic integrity, the life of the spirit, and that of social justice, "the palpable and obvious love of man for man."

December 1935.

A TYRANT OF TASTE [1]

BOOKS ABOUT DIAGHILEV ARE ALWAYS GOOD, BECAUSE ANYTHING about him can be read in two ways. There is the life of the genius, a genius who never himself created a single work of art yet whose genius was admitted by everyone; and there also is the showman, the caricature of the international homosexual aristocratic millionaire, the walking Charlus, with his quarrels and grievances, his "scenes" and his superstition. The tragedy of genius and the comedy of manners co-exist in everything that touches him.

Lifar's book is therefore appropriately divided into two halves. The first half is a Life of him up to his death—solid, rather dull, obviously the result of some painstaking collaboration (probably Kubitovitch or some old friend)—the second an account of his friendship with Lifar, in what is to all intents Lifar's autobiography. Lifar is a very good dancer and beautiful as a rare monkey, but he is not a genius, nor does he possess the self-knowledge of the true autobiographer. He is vain, pompous, humourless, spoilt, and exhibitionistic; consequently this second part is a fascinating, comic, and appalling volume, like Charlus' life written by Morel. Among tender tributes to Diaghilev's awe-inspiring genius and friendship appear shafts of malice and contortions of envy. Nijinsky, Massine, Dolin, and Marcievitch are especially sore subjects. For macabre comedy I have read nothing to equal the death scenes, in which Lifar, who had been cut out by Marcievitch, takes, amid scenes of genuine grief, his unconscious revenge. A main difficulty, and a very real one, was how to steal the limelight at Diaghilev's funeral, where strategically one would have thought the corpse occupied an almost impregnable position. Here, in his own words, is how his Id solved it.

At the church:

"But when we came to the church, now full of people, though I was supported on either side by Misia and Coco,

[1] *Diaghilev.* By Serge Lifar. Putnam's, London.

223

I found it utterly impossible to enter the church, for at every moment some unknown force seemed intent to prevent me. It was as though a wall had risen in front of the church which I was utterly unable to pierce. With every ounce of my will I strove to master the spell cast over me—but unsuccessfully. I was terrified: 'What could it be—was I about to go mad?' And this thought paralysed me still more completely. After a number of efforts, however, I finally succeeded in making a rush that forced me through the portals, as though I were crashing through something hard and indestructible which had raised itself like a barrier: then racing down the whole length of the church, I collapsed with a terrible scream by the altar, behind the iconostasis, as though I had gone completely out of my mind. . . .

I hated the idea of approaching the grave and was terrified of seeing the coffin lowered into it. . . . Then, picking up a small trowel, the priest cast a handful of earth on the coffin. How fearful was the sound it made! And I too took some earth, meaning to follow his example. But suddenly it was impossible to hold myself back. I was swept away by some unknown force which surged irresistibly up in me, which swept away all restraint, and I hurled myself into the grave . . . whereupon a dozen hands seized me, and with immense difficulty managed to drag me back, for my maniac delirium had endued me with herculean strength. Then I was led from the cemetery.

Quiet, solemn quiet, reigns on the Island of St. Michele where the mortal remains of Sergei Pavlovitch Diaghilev rest for ever—

'Venise inspiratrice éternelle de nos apaisements.'"

When the cigar smoke and incense have subsided, the gardenias withered, the quarrels been forgotten, the first-night audience, choice as his first editions, been dispersed, and the *wagon-lit* shunted home, what remains of Diaghilev? Was he more than an Impresario or a caricature of the Artist to whom everything was permitted for Art's sake? I think he was. He was a genius, a genius at collaboration, a genius at bringing out the genius in others, a genius at watering the most fruitful art-forms of his time. His tyranny, like Toscanini's, came from a love of art even stronger than his pupils', and an iron resolve to bring out the best in them. Although the only subject connected with the ballet in which he was supreme was lighting, in all the great ballets of his time the collusion of painters and composers without his aid came to nothing. From its Oriental remoteness, far away from Paris and London as the Royal Cambodian dancers, he took the Maryinsky ballet and developed it, against every kind of bureaucratic intransigence, and with no funds except what he could raise from his own self-confidence, into the most advanced cultural force in Europe, and accomplished this entirely on the strength of his faith and his personality.

As a man he seems to have been irresistible, overwhelmingly simple, kind, extravagant, and friendly. When Lifar is ill and depressed he dances lumbering *entrechats* for him. He borrows money like an aristocrat, and spends it like a king. His tribute to unknown talent is as deep and instantaneous as is his dropping of the same talent when it grows well known and shop-soiled. His Russian side, which includes his melancholy and superstition, is delightful. It is his cosmopolitan's homosexual character that deteriorates. It seems dominated, as are the lives of so many men of pleasure, by the fear of death—his own death, the death of movements, the slow decay of talent misapplied, the quicker decay of beauty. He is always hopping from sinking ship to sinking ship before even the first leak has appeared. "Jean, étonne moi!" is his favourite remark to Cocteau, and Jean embarks on that career of professional Astonisher that is to suit him so well. Nijinsky and Lifar, however, are expected to lead a monastic existence, and Massine spent "seven years in a gilded cage." His favourite quotation was one about ' seeing to-morrow's dawn in to-day's sunset,' and his fear of not being "in" on to-morrow is pathetic, when we look at the photos of him in this book, with his straw hat, his fur coat, his Edwardian suits, and his fatcat smile, all irretrievably dated. Fear maims genius, for all Diaghilev's love of life was not proof against the fear it compensated; fear of death, fear

of dying, fear of growing old.   Had he lived, had he obtained
the money for his artist's workshop monastery at Monte Carlo,
what would have happened?   But he could not have lived.
One disease or another would have inevitably been called upon
to remove someone who had given his life to being young, and
who, pursued by Age the invader, had relied on charm and
money as his Maginot Line.

March 1941.

PSYCHO-ANALYSIS [1]

PSYCHO-ANALYSIS LEADS TO THE MOST PROFOUND DIS-
coveries man has made about himself. Yet most people would
agree that its results have been disappointing. The cures are
few, and seem confined to certain extreme cases, while the
neurotic infirmities of human beings increase out of all proportion. Of the two or three hundred Londoners I know,
almost all between the ages of twenty-five and forty would be
improved by analysis in so far as they are neurotic cases. But
many border-liners are in a state of flux. When they are
absorbed in work or living in the country or with one type of
friend they get better; when they are lonely, poor, or tired
they get worse. In fact, they react to environment, and are
therefore capable of improving themselves. The tragedies of
infancy do not seem to remain ever present, ever re-enacted
by the inconsolable ego, or the ineluctable id. Dr. Horney
records fifteen years of relative therapeutic failure as a pure
Freudian, and has written a book in which she takes his theories
one by one and gives her verdict on them. Some she finds
unsubstantiated, others too limited in their refusal to allow
validity to cultural background. In fact, the gist of her book
is that education and environment do count, that the battle
of life and the part we are to play in it is not decided at the
breast or on the pot, but is fought out with constant reinforcements and changes of plan, many of which repeat the infantile
pattern, but are not for that reason strategically useless. The
trouble is that Freud, like all great geniuses, created his
universe: his theories dovetail together; it is impossible to
accept two or three without accepting them all. So beautifully
do they fit in and so magnificently are they presented to us
that we are slow to detect certain man-made aspects. That
lecture on the psychology of women—how Victorian! That
worship of science at the expense of all other methods not

[1] *New Ways in Psycho-analysis.* By Karen Horney. Kegan Paul,
London.

227

strictly scientific—how nineteenth-century! That contempt for rivals and that extreme pleasure in making his audience defy common sense, in getting them to swallow the most improbable explanation, on the slenderest evidence—how typical of the great artist! Yet his world is so incredible and so complete that when an Adler substitutes a banal desire for power or a Dr. Horney adds a craving for security to the basic instincts, we have a sense of disappointment, and we return to the preposterous claims of the great seducer himself, or to those of an orthodox disciple like Groddeck.

Yet Dr. Horney, though lacking in the graces and the art of surprise, may well be right. Psycho-analysis is in its infancy. It sets out to study the Nature of Mind with rudimentary instruments, it makes certain inferences as to that nature which seem to work—but the bits of the jigsaw puzzle which have been fitted together may not be arranged in the right way; it may still be necessary to try many combinations. The only favour psycho-analysis must demand is that we believe that the puzzle and its solution exist, that we realize that the mental is more powerful than the physical, that against the small amount of psycho-analytical cures must be set the enormous improvement in our dealings with each other which a general acquaintance with such ideas as the Oedipus complex, masochism, or the death-wish affords. Normalcy does exist and is desirable, and in proportion as we deviate from it we are unhappy and a cause of unhappiness; the abnormal remain abnormal because all the defences which they can erect, narcissism, masochism, perfectionism, etc., are sufficiently adequate for their normal needs. This does not mean, however, that such defences may not prove quite useless when an unforeseen danger arrives, and then the débâcle is all the more terrible. And the abnormal are not the neurotic few but the majority of the human race, all those who are unhappier than they need be, the discontented women and the defeated men, the faces in the tube, the sheep with the nasty side. It is a consolation of human life that the sick forget what it is like to feel well, or the miserable to be happy. They jog along. But, nevertheless, health and happiness exist, and may tend to grow identical, and it is a disaster that they seem to be outside the range of more than a few people and that anxiety, relieved only by cruelty or the opiate of indifference, is the lot of the rest. Even the masochist does not like being unhappy, and since he cannot make the efforts necessary for happiness he has to intensify his misery till it generates a stimulus—at the cost of getting farther and farther away from reality, where alone happiness is to be found.

Dr. Horney has some interesting things to say about masochism, which she is inclined to dissociate from the sexual basis insisted on by Freud. "Masochistic strivings are ultimately directed towards satisfaction, namely, towards the goal of oblivion, of getting rid of self with all its conflicts and limitations." As an amateur psychologist I would like to add that I have observed masochism in animals, who seem to be trying to avoid punishment by a kind of anticipatory acceptance of it, and that I believe masochism to be a process of ridding oneself of the fear of death by counterfeiting that sensation. In fact, there is an element of masochism in all acceptance of death, in fatalism, in many religions. This acceptance may be partly sexual, but it is also—since death must happen—the only logical strategy to adopt in face of it. For this reason most human beings are masochists and it would be a good thing if the word were freed from its connotation with sexual perversion and given a fuller meaning. There is even an element of courage in masochism, which we see in the tendency to embrace the fear of destruction in the hope that destruction thus will be evaded. The masochist is often one who was exposed to too many dangers in childhood, such as loneliness and the dark, and who, unable to defend himself, made use of others to protect him. Since then he retains both the anxiety and the need for protection, and as Dr. Horney points out, "relationships built on masochistic dependency are replete with hostility towards the partner." Often both partners are masochists, and hence the spectacle, which has done so much to discredit marriage, and indeed the whole system of the human couple, of the Babes in the Wood, escaping from their pursuers and clinging helplessly to each other in the bracken—by the throat.

Dr. Horney's book is easily read by the unscientific. In spite of her attrition the tremendous statue of Freud remains with only a few chips taken off it, but it is clear that she shows the trend of future investigation, which will be in the direction of helping patients to help themselves through an altogether thorough and complete analysis, rather than concentrating, fatalistically, on the therapeutic effects of the discovery of the initial error. We cannot be happy until we can love ourselves without egotism or our friends without tyranny. The issue, even in war-time, cannot be avoided, so any attempt to cast new light on the problem, especially from such a patient and humane angle, is to be encouraged and to be read.

March 1940.

THE ANT-LION

THE MAURES ARE MY FAVOURITE MOUNTAINS, A RANGE OF OLD
rounded mammalian granite which rise three thousand feet
above the coast of Provence. In summer they are covered
by dark forests of cork and pine, with paler interludes on
the northern slopes of bright splay-trunked chestnut, and an
undergrowth of arbutus and bracken. There is always water
in the Maures, and the mountains are green throughout the
summer, never baked like the limestone, or like the Southern
Alps a slagheap of gritty oyster-shell. They swim in a golden
light in which the radiant ebony green of their vegetation
stands out against the sky, a region hardly inhabited, yet
friendly as those dazzling landscapes of Claude and Poussin,
in which shepherds and sailors from antique ships meander
under incongruous elms. Harmonies of light and colour, drip
of water over fern; they inculcate in those who stay long in
the Midi, and whose brains are addled by iodine, a habit
of moralizing, a brooding about causes. What makes men
divide up into nations and go to war? Why do they live in
cities? And what is the true relationship between Nature
and Man?

The beaches of the Maures are of white sand, wide, with
a ribbon of umbrella-pines, below which juicy mesembrian-
themum and dry flowers of the sand stretch to within a yard
of the sea. Lying there amid the pacific blues and greens one
shuts the eyes and opens them on the white surface: the vague
blurred philosophizing continues. Animism, pantheism, images
of the earth soaring through space with the swerve of a ping-
pong ball circulate in the head; the woolly brain meddles with
ethics. No more power, no aggression, no intolerance. All must
be free. Then whizz! A disturbance. Under the eye the soil
is pitted into a conical depression, about the size of a candle
extinguisher, down whose walls the sand trickles gently,
moved by a suspicion of wind. Whizz, and a clot is hurled to
the top again, the bottom of the funnel cleared, in disobedience

to the natural law! As the funnel silts up it is cleared by another whirr, and there appears, at the nadir of the cone, a brown pair of curved earwig horns, antlers of a giant earwig that churn the sand upwards like a steam shovel.

Now an ant is traversing the dangerous *arête*. He sidles, slithers, and goes fumbling down the Wall of Death to the waiting chopper. Snap! He struggles up, mounting the steep banking grain by grain as it shelves beneath him, till a new eruption is engineered by his waiting enemy. Sand belches out, the avalanche engulfs him, the horny sickles contract and disappear with their beady victim under the whiteness. Mystery, frustration, tragedy, death are then at large in this peaceful wilderness! Can the aggressive instinct be analysed out of those clippers? Or its lethal headpiece be removed by a more equitable distribution of raw materials? The funnels, I observe, are all round me. The sand is pockmarked with these geometrical death-traps, engineering triumphs of insect art. And this horsefly might be used for an experiment. I shove it downwards. The Claws seize on a wing, and the struggle is on. The fight proceeds like an atrocity of chemical warfare. The great fly threshes the soil with its wings, it buzzes and drones while the sand heaves round its propellers and the facets of its giant projectors glitter with light. But the clippers do not relax, and disappear tugging the fly beneath the surface. The threshing continues, a faint buzzing comes from the invisible horsefly, and its undercarriage appears, with legs waving. Will it take off? The wings of the insect bomber pound the air, the fly starts forward and upwards, and hauls after it— O fiend, embodiment of evil! A creature whose clippers are joined to a muscle-bound thorax and a vile yellow armour-plated body, squat and powerful, with a beetle set of legs to manœuvre this engine of destruction. The Tank with a Mind now scuttles backwards in reverse, the stern, then the legs disappear, then the jaws which drag its prey. Legs beat the ground. A fainter wheeze and whirr, no hope now, the last wing-tip vanished, the air colder, the pines greener, the cone empty except for the trickle, the sifting and silting down the funnel of the grains of pearl-coloured sand.

Nature arranged this; bestowed on the Ant-Lion its dredging skill and its cannon-ball service. How can it tell, buried except for the striking choppers, that the pebble which rolls down has to be volleyed out of the death-trap, while the approaching ant must be collected by gentle eruptions, dismayed by a perpetual sandy shower? And, answer as usual, we do not know.

Yet the relationship between the Ant-Lion and the curving beaches of Pampelone suggests a parallel. This time at Albi. Here Art and Nature have formed one of the most harmonious scenes in Europe. The fortress cathedral, the Bishop's Palace with its hanging gardens, and the old bridge, all of ancient brick, blend into the tawny landscape through which the emancipated Tarn flows from its gorges to the Garonne. Here again one wanders through this dream of the Middle Ages, by precincts of the rosy cathedral where the pious buzz like cockchafers, to be brought up by a notice on the portcullis of the Bishop's Palace. "Musée Toulouse-Lautrec." Tucked in the conventional Gothic of the fortress is a suite of long rooms in which the mother of the artist, using all her feudal powers, forced the municipal authorities to hang the pictures of her son. Less fortunate than those of Aix, who refused Cézanne's request to leave his pictures to the city, the fathers were intimidated by the Countess into placing them in this most sacred corner, lighted and hung in salons whose decoration has concealed all traces of the unsightly past.

The concierge turns proudly to the Early Work—pastoral scenes and sentimental evocations of Millet—these he likes best; they are what the Count was doing before he left his home and was corrupted by the Capital. Then come the drawings, in which emerges the fine savage line of the mature artist, that bold, but not (as in some of the paintings) vulgar stroke, which hits off the brutality of his subjects, or the beauty of those young girls doomed to such an inevitable end. In the large room beyond are the paintings, a morgue of End of Century vice, a succession of canvases in which there is hardly daylight, and where the only creature who lives by day is the wizened little Irish jockey. The world of the hunchback Count is nocturnal, gas-lit, racy, depraved and vicious; the shocked

Albigeois who pass through the gallery are riveted by the extraordinary picture of the laundress who checks over with the *sous-maîtresse* the linen from her Maison. As one goes from picture to picture the atmosphere intensifies, Valentin le Désossé and La Goulue become familiars, and the lovely girls blur into the dark of the Moulin Rouge, where one distinguishes a favourite figure, the long, sad, nocturnal, utterly empty but doggedly boring face of "L'Anglais,"—some English habitué to whom constant all-night attendance has given the polish of a sentry at his post.

At the end of the gallery is a door before which the concierge smiles mysteriously, as if to prepare us for Pompeian revelations. He opens it, and we emerge on a small terrace. The sun is shining, the sky is blue, the Tarn ripples underneath. Beyond the ancient brick of the bishop's citadel and the arches of the bridge stretches the landscape of the Albigeois—foothills of green corn delicately crowned by pink hill villages, which merge into the brown of the distant Cevennes under the pale penetrating light of the near-south, the transitional-Mediterranean. A lovely and healthy prospect, in which fields and cities of men blend everywhere into the earth and the sunshine. One takes a deep breath, when obstinately, from behind the closed door, one feels a suction; attraction fights repulsion as in the cold wavering opposition between the like poles of a magnet. Deep in his lair the Ant-Lion is at work; the hunchback Count recalls us; the world of poverty, greed, bad air, consumption, and of those who never go to bed awaits, but there awaits also an artist's integration of it, a world in which all trace of sentiment or decadence is excluded by the realism of the painter, and the vitality of his line. In the sunlight on the terrace we are given the choice between the world of Nature and the world of Art. Nature seems to win, but at the moment of victory there is something lacking, and it is that lack which only the unnatural world inside can supply—progress, for example, for the view from the Palace has not altered, except slightly to deteriorate, for several hundred years. The enjoyment of it requires no more perception than had Erasmus, while the art of Lautrec is modern, and can be appreciated only by those who combine a certain kind of aristocratic satisfaction at human beings acting in character, and in gross character, with the love of fine drawing and colour.

Not that Lautrec was a great artist; he is to Degas what Maupassant is to Flaubert, one who extended the noble conception of realism by which a great master accepts the world as it is for the sake of its dynamism, and for the passive, extraordinarily responsive quality of that world to the artist who has learnt how to impose his will on it. The world of Lautrec is artificial because it excludes goodness and beauty as carefully as it excludes the sun. But it is an arranged world, a world of melancholy and ignorance (figures melancholy because ignorant, patient in the treadmill of pleasure), and so the artist drags us in from the terrace because force and intelligence dominate that arrangement. And once back, we are back in his dream, in a hunchback's dream of the world; the sunlight seems tawdry, the red brick vulgar, the palace ornate; the crowd who stand in their tall hats gaping at the blossoming Can-Can dancers are in the only place worth being.

Now I understand the Ant-Lion. It is in Nature and with a natural right to its existence. There is no conflict between them; it is an advanced gadget in the scheme which includes the peaceful hills and the beach with its reedy pools of brackish water. Nor is there any opposition between Lautrec and the landscape of Albi. Albi was the oyster, and the contents of the museum are the Pearl. The irritant? The action of a physical deformity on an aristocratic, artistic but unoriginal mind which was happiest in the company of its inferiors, and which liked to be surrounded by the opposite sex in places where the deformity could be concealed by potency, or by the distribution of money. The result, a highly specialized painter, one of Nature's very latest experiments. And yet even that peaceful landscape was the home in the Middle Ages of a subversive doctrine, the Albigensian heresy; a primitive anarchism which taught that men were equal and free, which disbelieved in violence and believed in a chosen priesthood, in the Cathari who attained purity by abstinence, while they encouraged the Count's royal ancestors to come through excess and indulgence to heavenly wisdom. It was they who believed that the human race should cease to procreate, and so solve the problem of evil, who were massacred at Muret and Lavaur, and whom Simon de Montfort slaughtered with the remark, "The Lord will know his own." And the Heretics were right. Had a revolt against procreation spread outwards from Albi the world would have become an empty place, nor would such obstinate human beings who survived have been driven to kill each other for living-room, victims, for all we may know, of some deeper instinct of self-destruction which bids them make way for a new experiment, the civilization of the termite or the rat.

Much has happened since the summer. To-day the Maures are out of bounds, the Museum closed, and many generalizations based on incorrect assessment of the facts fallen to pieces, but (since the operations of the Ant-Lion have now been extended) it seems worth while to recall that the statements on the life of pleasure which Lautrec took from his witnesses at the Tabarin and the Moulin de la Galette, and which he so vigorously recorded on canvas, are still available to the traveller of the future, and assert their truth.

December 1939.

"1843"

LET US ESCAPE FOR A MOMENT TO THE YEAR 1843, AND SEE
what can be learnt from it. "What I call trifles are often read
with curiosity and avidity a hundred years later, even though
the writer may be a very commonplace, ordinary person like
myself," wrote Greville, on May 7 of that year, and in order
to recapture the flavour of that summer exactly a century ago,
we can begin with no richer authority. But we must not
confine ourselves to him, for Greville is one of those writers
whose mind is set in the rigidity contracted from his early
surroundings: he belongs in spirit to the Regency, and to the
eighteenth-century Whig tradition. In reading his journal
for 1843, in spite of his proximity to the centre of politics, we
feel him to be old-fashioned, and the great people who appear
in his pages seem already out of date:

"Another night, Moore sang some of his own Melodies,
and Macaulay has been always talking. Never certainly was
anything heard like him. He is inexhaustible, always
amusing and instructive, about everybody and everything.
. . . The drollest thing is to see the effect upon Rogers, who
is nearly extinguished, and can neither make himself heard,
nor find an interval to get in a word. He is exceedingly
provoked, though he can't help admiring, and he will revive
to-morrow when Macaulay goes. It certainly must be rather
oppressive after a certain time, and would be intolerable,
if it was not altogether free from conceit. . . . He said that
he read no modern books, none of the works or travels
that come out day after day. He had read *Tom Jones*
repeatedly, but *Cecil a Peer* not at all; and as to *Clarissa*, he
had read it so often that, if the work were lost, he could
give a very tolerable idea of it, could narrate the story
completely, and many of the most remarkable passages and

expressions." . . . "Subjects are tapped and the current flows without stopping."

"Macaulay went away the day before Christmas Day, and it was wonderful how quiet the house seemed after he was gone, and it was not less agreeable. Rogers was all alive again, Austin and Dundas talked much more than they would have done, and Lord Lansdowne too, and on the whole we were as well without him."

Macaulay's *Essays* were published in 1843, and they form one of the dozen important books to come out in that year. He is the only writer with whom Greville seems in touch, for politicians are notoriously reactionary in their literary tastes, and Greville moves only in the exclusive society of Holland House, the great country houses, and the racing stables of Newmarket, where his sense of guilt (after politics and gambling his strongest passion) is not slow to pursue him. "And this is the sort of society which I might have kept instead of that which I have," he writes of the Bowood Christmas just mentioned, and on October 31, 1843, crippled with gout, he returns to the theme:

"And this is called society; and amongst such people I have lived, do live, and shall live—I who have seen, known, and had the choice of better things. Eating, drinking, and amusement is the occupation of these people's lives, and I am ashamed to say such has been mine. I was reading Charles Lamb's Letters in the carriage, and very remarkable they are, among the very best I think I ever read. I was struck by one passage, which I applied to myself: 'I gain nothing by being with such as myself; we encourage one another in mediocrity.' This is it. We go on herding with inferior companions, till we are really unfit for better company."

Yet a few days before he had been present at an unsuccessful lunch where Macaulay met Ranke (whom many think the greatest of historians) and had been on a visit to Richmond to Mary Berry, the old friend of Horace Walpole:

> "She said nothing could be more beautiful and touching than his affection for her, devoid as it was of any particle of sensual feeling, and she should ever feel proud of having inspired such a man with such a sentiment."

In August he had visited the new royal yacht *Victoria and Albert*, "luxuriously fitted up, but everything is sacrificed to the comfort of the Court, the whole ship's company being crammed into wretched dog-holes, officers included," and on August 8 he had recorded a conversation with the Duke of Wellington at which one would have given much to be present. The Duke had given his opinion on the Duke of Marlborough, and defended his spelling, his morals, and his communications with the Pretender, the acting of a double part "that was no more than many men in France did during Napoleon's reign."

> "The Duke then talked of the military genius of Marlborough, and said that though he was a very great man, the art of war has so far advanced since his time that it is impossible to compare him with more modern generals; and unquestionably Napoleon was the greatest military genius that ever existed. . . ."

Among other interesting old men, there were, of course, Beckford, wrapped up in ancestor worship in his tower above Bath (he died in the following year); Landor, whose *Imaginary Conversations* were then appearing; Sydney Smith, and Wordsworth, who became Poet Laureate in that year; but doubtless Rogers would have been the most worth meeting, for alone he seems to have cultivated that art of living in the present which robs old age of so much of its terror. The Banker-Bard of St. James's Place, famous for his malice, his whisper, his corpse-like face, his breakfasts, his expensive editions of his mediocre works, his friendship for Byron and Wordsworth, for Porson and the family of Fox—this old man of over eighty, who had once rung Johnson's door-bell and run away in panic, kept all the latest books on his table, and made friends with their authors. Tennyson in particular, whose most important volume of poems had come out in the previous year, and been reprinted in 1843, was often invited, and seldom came. Aubrey de Vere describes a typical meeting between them.

"'Wordsworth,' he [Tennyson] said to me one day, 'is staying at Hampstead in the house of his friend Mr. Hoare; I must go and see him; and you must come with me; mind you do not tell Rogers or he will be displeased at my being in London and not going to see him.' We drove up to Hampstead, and knocked at the door; and the next minute it was opened by the Poet of the World, at whose side stood the Poet of the Mountains. Rogers' old face, which had encountered nearly ninety years, seemed to double the number of its wrinkles as he said, not angrily but very drily: 'Ah, you did not come up the hill to see *me*. . . .' As we walked back to London through grassy fields not then built over, Tennyson complained of the old poet's [Wordsworth's] coldness. He had endeavoured to stimulate some latent ardours by telling him of a tropical island where the trees, when they first came into leaf, were a vivid scarlet, 'Every one of them, I told him, one flush all over the island, the colour of blood! It would not do, I could not influence his imagination in the least!'"

The anecdote reveals Tennyson's own preoccupation with the exotic, with those tropics he never visited and indeed increasingly disapproved of, but which were his symbol of the wild, natural, unrepressed, and truly poetic life, free from politics, marriage, and duty—tropics which played such a lovely rôle in the imagery of his poems, in the *Lotos Eaters*, in the *Voyage of Maeldune*, in *Enoch Arden*, and in *Locksley Hall*.

. . . Slides the bird o'er lustrous woodland, droops the trailer from the crag,
Droops the heavy-blossomed bower, hangs the heavy-fruited tree—
Summer isles of Eden lying in dark-purple spheres of sea.
There methinks would be enjoyment more than in this march of mind,
In the steamship, in the railway, in the thoughts that shake mankind.
There the passions cramp'd no longer shall have scope and breathing space ;
I will take some savage woman, she shall rear my dusky race.

One might say, in fact, that *Locksley Hall* and *Ulysses* are the two poems most typical of young England in 1843, of the conflict, on the one hand, between Victorian optimism, the belief in progress, science, industrialization, and the white man's burden, and those other feelings which were opposed to it—the doubts and misgivings, religious, philosophic, and political, which we find in the Oxford Movement, in Chartism, in Clough and Arnold, in the unprogressive behaviour of Irish and Indians, or the events of 1848. Tennyson, our greatest poet of the last hundred years, might have been one of the greatest poets of the world if he had listened to his instinct alone, if he had not permitted his reason to enforce the doctrines of the day, not felt it his duty to be a philosopher-bard, a State-mouthpiece, rather than a wild and sensual voice of protest, a dying swan. The core of Tennyson's genius is voluptuous, surcharged with indolence and passion, and heavy with decay. The two *Marianas*, the *Lotos Eaters*, and many others of the early (1830) poems show this. By 1842 the new poems were becoming orthodox and didactic, till in *In Memoriam* the triumph of the official poet over the bereaved lover is finally assured. [*Maud* represents a rebellion against the age, a desperate rearguard action, yet the madness of the principal character robs his criticism of the power which it might have had if backed by all Tennyson's authority.] FitzGerald was the first to withdraw his admiration, and to hint that he considered the 1842 volumes to be the high-water-mark of his poetry. Meanwhile the Tennyson of 1843, under forty and enjoying his first real literary success, must have been unconscious of the conflict which was expressing itself in him, and which was to work itself out in *In Memoriam* and set the diamonds of his lyrics in the cheap paste of his argument, an argument never on the unpopular side. He was still melancholy and somewhat ascetic, even at his dinners at the Cock, where a "perfect dinner was a beef-steak, a potato, a cut of cheese, and a pint of port, and afterwards a pipe (never a cigar)." Among his friends at that time with whom he discussed the new inventions of science and their political implications, or the role of the poet, were Carlyle, Rogers, Barry Cornwall,

Thackeray, Dickens, Forster, Savage Landor, Maclise, Leigh
Hunt, and Tom Campbell. Carlyle, in a letter to his new
friend Emerson [*circ.* 1843], thus describes him:

> "One of the finest-looking men in the world. A great
> shock of rough dusky dark hair; bright laughing hazel eyes;
> massive aquiline face, most massive, yet most delicate; of
> sallow brown complexion, almost Indian looking, clothes
> cynically loose, free-and-easy, smokes infinite tobacco. His
> voice is musical, metallic, fit for loud laughter and piercing
> wail, and all that may lie between; speech and speculations
> free and plenteous; I do not meet in these late decades such
> company over a pipe! We shall see what he will grow to."

One of his most prized letters of the year must have been
from Dickens (March 10, 1843):

> "For the love I bear you as a man whose writings enlist
> my whole heart and nature in admiration of their Truth
> and Beauty, set these books upon your shelves; believing that
> you have no more earnest and sincere homage than mine."

These works were to be enriched during the year by *Martin
Chuzzlewit* and *A Christmas Carol*, novels which added the
words gamp (from Mrs. Gamp's umbrella), Pecksniffian, and
Scrooge to the English language. Thackeray was not at his
best in this year, for he produced only his *Irish Sketch Book*,
and in the year following *Barry Lyndon*. It was, however, a
very fine year for solid and profitable novels: Ainsworth
published *Windsor Castle*, Lytton *The Last of the Barons*,
Lever *Jack Hinton*; and Mr. Jorrocks set off for his earthbound
immortality in Surtees' *Handley Cross*. Lover's *Handy Andy*
came out in 1842, and Disraeli's *Coningsby* in 1844, while the
young Brontë sisters were still learning and teaching in Brussels.
Of the other poets besides Tennyson, Browning published
A Blot on the Scutcheon, Southey died, and Wordsworth became
Laureate. Eighteen hundred and forty-two saw, besides
Tennyson, Wordsworth's poems, *Early and Late Years*, and
Macaulay's *Lays of Ancient Rome*. Eighteen hundred and
forty-four brought Elizabeth Barrett Browning's *Poems*, and

also those of Milnes and William Barnes. Perhaps the best-
known poem of our year was Hood's *Song of the Shirt*,
which appeared anonymously in the two-year-old *Punch* and
set it on the road to financial success. The most impressive
poem, however, was surely Richard Horne's epic *Orion*,
published at a farthing "to mark the public contempt into
which epic poetry had fallen." The epic told an Orion myth
of a struggle between the senses and the intellect somewhat
similar to that of Prometheus, and according to Gosse was "an
attempt to re-establish the union which had existed in ancient
time between philosophy and poetry." Three editions at a
farthing and three more at a higher price were exhausted
within a year, and Poe pronounced *Orion* "superior even to
Milton's *Paradise Lost*." Who will exhume it?

In other works of the intellect the year is outstanding. The
most important work of this kind was John Stuart Mill's *System
of Logic*, Darwin's *Structure of Coral Reefs* came out in 1842,
and Newman's *Essay on Miracles* in 1843. The essayists were
busy. Carlyle's *Past and Present* heads the list, for those who
can read him; Landor, Leigh Hunt (*Imagination and Fancy*),
De Quincey, FitzGerald, Beddoes were all in bloom, and Wilson
in Edinburgh published his *Recreations of Christopher North*;
two remarkable travel books appeared, Borrow's romantic
Bible in Spain (1843) and Kinglake's more robust *Eothen* (1844),
but the work of the imagination which most breathed a new
spirit was the first volume of *Modern Painters*, "by a graduate
of Oxford," which came out in 1843 when Ruskin was twenty-
four. The graduate (he had taken "an honorary fourth") had
originally intended to call the book "Turner and the Ancients,"
but even so his defence of Turner, then painting his most
exaggerated works, and of Nature and the Gothic against
all comers was an immediate success. The poet Rogers allowed
the book to lie on his table. Tennyson, supreme Nature-lover,
begged for the book, and Sydney Smith in the *Edinburgh
Review* rightly declared that "it was a work of transcendent
talent, presented the most original views, and the most elegant
and powerful language, and would work a complete revolution
in the world of taste." Those talent-spotters who feel that

even twenty-four is rather old may like to wonder if they would have helped to take the chill off the reception of Ebenezer Jones' "morally unwholesome" and "youthfully defiant" poems, *Studies of Sensation and Event* (1843), or if they would have noticed anything special about the poem on Cromwell with which an undergraduate won the Newdigate that year. They might indeed have noticed Matthew Arnold. But what about Cory who was twenty, Meredith who was fifteen, Butler who was eight, and Swinburne who was six? Would they have been guided to them?

* * *

There is no space to treat of literary events outside England at much length, but to complete the picture of the year's output one might mention that the tales of Poe and Hawthorne were appearing in America, as well as Emerson's *Essays* and Prescott's *Conquest of Mexico*. Melville was in the South Seas, Longfellow had just been the guest of Dickens, Irving had gone to Spain, Whitman was twenty-four, Henry Adams was five, and Henry James new-born.

In France the prospect is more exciting. Hugo, Lamartine, Musset, Gautier, Sainte-Beuve were all in spate, George Sand was producing some of her best work (which Thackeray was shocked by), Balzac, after his famous preface of 1842, was bringing out the whole *Comédie Humaine* as a work complete in itself (*Eugénie Grandet* and *Le Lys dans la Vallée* belong to 1843-44); while three young men, two born in 1821, reached crises in their lives; Baudelaire came back from India, Flaubert had a nervous breakdown, and Renan went to the Saint-Sulpice Seminary to train for the priesthood. During the year 1843 appeared one of the most mysterious poems ever written, so much the best poem of the year, so prophetic in instinct, so modern in feeling, so guileless in form, that it is worth printing entire, if only to suggest an English translation.

DELFICA

Ultima cumaei venit jam carminis aetas.

La connais-tu, Dafné, cette ancienne romance,
Au pied du sycomore, ou sous les lauriers blancs,
Sous l'olivier, le myrte, ou les saules tremblants,
Cette chanson d'amour qui toujours recommence ? . . .

Reconnais-tu le Temple au péristyle immense,
et les citrons amers où s'imprimaient tes dents,
et la grotte, fatale aux hôtes imprudents,
Où du dragon vaincu dort l'antique semence ? . . .

Ils reviendront, ces Dieux·que tu pleures toujours !
Le temps va ramener l'ordre des anciens jours :
La terre a tressailli d'un souffle prophétique . . .

Cependant la sibylle au visage latin
Est endormie encor sous l'arc de Constantin
et rien n'a dérangé le sévère portique.

GÉRARD DE NERVAL.

*　　*　　*

But if one could assign any one movement in France to the year 1843 it would be not so much a literary one as the birth of a myth: the myth of Paris. It was in 1843 that the idea first took shape of Paris as the capital of the world, luxurious and elegant, yet also mysterious; the sprawling industrial Babylon with its romantic underworld of squalor and vice. *The Murders in the Rue Morgue* (1841) began to yield its fruit. The supreme example of the myth is Eugène Sue's *Mystères de Paris* (1843), an interminable serial of high life and the under-world whose illustrations gave Max Ernst his *collages*, and show us for the first time the spread-eagled bourgeois corpse on the street corner, or the drowned prostitute floating just under the surface of the newly constructed St. Martin's Canal. Hugo's *Notre-Dame* and *Les Misérables* were historical novels inspired by this feeling. Vidocq's *Les Vrais Mystères de Paris*, *Les Mystères du Grand Opéra* (Lespes), *Les Mystères de Londres* (Feval), *Les Rues de Paris* (Kugelmann)—all appeared in 1843-44, as well as that extraordinary compilation of Gavarni, Nerval, Sand, Balzac, Gautier, and others, *Le Diable à Paris* (1845). It was still the golden age of the romantic illustrator— Nanteuil, Tony Johannot, Gavarni, Lami, Dévéria, and of that surrealist genius, Grandville. His *Un Autre Monde* (1844), recently the subject of an article in the *Architectural Review*, is the book of all this period that it is most delightful to possess in its original form.

From 1846 onwards Baudelaire was to give himself up to this cult of Paris and of modern life which was inspired by his youthful enthusiasms for Balzac and Guys. He saw both the romance, the aesthetic possibilities, and also all the boredom and horror of urban life on a grand scale, "la noire majesté de la plus inquiétante des capitales." The current of modern sensibility which was to lead to *Lautréamont*, *A Rebours*, *Dorian Gray*, *Ulysses*, *Voyage au bout de la nuit*, *Mrs. Dalloway*, the London scenes of *Prufrock* and of *The Waste Land*, and to so many of our best detective stories and films, which was to compel Chirico to paint his grief-stricken and sonorous colonnades, the poetry, in fact, of the city grown large enough to devour those who live in it, no longer a mere flowering into stone of the surrounding landscape, but a monster which men have created out of their greed to feed on them: all this lyrical realism, this pride in their destroyer, comes from the research into Babylon engendered by the genius of Baudelaire operating on the more innocent enthusiasm of the authors and illustrators of 1843, compelling the Balzac of Vautrin or of the *Histoire des Treize* to answer Baudelaire's own question, whether the poet's own time possessed "une beauté particulière, inhérente à des passions nouvelles."

*   *   *

And yet, so luminous is the spirit of an age, we can see now, looking back to 1843, as if looking at children in a class-room, which artists are creating and which are marking time, which, like Baudelaire, Grandville, and Nerval, are of our period; which, like Hugo and Tennyson, Balzac and Dickens, are of their own; and which belong in fact to the past, despite their illusion that they were of their so vigorous present, like the French gourmet-writers or Macaulay and Greville. Past, present, and future exist in the arts simultaneously. According to our courage or to our inclination we are all free to choose. Thus, while the Paris of 1843 was fermenting with talent and forward-looking inspiration, while "Delfica" was being written, a hundred and fifty miles away Greville was taking his summer holiday on the Rhine, admiring the brand-new railway and the food on the steamer, the volume of the water, but not the scenery ('inferior to the Wye'), and, after many pleasant *tables d'hôte*, was reposing in Baden. The past surrounded him, he seemed to bring it with him, to smell it out, even being so fortunate in Frankfort, when visiting the dilapidated ghetto whose streets were once locked at night, as to come across

> "in this narrow gloomy street and before this wretched tenement, a smart *calèche* fitted up with blue silk, and a footman in blue livery at the door. Presently the door opened, and an old woman was seen descending a dark narrow staircase, supported by her granddaughter. Two footmen and some maids were in attendance to help the old lady into the carriage, and a number of the inhabitants collected opposite to see her get in."

It was the old mother of the Rothschilds, then aged ninety-four, who all her life had never been out of Frankfort nor inhabited any other house there than the one in which she had resolved to die—and so back again to the life at Baden, the newspapers in the club, the dinners and the drives, the evenings in the gardens:

> "Then I sit with any friends I find at a little round table, in the cool of a delicious evening, eating ice and drinking what I please, a band of music playing, and the odours of new-mown hay, orange trees, limes, and roses, wafted on every gale. . . . Every now and then one saunters into the magnificent rooms where the eternal play goes on, and the monotonous voice of the *croupier* 'Le jeu est-il fait? Messieurs, faites vos jeux' wearies the air. These creatures sit hour after hour, peddling with their florin stakes, and assiduously marking cards with pins, till between ten and eleven the gardens are gradually deserted, and at eleven a kind of curfew tolls the knell of day departed, and gambling ends. A bell rings, which is the signal for general dispersion and the closing of houses of resort. The lights in the rooms are extinguished, and the weary *croupiers* retire. The police drive people even out of the hotels, and long before midnight no sound is heard in Baden but the waters of the river gurgling over their pebbled bed."

Such is the life of pleasure. Outside time, exempt from time, the same in any age, an invaluable trance in which those worn out by the battles of time can for a little take their convalescence. "Messieurs, faites vos jeux": which shall we choose?—a life-time of pleasure, immune from all the horrors of life except the one supreme horror of finding that life has by-passed us, and of finding it out only at the last moment, when the unused potential of the mind is about to crumble into dust—or a life-time of belonging to the age, fighting its battles, espousing its causes, wallowing in its optimism, or its fashionable pessimism, enjoying its respect and gathering its praise? We can be Browning or Tennyson, Ruskin, Carlyle, Herbert Spencer. Or a life altogether outside the age, a life of epicureanism like FitzGerald's, renouncing everything except Horatian comfort, taste, and a kind heart, and unloading a few copies, sold for fourpence on a barrow, of a chance translation from the Persian which will captivate posterity and place all that selfish life above reproach? Nobody need be anything they do not want to: they can spend their whole life (like John Allen, who died in 1843) in being a perpetual guest, with no private residence at all, at whatever is the modern equivalent of Holland House—or they can live like Lord Hertford (died 1842), who was driven round London in his last illness and carried every after-noon by two footmen up the steps of a brothel, or die in 1843 like Hölderlin after forty years of quiet insanity. And yet there is always the other life which does not hide from time behind the skirt of pleasure, nor, underneath the umbrella of duty, ignore it, but which defies it, and defies it intelligently, to triumph in the end over time. This is the life of those artists who are ahead, who so identify themselves with reality, the reality of the spiritual discoveries of their age, that they achieve a complete timelessness in their art and through the intensity of their vision become identified with the future. It is to this visionary class that Baudelaire, Nerval, and Kierkegaard, whose "Repetition" and "Fear and Trembling" came out in 1843, belonged, and to which Tennyson and Brown-ing just failed to belong, through a certain cowardice and back-sliding which made them draw away into the conventional

world of Victorian optimism when they divined in what
direction they were going, and what the consequences would
be. A period in which the conception of life as it might be is
hurled against reality like a wave which breaks against a black
rock into a scintillation of diamonds—such is the century of
Flaubert and Baudelaire. It is indeed a terrible choice, to
decide whether one would have preferred to be Baudelaire with
his syphilis or "Lawn" Tennyson with his country houses.
But, if 1843 has a lesson for us to-day, it should be that of all
forms of appeasement the most tragic is the appeasement by
an artist of his own genius, when, after the compromise, only
talent remains.

Yet there is one other lesson which 1843 seems to ram home
somewhat uncivilly for us writers of to-day. Of course this is
a bad year—we are at the most exhausted moment of a war, the
moment before victory, and our writers are mostly otherwise
occupied—yet we are also, or so all of us under forty believe,
products of a peculiar and unique process: the modern movement—a renaissance to which we belong by birth and which
has put us in quite a different position to all those who have
preceded us and who have not had our advantages in being
post-war, post-Freud, post-Einstein, post-twentieth century.
I do not wish to say anything against the period to which I
belong, a period which has had the unique experience of
beginning where all other periods have left off, nor do I wish
to find fault with the generation which has succeeded it. Only,
after comparing the year we live in with the one of which it
is the centenary, I seem to hear Time, like Greville's weary
croupier, cry "Faites vos jeux" and to feel a wish to cry out,
to the chosen and privileged generation of 1900-10, and to
the still more privileged generation of 1910-20 who are coming up for air, "We are unique, I know, but there may be
someone—shall we say in 2043?—who might conceivably
wish to write an article like this. You do see what I mean?
Not that there's any real hurry."

August 1943.

THE ART OF BEING GOOD

A NOTE ON MAUGHAM AND FORSTER

I. The Razor's Edge. By W. Somerset Maugham. (Heinemann, 12s. 6d.)

THIS IS MR. MAUGHAM'S BEST NOVEL SINCE "CAKES AND ALE," and, appearing at a time when the decline in literary quality is fairly matched by the decline in literary taste, it breathes the atmosphere of another world.

The novel is a considerable addition to the literature of non-attachment, and ranks with Huxley's *Grey Eminence* and Heard's *Man the Master* as powerful propaganda for the new faith or, rather, new version of an old faith, which is called by various names—neo-Brahmanism, or the Vedanta of the West—and which has made its home in somewhat macabre proximity to Hollywood. This does not mean that Mr. Maugham "has been converted by Gerald Heard" and so forth, for in all his previous work there has always been a strong inclination to mysticism and an ill-concealed sympathy for those who turn their back on the world. Mr. Maugham's gallery of bums and beachcombers, his sanguine study in *The Moon and Sixpence*, his interest in the Spanish mystics in *Don Fernando* and in various Eastern types of holy man, proclaim this obsession through all his work. He is the worldliest of our novelists, and yet is fascinated by those who renounce the world, whether to do nothing, to become artists, to be a Communist as in *Christmas Holiday*, or a Saint as in *The Razor's Edge*. The book is indeed a study in pre-sanctity in the early years of a man whom the author hints is capable of saving the world, if it will ever listen—and it is part of his sanctity that Larry should be in many ways very like everybody else, a delightful, simple, single-minded Krishnamurti from the Middle West. Since he is to be tempted, we have also pictures of the World and the Flesh: the world in the form of Elliot Templeton, most perfectly drawn of all the characters; the genial, infinitely

painstaking romantic snob, with Catholic and discreetly homosexual leanings, whose magnificent but empty career of social
success Mr. Maugham paints with lingering tenderness, right
down to the wonderful death-scene which is a kind of farewell
offering to his old corrupt world of Paris and the Riviera, whose
eclipse he would seem here both to acknowledge and to regret.

The flesh appears in the guise of three women: Isabel,
Elliot's niece, an admirably drawn American girl, charming
and sensitive when first engaged to Larry, but moulded by
the conditions of moneyed American life into a chic, beautiful,
greedy, heartless woman, typical of all well-dressed, noisy, yet
withal warm and honest, machine-tooled cosmopolitans. It is
Isabel's tragedy to know that Larry, whom she rejected as a
suitor because he was poor, is the only man who really attracts
her and can bring out her own potentialities. The two other
women are Sophie Macdonald, the type of American girl gone
to the bad—drink, drugs, sailors—out of the violence of her
disappointment with life; and Suzanne Rouvier, Mr.
Maugham's familiar female character, the honest whore.
She represents the charm and common sense, the fundamentally
worth-while values of French civilization, as contrasted with
the depravity of American, as typified by the worldly Elliot,
the savage Isabel, the nymphomaniac Sophie, and Isabel's
simple, money-making husband Gray. These are the material
the young saint (who, however, is also an American) must get
to work on. On the whole, he is not a success, for in this pre-
sanctity stage, in his commonplace, somewhat priggish, larval
form, he is chiefly concerned with getting away from people
like these and trying to find the truth by reading and travel,
manual labour and meditation. He is enlightened by a holy
man in Southern India, and the lovely descriptions of this
country make some of the pleasantest reading in the book.
They also present Mr. Maugham with his hardest problem,
that of conveying the mystical experience, that explosive which
has so far defied all rational analysis. I think that, on the
whole, for a writer who is not a mystic, he has managed to
do this: he conveys well the passionate quest for truth which
consumes Larry's whole life and which originates in his

experiences as a pilot in the last war, when he made the discovery that "the dead look so terribly dead when they're dead." Thus the moment of faith to which it leads up comes as no surprise. But of what faith? This seems to me the real difficulty: to a sceptical mind it seems doubtful whether human beings actually possess the apparatus which can discover truth, and when they pin it down in a doctrine there is always a sense of disappointment. Now, the neo-brahmins of Hollywood have a doctrine, and that doctrine embraces a considerable amount of Hindu religion and Yoga mysticisms, so Larry has to believe in the transmigration of souls, in Brahma, Vishnu and Siva, and Mr. Maugham's attempt to make this convincing seems far more disastrous than his penetrating criticism of Christianity or the mystical experience which he previously described. A ridiculous hypnotic trick, an example of suggestion, is made use of as a "sign" of power, and the vision of Larry's previous selves also fails to convince. It would have been better for the novel not to have confined Larry to any known religious system: to let him have his revelation and then leave it at that.

The Razor's Edge shows a great technical improvement on the author's recent novels. He handles his four or five characters to perfection, and includes himself—not as a fictional character—but as the flesh-and-blood Willie Maugham of real life, with complete mastery. Here is a novelist right inside his own novel—not a mere stooge or onlooker, or larger than life, as a *deus ex machina*, but on the same plane as all the other characters, not more real nor less—a brilliant feat, carried off with quiet mastery. The too short staccato sentences which often mar his style have also been expanded; there is less of "I have a notion," and the writing is delightfully flexible, vivid and easy. Everything appears haphazard, yet everything is to the point. Maugham is the greatest living short-story writer, and so one expects his handling of plot to force one into a breathless, non-stop reading from the first page to the last, and his character-drawing and observation to be in the fine tradition—but one would not expect to be so captivated by the brilliant fluency of the writing. Here at last is a great writer, on the threshold of old age, determined to tell the truth in a form which releases all the possibilities of his art. His comments and asides excite us in their justice and sometimes by their rancour. He has, for example, a note of particular asperity whenever there is any question of the standing of writers in the social world. If there is one thing to regret about this novel it is that it is written not for us but for Americans: one detects a considerable amount of playing down to the trans-atlantic common man and a faintly disapproving attitude to Europe and this country. Mr. Maugham has never been a master of words; he has always preferred the *mot moyen* to the *mot juste*; he is incapable of those flights of vocabulary which we find in the great living stylists: Logan Pearsall Smith, E. M. Forster, Max Beerbohm ; but even he should know better than to use "exquisitely gowned" or various slangy expressions (not in dialogue but in the author's musings) which are already out of date. Yet if his book is written for Americans, it is certainly a tract for them! Never have their weak points been so tactfully yet remorselessly suggested—Mr. Maugham never forgets the spiritual dust-bowl which every American carries within him, and which he vainly tries to irrigate with alcohol, statistics, or labour-saving devices. "I have a notion," Mr. Maugham seems to say, "that the new Messiah is going to have his work cut out." Here is his final judgment:

> Larry has been absorbed, as he wished, into that tumultuous conglomeration of humanity, distracted by so many conflicting interests, so lost in the world's confusion, so wishful of good, so cocksure on the outside, so diffident within, so kind, so hard, so trustful and so cagey, so mean and so generous, which is the people of the United States.

It has puzzled me, considering the sheer delight that I and all my friends have received from this novel, that it has been so uncharitably reviewed. Are we becoming incapable of recognizing excellence when we see it? I think prejudice is to blame—prejudice against any book which so perfectly recaptures the graces that have vanished, and against any writer who is so obviously not content with the banal routine of self-esteem and habit, graced by occasional orgies of nationalism and herd-celebrations, with which most of us, from the lovely Isabels and exquisite Elliot Templetons, down to the tame gravel-throwing apes of Fleet Street, fidget away our one-and-only lives.

II. The Undeveloped Heart.

"To write simply," says Mr. Somerset Maugham, "is as difficult as to be good." One might add that to write badly is as natural as to do evil, if we accept Baudelaire's definition: "Le mal se fait sans effort, naturellement, le bien est toujours produit d'un art."

But supposing the connection is even closer—supposing it were true, as the Victorians and some of the ancient Greeks believed, that to write simply it is necessary to be good; that virtue has the best style—what a burden of right conduct would be laid on the already overburdened tribe of authors! Yet that, I think, is what Mr. Forster believes, and certainly it is the secret of his art. For Mr. Forster, whose great-grandfather was a pillar of the Clapham Sect, is in everything he writes a moralist, a militant tractarian who in all his novels and stories not only blatantly rewards the good and punishes the wicked, but (in a long series of personal asides) distributes marks and awards points on his characters' behaviour and actions.

So much is clear; here in an age whose values are blurred is a writer with a creed—not a creed, like Mr. Maugham's, of oriental fatalism—but a vigorous and clear-cut ethical system. What is not so clear is how it may be defined. But it is through such a definition of this creed that we can best understand Mr. Forster, and a very clear one has just been advanced by Dr. Trilling, an American professor of English literature and author of a book on Matthew Arnold, whose *E. M. Forster* is now published in England by the Hogarth Press.

Sawston-Tonbridge [he writes] may have made Forster miserable, but it gave his thought its great central theme. This is the theme of the undeveloped heart. In his essay, "Notes on the English Character," Forster speaks of the

public school system as being at the root of England's worst
national faults and most grievous political errors. For, he
says, the faults of England are the faults of the middle
classes that dominate it, and the very core of these middle
classes is the English public school system, which gives its
young men a weight out of all proportion to their numbers
and sends them into a world "of whose richness and subtlety
they have no conception," a world into which they go "with
well-developed bodies, fairly developed minds, and undeveloped hearts."

The theme is almost obsessive with Forster. It is not the
unfeeling or perverted heart that absorbs him, but the
heart untrained and untutored, the heart checked too early
in its natural possible growth. His whole literary effort is
a research into this profound pathology.

Bearing this interpretation in mind let us continue our
inquiry into Mr. Forster's religion. Here is the first sentence
of one of his early stories, a sentence which also illustrates what
is meant by writing simply and writing well.

Few things have been more beautiful than my notebook
on the Deist Controversy as it fell downward through the
waters of the Mediterranean. It dived, like a piece of black
slate, but opened soon, disclosing leaves of pale green, which
quivered into blue. Now it had vanished, now it was a
piece of magical india-rubber stretching out to infinity, now
it was a book again, but bigger than the book of all knowledge.
It grew more fantastic as it reached the bottom, where a
puff of sand welcomed it and obscured it from view. But it
reappeared, quite sane though a little tremulous, lying
decently open on its back, while unseen fingers fidgeted
among its leaves.

"It is such a pity," said my aunt, "that you will not
finish your work in the hotel. Then you would be free to
enjoy yourself and this would never have happened."

What can we conclude from this passage? First let us notice
the rapid vivid impressionist character of the writing. This is
typical of all his work. Then the exactness of his observation

and the felicity of his imagery—"like a piece of black slate"—
"magical india-rubber stretching out to infinity"— and so on.
Then a kind of ascetic delight which is the particular hall-mark
of his sensibility: Mr. Forster sees the world not so much as
a child but as a poet who is in training, who neither drinks
nor smokes nor obscures his vision with any form of self-
•indulgence; his eyesight is extraordinarily good, whether he
is looking at the Blue Grotto or at the hypocrisy which lurks
concealed in a cluster of mixed motives. Now we come to the
ethical content. What happens in this sentence? A notebook
(full of obsolete academic information obtained in a northern
university) falls into the blue southern sea and becomes, for
the first time in its existence, an object of beauty. The owner
of the notebook experiences a sense of release and exhilaration
in which the author obviously shares; an Anglo-Saxon aunt,
however, misses the point and immediately makes a reproving
remark.

Here already is much of Mr. Forster's religion. The notebook is Culture (Culture not so much for its own sake as for
some academic preferment), the sea is Life, the owner of the
notebook is English Youth, and the Aunt is English governing-
class authority. On the next page the naked Italian boatman
dives for it, and he will then represent the pagan element of
beauty and natural desire. Forster is always on the side of
life; always against authority, puritans, prigs, and pedants—
he is continually making clear to us the choice between life
and the cultivation of class or money, comparing the spontaneous and living with the neatly fossilized dead. For
culture-prigs, those who exclaim "procul este profani!" or
"oh, what a good boy am I!" he reserves his most vibrant
arrows.

His religion, in fact, in its early stage is an Hellenistic
paganism in which there are no dualities; death is a friend—
beauty and goodness and impulse are one. Youth, helped
perhaps by a sensitive old lady, is right, and age, convention,
privilege and success are generally wrong. The Aunt (or
Uncle), the Italian Diver, the Youth torn between the South
and the demands of his family, constantly reappear. One

might say that Mr. Forster's religion is a primitive pantheistic paganism to which has been afterwards added an oriental preoccupation with non-attachment and abnegation, all worked upon by his inherited moral temperament. Pan is led by conventional English standards of decency to the Krishna of the Bhagavad-gita; the Greek religion whose origins were in the East is traced back to its source.

Dr. Trilling writes at length of one of Forster's short stories, *The Eternal Moment*, which is also one of his most perfect works, stamped throughout with his moral insight, his lyricism, and ascetic vitality. It is an attack on our civilization; on its well-meaning destructiveness and its money-values. Miss Raby, a successful novelist, with an admiring and sensitive friend, Colonel Leyland, returns to the village in which she had once been made love to by her Italian guide. The village, now grown popular through her book, has become a tourist-ridden and corrupt Dolomite capital. The Italian guide has evolved into the concierge of the big hotel: she realizes that, for an eternal moment in the past, she had loved him, and tries to tell him so. The concierge is deeply embarrassed and alarmed by her. Colonel Leyland, even more shocked at her class betrayal, opens his wallet, taps his head and so connives in the idea that she is mad. If we think how Proust, or Maugham, or Hemingway, or other male novelists would have treated this story we see that they would all really have thought such an elderly lady insane, victim of a temporary sexual aberration, and that none of them would have seen anything vile in the colonel's gesture, nor anything inherently ignoble in the concierge's position. To Proust a concierge was a kind of fashionable cardinal. But to Forster, who is a moralist, a concierge is a wicked thing. Miss Raby, who by writing her best-seller has made it possible for the mountain guide to become a plump concierge, has indeed betrayed life, and has every reason to take the blame.

He opened the windows, he filled the match-boxes, he flicked the little tables with a duster, always keeping an eye on the door in case anyone arrived without luggage, or left without paying. . . . She watched the man spreading out the postcards, helpful yet not obtrusive, alert yet deferential. She watched him make the bishop buy more than he wanted. This was the man who had talked of love to her upon the mountain. But hitherto he had only revealed his identity by chance gestures bequeathed to him at birth. Intercourse with the gentle classes had required new qualities—civility, omniscience, imperturbability. It was the old answer: the gentle classes were responsible for him. It was absurd to blame Feo for his worldliness—for his essential vulgarity. He had not made himself.

This leads us on from Forster's ethical to his political sense. For he is a political writer who prefers unpolitical themes: his two best novels, *Howard's End* (which Dr. Trilling says is about "who shall inherit England") and *Passage to India*, are, for all their romantic interest, tales of the barricades and the class war, and Forster, acutely though he sees the weaknesses of the under-privileged, remains unquestionably on their side. What Miss Raby hated about Feo's hostelry, the *Grand Hôtel des Alpes*, were "the ostentatious lounge, the polished walnut bureau, the vast rack for the bedroom keys, the panoramic bedroom crockery, the uniforms of the officials, and the smell of smart people—which is to some nostrils quite as depressing as the smell of poor ones."

"The uniforms of officials, and the smell of smart people"— all his life Forster will detest these, for he is somewhat more than a liberal in politics: he is a libertarian. Though he believes in original sin and feels the contempt of those who share this belief for those who don't, he also believes in human dignity, courage and freedom—given the right conditions. "Death destroys a man," he says in *Howard's End*, "but the idea of death saves him—that is the best account of it that has yet been given." As a philosopher Forster may be sceptical about progress; as a political being he is much more than sceptical about reactionaries, militarists, millionaires, pharisees, and bureaucrats. We are lucky to possess what amounts to the creed of this artist-philosopher, in his pamphlet *What I believe* (Hogarth Press, 6d.). He "doesn't believe in Belief," but he does believe in (1) Personal Relations; (2) Democracy; (3) Aristocracy, "an aristocracy of the sensitive, the considerate, and the plucky. Its members are to be found in all nations and classes, and all through the ages, and there is a secret understanding between them when they meet. They represent the true human tradition, the one permanent victory of our queer race over cruelty and chaos."

In his golden pamphlet Forster also mentions what he does *not* believe in—heroes, great men, leaders, Christianity, autocracy, asceticism, intolerance, and the State—and here too he enounces his slogan—his act of faith. "The people I respect must behave as if they were immortal and as if society were eternal. Both assumptions are false: both of them must be accepted as true if we are to go on working and eating and loving, and are to keep open a few breathing holes for the human spirit."

In a world of masters and slaves both Maugham and Forster have escaped to the minority of the free. Maugham, the cynic, is sentimental about his hero's goodness; Forster, the progressive liberal, sees virtue warily as something which, so lax have we become, has to be punctiliously enforced, like vaccination. Maugham has bought his freedom through hard work and popular success. "The value of money," he remarks, "is that with it we can tell any man to go to the devil." It is "the sixth sense which enables you to enjoy the other five." Forster's freedom is based on money also, for he has never had to earn his living, but he has also learnt to make do with very little, to purchase freedom through an exacting conscience, a detached passion for the life of the spirit and (this is common to Maugham also) an attitude to the State which can best be described as one of quiet effrontery. Long life to them!

WRITERS AND SOCIETY, 1940-3

THE POSITION OF THE ARTIST TO-DAY SHOULD OCCASION GENERAL concern were it not that the whole human race seems threatened by an interior urge to destruction. He occupies, amid the surrounding dilapidation, a corner even more dilapidated, sitting with his begging bowl in the shadow of the volcano. What can be done to help him? In the event of the defeat of England and France, nothing. We are accustomed to the idea that there is no art worth the name in Germany and Italy (although Italy possesses a high standard of taste—witness her pavilions in recent exhibitions, and a group of interesting young painters), but we are less familiar with the fact that literature and painting are becoming more and more confined to the Western democracies, the countries where wealth and appreciation survive, and where the environment is friendly. A defeat of those countries would mean the extinction of the "liberal" arts in Western Europe, as much as of liberal opinions.

But in the democracies themselves the artist finds himself tolerated rather than appreciated. Unless he is a purveyor of amusement or a mouthpiece of official cliché he is there on sufferance, and before suggestions for the betterment of his condition can be made, we must consider his ideal status in life. Just as education cannot improve until the world for which children are educated improves, so the artist cannot receive his due until the society in which he lives fundamentally revises its conception of the objects of existence. Many people would accept the idea of a benevolent world Socialism as their political aim, a world in which all the resources were available to its inhabitants, in which heat and fuel and food were as free as air and water, in which Marx's familiar definition of an ultimate civilization, "to each according to his needs, from each according to his ability," was realized. But this world does nothing for the spiritual life of humanity except to provide for its inhabitants the material comfort and security which has hitherto provided the point of departure only for the spiritual life of the few. The final happiness of humanity must depend on its capacity to evolve, on the use it makes of the capacity—found only in human beings—of getting outside itself, of extending human consciousness to include the perception of non-human phenomena, till it is not only aware of, but able to transcend, the laws by which it is governed. Otherwise to achieve a material Utopia, however difficult and desirable, is still to doom the race to the disintegration of satiety, and to the decay inherent in its own limitations.

There are certain types of human beings who are especially equipped for the extension of human consciousness and for the domination of the in-human world. They are the scientist, the mystic, the philosopher, the creative artist, and the saint. Of these, only the scientist receives the partial appreciation of the world, because by subsidizing his researches the world will grow the richer by such by-products as the aeroplane or the telephone. Einstein and Freud, the physicist and the psycho-analyst whose inventions were of doubtful value, were exiled by their immediate public. These five types, the pure scientist who uses measurement in his investigation of natural laws, the philosopher who uses mind, the saint and the mystic who make use of extra-sensitive emotional machinery, and the artist with his dark lantern, form the aristocracy of a more perfect world, in which the second order is composed of those who, without seeking to expand human possibilities, work at improving their condition. These would include the reformers and administrators, the practical scientists and inventors, the educators, the alleviators, the doctor and nurses, the practical artists, actors, singers, journalists and entertainers, and the men of law. Then would come the middle-men, the keepers of order and the pillars of trade, and then the great mass whose progress towards intelligence and happiness is the concern of the others, and lastly the "blind mouths," the invincibly ignorant, the obstructive and destructive, the power-grabbers, the back-street Napoleons, the incurable egoists and prima donnas, the gangsters, whether poor or rich.

While the greatest explorations of the world beyond our boundaries have been made by scientists, never have writers

been so preoccupied as now with the investigation of spiritual
possibilities, and this alone justifies the artist's claim to the
respect of mankind. At the moment Wells, Maugham, Joyce,
Virginia Woolf, Huxley, Heard, Priestley, Eliot may all be
said to be working on it, and, among young writers, a deepening
sense of spirituality characterizes the recent poetry of Auden
and Spender. There is no escapism from a political present in
this, and the best analysis of it is to be found in the opening
chapters of Heard's *Pain, Sex and Time*, in which he describes
human beings as the prisoners in a submarine who can only
escape the fate of the unadaptable species by concentrating all
their evolutionary energy on a dangerous and difficult escape
by a spiritual Davis apparatus. The value of Picasso's *Guernica*,
of the work of Proust, of the landscapes of Cézanne, is to
penetrate the darkness which surrounds the human camp-fire,
and reveal something of the landscape beyond it. The artist
lacks the training and the profound comprehension of a Freud
or an Einstein, nor does he make a good philosopher according
to academic standards, but his intuitive intensity, his patient
obsession, and the quality of his imagination entitle him to
rank with the great disappointed Prometheuses of our age,
those who are bent on changing the world as inexorably as
their rulers appear set on its destruction.

That is the ideal picture. And even there it will be noticed
that most of the artist-sages I have mentioned have accumulated
their fame and fortune as artist-entertainers. To-day the
scientist is subsidized, but the saint is expected to live by his
sanctity, the mystic on his mysticism, the artist by his popularity
with his sitters, or with the twopenny libraries. Only the
entertainer receives his due, which nobody grudges him, but
which hardly compensates for the squalor and penury in which
the serious poet or painter is permitted to rot. To-day the most
precariously situated in any society are that abandoned trio,
the writer, the painter, and the liberal intellectual. The
intellectual is the most unfortunate, for he has no creative
power to absorb him, he is the Cassandra of our age, condemned
to foresee the future and to warn, but never to be listened to,
nor to be able to profit from his foresight. Without power and

without money he has spent the last ten years prophesying a disaster in which he will be the first to perish. For the world has disproved the liberal axiom, that persecution defeats its object; it has been shown that an efficient secret police, a concentration camp, or an invasion with tanks and machine-guns can silence any opposition, can stop the intellect from questioning or the poet from affirming, and thus reduce his historical potency to that of the Redskin or the Carib. In any case, artists are easy to suppress; adaptability and subservience to the powers that be, a happy tropism, characterize them as often as inflexible courage and integrity. They recant more merrily than they burn.

What can be done to improve their position? They must, like every defenceless minority, unite, and learn to help each other, to present their case to the public. They must respect their creative mission more than they do now, and they must force their rulers to respect it, they must understand that their position is desperate, and will become intolerable, that, outside the Western democracies, they are surrounded by enemies, while their friends are dwindling within them. Like the Pet-World, they are the first to feel the rationing and the change in the standard of living; they will be hard hit if the rentier class, on which many of them are remittance men, goes under, nor is there any political party likely to come to power to whom the artist and the intellectual are not at best but means to be exploited.

But it is not easy for artists to help themselves. They are not a class for whom co-operation is pleasant. Besides being envious and bitter, as are the economically under-privileged, many often work better through an inability to appreciate the art and aims of their contemporaries. When success permits them, both writers and painters prefer to barricade themselves deep in bourgeois country, like those birds which we admire for their colour and song but which have divided our woods into well-defined gangster pitches of wormy territory. The artist and intellectual are a kind of life-giving parasite on the non-artist and the non-intellectual, and they are not to be criticized for being slow to combine with each other.

Therefore it is the public who must be educated, and the rulers who must be mollified; and here the artists can combine, for the smug hostility of the English is indiscriminately extended to all forms of art. In a number of *World Review* Sir Thomas Beecham brilliantly attacks the musical apathy of the nation; the attack must be sustained by artists and writers. The public must be asked to distinguish between the serious writer and the potboiling entertainer, between the poet and the prima donna journalist; the ruling class must be seduced into recognizing the importance of the great dollar-producing invisible export of our literature, not only the Mr. Chips, Gracie Fields, Peter Wimsey brands, which go wherever a bottle of Worcester sauce can penetrate, but the difficult, conscientious, and experimental work for which England and France are uniquely adapted, the delayed-action art and literature which survives indifference and slowly dominates—as Rimbaud or Hopkins have dominated—the creative minds of a generation. The idea of quality is an Anglo-French obsession; where the quality is not easily apprehended, the judges should be lenient. Here is a black list of some who are not.

Lord Beaverbrook. This nobleman injects into the jaunty philistinism of his papers a breath of the great art-hating, art-fearing open spaces. "You do not often see a writer mentioned on this page" complacently remarks an article in the proprietor's breezy biblical style. What information about art and literature there is in his papers is intelligently but stealthily purveyed by the younger gossip - writers. The popular press as a whole, when not content to ignore art and literature, fosters such absurd distinctions as that between highbrow and lowbrow, which has done more harm to both serious and popular art than any other false classification.

But there are other circles as much to blame. There are the private and public schools which, under the cloak of a genial obscurantism, do so much to warp the talent that passes through them, and to harden the untalented in their own conceit. Then there is the Government, who, as Sir Hugh Walpole has recently pointed out, do nothing for literature, except to grant occasionally a miserable pittance for some half-starved veteran. Then there are the increasingly illiterate rich, often the descendants of those patrons who willingly gave a hundred pounds away, not for a picture or for a dedication, but to enable an artist to carry on. This practice is almost extinct, and a poet who was given a sum of money for being a poet rather than for writing copy for underclothes would be regarded as an undesirable. A useful remedy for this would be to let it be known that any benefactions already made to the arts, to the furtherance of research, or to the betterment of conditions in any form would be deducted from tax. But this implies a bureaucracy friendly to the arts, and we are a long way from it. Freud mentions tidiness, parsimoniousness, and obstinacy as the three characteristics of the Anal Type, and it is engaging that they also symbolize what is called the Official Mind.

Then there are the traitors among the artists themselves: the Publisher, with his Cold Feet; those who are ashamed of their vocation, who accept the enemy's estimate of it and become horse-painters or country gentlemen; those who clown for the philistines or who throw away their genuine talent through fear of being unpopular; or those defeatists who enjoy with Oriental relish the ignominy to which they are subjected and pretend that to starve and to be bullied by bank managers and passport authorities is part of the state to which artists are called, and which they must accept without question.

It is true that the artist is drifting into becoming a disreputable member of the lower middle classes waiting, in a borrowed mackintosh, for the pubs to open, but the privations which improve his talent must be imposed not by society but by himself—and any investigation of the artist's circumstances reveals that by far the most favourable conditions for him are neither at the top nor the bottom, but snug in the heart of the bourgeoisie, with a safe middle income, such as nineteenth-century capitalism (the golden age of the remittance man) provided, and such as some other system will now have to be dragooned into paying.

An opponent particularly dangerous in these times is the near-artist, or Pinhead. Pinheads are a race apart, they are generally tall and bony, anal to the nth degree, but sometimes small and foxy. They are obsessed by a profound hatred of art and are prepared to devote their lives to gratifying it. To do this they occupy a fortified position, either at a university, or in an advanced political party, or as a publisher, and then proceed to castigate the artist, if from the university, on grounds of faulty taste or scholarship, if from a party, on grounds of political unorthodoxy or loose thinking. Every artist is an exhibitionist. The tragedy of a Pinhead is that he is a repressed exhibitionist, a guilty character whom a too strict censor is punishing for his wicked desire to undress and dance. The Pinhead is consequently attracted to the artist, whose generous immodest antics excite his own, but he is also consumed with envy and disgust for them. The ultimate enemy of art is power. One cannot desire both beauty and power, so the Pinhead, lacking as he does all aesthetic sense, usually obtains power and then becomes one of those Puritan commissars of the arts who see nothing in Picasso, who do not "understand" modern poetry, who examine art through the wrong end of the scientific telescope and see very little, or find no basis for it in Logical Positivism. They wear their Marxism like a hair-shirt, and their triumph is when they have persuaded a painter to abandon colour for abstraction, or a poet to write a political pamphlet, or to suppress a novel "for personal reasons." Fortunate is the artist to-day who is able to follow his invention without one of these poor bald old homo-puritan Pinheads blowing down his neck.

For the time being, the outlook is black. The painter, the writer, the liberal intellectual are in for a bad time; if they can co-operate, if they can assert themselves, if they can survive to the incredible period when nations are not afraid of each other, they will come into their own, for they have powerful allies. The working class, for instance, has not the deep-rooted animosity of the others towards artistic creation. Lawrence was not persecuted by it for his secession, but by his betters. The success of the *Penguin* library or of *Picture Post* or *The March of Time* show what a great potential benefactor an increasingly educated working class can be. Those who visited Azaña's Spain, our Lost Ally, will recall how pathetically friendly to culture were its masses, and there are many parts of the world where it is still a compliment to call someone an educated man. Even the Court is emerging from two centuries of Hanoverian apathy. Then the technocracies of the future are well disposed, the most powerful of all, the army and navy, show less of that hostility to art which is found in commerce and the Cabinet, and when the war is over they will hardly allow themselves to be quietly deprived of their influence, and handed a gratuity, as before. Revolutions do not happen in this country, but every now and then the public gives a great heave of boredom and impatience and something is done with for ever. When that happens, the artist must be on the crest of the wave, not underneath it, for art occupies in society the equivalent of one of those glands the size of a pea on which the proper functioning of the body depends, and whose removal is as easy as it is fatal.

Meanwhile the almond blossom is out, the sun shines, the streets look shabbier and the shops emptier, and the war slowly permeates into our ways of living. It is a war which seems archaic and unreal, a war in which eighty million people are trying to kill us, a war of which we are all ashamed—and yet a war which has to be won, and can only be won by energetic militant extroverted leaders who are immune from the virus of indecision. And the intellectuals recoil from the war as if it were a best-seller. They are enough ahead of their time to despise it, and yet they must realize that they nevertheless represent the culture that is being defended. Abyssinian intellectuals, Albanian intellectuals, Chinese intellectuals, Basque intellectuals, they are hunted like the sea-otter, they are despoiled like the egret. Our own are the last to survive. Granted the whole cumulus of error in the last twenty years, the greedy interlocking directorship of democratic weakness and Cabinet stupidity, then the war is inevitable. It is a war which dissipates energy and disperses friends, which lowers the standard of thinking and feeling, and which sends all those who walk near emotional, mental, or financial precipices toppling over; it is a war which is as obsolete as drawing and

quartering; which negatives every reasonable conception of
what life is for, every ambition of the mind or delight of the
senses; and which inaugurates an era of death, privation,
danger, and boredom, guaranteeing the insecurity of projects
and the impermanence of personal relations. But there it is.
We are in it: for as long as Hitler exists we must stay there.
The war is the enemy of creative activity, and writers and
painters are wise and right to ignore it and to concentrate
their talent on other subjects. Since they are politically
impotent, they can use this time to develop at deeper emotional
levels, or to improve their weapons by technical experiment,
for they have so long been mobilized in various causes that
they are losing the intellectual's greatest virtues: the desire
to pursue the truth wherever it may lead, and the belief in
the human mind as the supreme organ through which life can
be apprehended, improved, and intensified.

But they must also understand that their liberty and security
are altogether threatened, that Fascism is against *them*. The
Anglo-French artist and the intellectual are lucky to be alive.
They must celebrate by creating more culture as fast as they
can, by flowering like the almond blossom; for if they take
a vow of silence till the war is over, or produce as little as do
some of our lords of language, they will disappear: and their
disappearance will provide further evidence that the human
race has outstayed its welcome.

Several times a year articles arrive called "Where are
our war poets?" The answer (not usually given) is "Under
your nose." For war poets are not a new kind of being, they
are only peace poets who have assimilated the material of war.
As the war lasts, the poetry which is written becomes war
poetry, just as inevitably as the lungs of Londoners grow black
with soot. It is unfortunate from the military point of view
that war poetry is not necessarily patriotic. When the articles
ask "Where are the war poets?" they generally mention
Rupert Brooke, because he wrote some stirring sonnets and
was killed in action, though his poems were mostly nostalgic
or amorous. They want real war poets and a roll of honour.

That we lack patriotic poetry at the moment is a healthy sign, for if it were possible to offer any evidence that civilization has progressed in the last twenty years, it would be that which illustrated the decline of the aggressive instinct. This absence of aggressiveness, a danger in the war, is the healthiest of all symptoms for the peace, and makes possible the hope that, once we have had sufficient victories to remove self-confidence from our enemy, the awareness of the whole idiotic archaic process of war, with its boredom, its slaughter, its privations, and its general clumsy uselessness, may sweep over the world and induce people to give it up.

There is another aspect of the war and culture which it is refreshing to notice. Although there is very little new being written, there is a vast amount of old that is being forgotten. Blake told us to 'drive our harrow over the bones of the dead,' and such a silent revolution is happening. The vast top-heavy accumulation of learning, criticism, scholarship, *expertise*, the Alexandrian library of nineteenth-century Liberal capitalism, is falling to decay. Human beings have a tendency to over-civilization, they cannot tear up old letters, they collect and catalogue up to the edge of insanity. A burning of the books becomes at times a necessity; it was necessary to think Milton, or Pope, or Tennyson, or Proust, or James, bad writers, if writing was to go on. Before the war the stream of creative writing was choked with the leaves of exegesis; writers were bowed down with their intellectual possessions, with their names and dates, their sense of the past, their collection of unspoilt villages, their knowledge of cheese, beer, wine, sex, first editions, liturgy, detective stories, of Marx and Freud. It was a Footler's Paradise, a world in which, as on a long sea voyage, those came to the top who could best kill time. Culbertson, Torquemada, Wodehouse, Dorothy Sayers, Duke Ellington; the hobby dominated the art, the artists were artists in spite of them-selves, or they worked in second-rate and inartistic material. In the realm of criticism the sense of the past dominated, the aunts and uncles of the great were exhumed, the load of material bore down on its inheritors, making them carping and irritable, while the ignorant but talented were forced to suffer for their ignorance, or waste their talent in catching up. The fear of democracy is the fear of being judged for what we are, instead of for what we have. Now that so many of us have no possessions, no houses or books or cars or notes, we find it less terrible than we thought. Let us also have no theories and no facts, let us forget our great names, who had so much more patience, talent, and leisure than we had, and declare a cultural moratorium. The sooner we accept the Dark Ages the faster they will be over. In the streets round this office, where the exposed green of fourth-floor bathrooms shines against the blue winter sky, an enormous Rolls-Royce often passes. Each time one sees this mammoth of luxury, one wonders to whom it belongs; some fatcat of Bloomsbury? A ground landlord? A member of the Corps Diplomatique? But as it glides past it becomes transparent, and reveals on well-oiled bearings its only passenger, a neat wooden coffin. The limousine belongs to the last people who can afford it: the luxurious dead.

Invasion and You! As I write these words I hear on unexceptionable authority that the enemy is on his way, following that route, old as the seasons, by which he has brought off all his most audacious infiltrations. He landed at Europe's extreme south, the sandy scab of the Punto de Tarifa, and at once opened a pincer movement round the Atlantic and the Mediterranean seaboard, with a central thrust up the valley of the Guadalquivir. The cork-woods of Algeciras, the cotton-fields of Estepona, the blue sugar-canes and custard apples of Almuñecar were the first to be penetrated, and in the west he reached that botanist paradise, the Sierra de Aracena and the Sierra de Monchique, at the same time as he encircled, on the east, the Contraviesa and the Gadór. The villages with their moorish walls, their goats and their aloes, surrendered on the hill-tops. Soon after fell the provincial capitals, Huelva, Cadiz, Seville, Granada, Almeria, Málaga, Jaen, and Córdoba, all of Andalusia along the river, till the green corn sprouted on the white soil, the Sierra Morena became a creaming waste of cistus, and New Castile and Estremadura were threatened, until even the places with the coldest names, Fregenal, Tembleque, Javalambre, surrendered, and the Duke of Frias betrayed his title. And what has happened in the Peninsula will happen in France: the country is ripe for it, all resistance is undermined, the asphodel blossoms are frothing over the Eastern Pyrenees, the catkins are on the willows, the poplars of the west are covering with new green leaves their balls of mistletoe, the chestnut buds and the outdoor tables have climbed to the Loire. At the longest we have only a fortnight to prepare against the malice and ingenuity of our hereditary enemy, the unsound, unprogressive, uneconomical, unpatriotic, unmechanized, non-belligerent Spring. "Make no mistake about it," said a High Official who is in his free time a Military Spokesman, "Spring will try us hard, but, buttressed in this island bastion, we will withstand him. The enemy will use gas. 'Aires, vernal aires,' 'Banks of violets,' 'Delicious South.' We have a filter for all of them. 'April is the cruellest month.' Green grass, blue sky, white clouds, primroses; everything will be tried that may distract our attention and sap our resolve. Don't look at 'em. Wear dark glasses. Stay put. What did Gamelin say to Ironside? 'Pas bouger!' Stay put!" "And bacteriological warfare?" "Ah, yes, Spring fever, glad you mentioned it, very important. When you get that pushover feeling, that false sense of well-being or euphoria, 'young man's fancy,' desire to receive or bestow affection, to crowd roads and railways, to change domicile; don't give way. If it gets too strong, consult your Mr. Sensible. And remember, now as always: win the Spring is win the war. We know what short shrift was meted out to the guzzlers in restaurants, now is the time to punish mental and emotional guzzling. We have got the measure of the food-hog. We must destroy the day-dreamer, the memory-hoarder, the escapist, the beauty-wallah, the reading man. Then and then only, bastioned in this island buttress, will we be totally conditioned to total war, and when victory is ours, when the war has swept the world, when nobody anywhere gets more to eat than the poorest Spaniard or the most starving Chinese, when nobody can read or write, when nobody has anything, nobody wants anything, nobody does anything except work, work, work—when we've

got the race war, the class war, the age war, the sex war, going
simultaneously, when we look back at to-day as the happiest
period of our lives, and when happiness is recognized everywhere for what it is, a dull and dishonest evasion of necessary
pain; when we have reduced humanity to its lowest denomin-
ator—then the sacrifices we have made in conditioning ourselves
against the daffodil and the blackbird will not have been worthless. Good morning. Stay Put." "Good morning. Go to it."

It is sad on a spring evening to walk through the bombed
streets of Chelsea. There are vast districts of London—
Bayswater, for example, or Kensington—which seem to have
been created for destruction, where squares and terraces for
half a century have invited dilapidation, where fear and
hypocrisy have accumulated through interminable Sunday
afternoons until one feels, so evil is the atmosphere of unreality
and suspense, that had it not been for the bombers, the houses
would have been ignited one day of their own accord by
spontaneous combustion. Behind the stucco porches and the
lace curtains the half-life of decaying Victorian families guttered
like marsh-gas. One has no pity for the fate of such houses,
and no pity for the spectacular cinemas and fun-places of
Leicester Square, whose architecture was a standing appeal to
heaven to rain down vengeance on them. But Chelsea in the
milky green evening light, where the church where Henry
James lies buried is a pile of red rubble, where tall eighteenth-
century houses with their insides blown out gape like ruined
triumphal arches, is a more tragic spectacle. For here the life
that has vanished with the buildings that once housed it was
of some consequence: here there existed a fine appreciation
of books and pictures, and many quiet work-rooms for the
people who made them. Here was one of the last strongholds
of the cultivated *haute bourgeoisie* in which leisure, however
ill-earned, has seldom been more agreeably and intelligently
made use of. Now when the sun shines on these sandy ruins
and on the brown and blue men working there one expects
to see goats, and a goatherd in a burnous—"sirenes in delubris
voluptatis"—pattering among them.

Meanwhile the bombs, which have emptied so many drawing-rooms, have also been blasting the reputations made in them. Our literary values are rapidly changing. War shrinks everything. It means less time, less tolerance, less imagination, less curiosity, less play. We cannot read the leisurely wasteful masterpieces of the past without being irritated by the amount they take for granted. I have lately been reading both Joyce and Proust with considerable disappointment; they both seem to me very sick men, giant invalids who, in spite of enormous talent, were crippled by the same disease, elephantiasis of the ego. They both attempted titanic tasks, and both failed for lack of that dull but healthy quality without which no masterpiece can be contrived, a sense of proportion. Proust, like Pope, hoaxed his contemporaries; he put himself over on them as a reasonable, intelligent, kind, and sensitive human being, when his personality was in fact diseased and malignant, his nature pathologically cruel and vacillating, his values snobbish and artificial, his mind (like a growth which reproduces itself at the expense of the rest of the body) a riot of alternatives and variations, where both the neurotic horror of decision and the fear of leaving anything out are lurking behind his love of truth.

For Joyce there seems almost less to be said; Proust's endless and repetitive soliloquies are at least the thoughts of an intelligent man, while those of Joyce reflect the vacuous mediocrity of his characters; both relive the past to the point of exhaustion. Both are men of genius whose work is distorted by illness, by the struggle of one to see and of the other to breathe; both seem to us to have lacked all sense of social or political responsibility.

Yet we must remember that the life which many of us are now leading is unfriendly to the appreciation of literature; we are living history, which means that we are living from hand to mouth and reading innumerable editions of the evening paper. In these philistine conditions it is as unfair to judge art as if we were seasick. It is even more unfair to blame writers for their action or inaction in the years before the war, when we still tolerate in office nearly all the old beaming second-rate faces, with their indomitable will to power, and their self-sealing tanks of complacency.

It would not be unfair to say that the England of Baldwin, MacDonald, and Chamberlain was a decadent country— "Cabbage Land," "Land of lobelias and tennis flannels," "This England where nobody is well"—its gods were wealth and sport; from any unpleasant decision it flinched in disgust; though assailed by critics from the right and left, it still wallowed supinely in a scented bath of stocks and shares, race-cards and roses, while the persecuted, who believed in the great English traditions of the nineteenth century, knocked in vain at the door.

Since Dunkirk we have seen the end of the political and military decadence of England. Whatever residue of complacency, sloth, and inefficiency there may be left, England is now a great power, and able to stand for something in the world again. When the war is over we shall live in an Anglo-American world. There will be other great powers, but the sanctions on which the West reposes will be the ideas for which England and America have fought and won, and the machines behind them. We had all this in 1918 and made a failure of it. The ideas expired in the impotence of Geneva. The machines spouted Ford cars, Lucky Strike, Mary Pickford, and Coca-Cola. The new masters of the world created Le Touquet and Juan les Pins, fought each other for oil and reparations, blamed each other for the slump, and wandered blandly and ignorantly over Europe with a dark blue suit, letter of credit, set of clean teeth, and stiff white collar. Fascism arose as a religion of disappointment, a spreading nausea at the hypocrisy of the owners of the twentieth century. It is important to see that Fascism is a disease, as catching as influenza; we all when tired and disillusioned have Fascist moments, when belief in human nature vanishes, when we burn with anger and envy like the underdog and the sucker, when we hate the virtuous and despise the weak, when we feel as Goebbels permanently feels, that all fine sentiment is ballyhoo, that we are the dupes of our leaders, and that the masses are evil, to be resisted with the cruelty born of fear. This is the theological sin of despair, a Haw-Haw moment which quickly passes, but which Fascism has made permanent, and built up into a philosophy. In every human being there is a Lear and a fool, a hero and a clown who comes on the stage and burlesques his master. He should never be censored, but neither should he be allowed to rule. In the long run all that Fascism guarantees is a Way of Death; it criticizes the easy life by offering a noisy way of killing and dying. The key philosophies which the world will need after the war are, therefore, those which believe in life, which assert the goodness and sanity of man, and yet which will never again allow those virtues to run to seed and engender their opposites.

The greatest discovery we can make from this war, the one without which no Renaissance is possible, is what human beings are really like; what is good for them, what standard of living, what blend of freedom and responsibility, what mixture of courage and intelligence, heart and head makes for progress and happiness. We find out what we need by having to do without what we think we need. All words and ideas must be tested and built up again from experience. When we have learnt what kind of life we want, what kind of man should live it, a Renaissance becomes possible. Here are some conditions for it.

An artistic Renaissance can only take place where there is a common attitude to life, a new and universal movement. By the time Anglo-American war aims have crystallized from the philosophy behind them, this should be in existence. But no political movement can have the art it deserves until it has learnt to respect the artist. The English mistrust of the intellectual, the brutish aesthetic apathy and contempt for the creative artist must go. Bred of the intolerance of public schoolboys, the infectious illiteracy of the once appreciative gentry, the money-grubbing of the Victorian industrialists and the boorishness of the Hanoverian court, our philistinism (which also expresses the English lack of imagination and fear of life) should be made a criminal offence. There can be no dignity of man without respect for the humanities.

A Renaissance also requires a belief in spiritual values, for materialism distils nothing but a little rare dandyism, an occasional Watteau, and that will not be enough. The most sensible cure for materialism is a surfeit of it, which post-war science and economics should assure us. Yet we cannot get such a spiritual revival until the religious forces and the spiritual humanistic forces come to terms together, as did the Basque priests and the Spanish Republicans, as have Bernanos, Maritain, and the French Left. This is the hardest bridge to erect, but it will have to be done, and should not be impossible; for our civilization is impregnated with Christianity even where it seems unchristian; the foundations of our beliefs are those of Christianity and Greece, however those beliefs may have become distorted.

Regionalism, after the war, must come into its own. There is already a Welsh Renaissance in being; there is activity in Ireland and Scotland. Regionalism is the remedy for provincialism. Only by decentralizing can we avoid that process which ends by confining all art to the capital, and so giving it a purely urban outlook. England is one of those mysterious geographical entities where great art has flourished. We have the racial mixture, the uneven climate, the European tradition, the deep deserted mine-shaft. We must reopen the vein.

The greatest danger, let us hope, to the artist in the England of the future will be his success. He will live through the nightmare to see the new golden age of the West, a world in which no one will be unwanted again, in which the artist will always be in danger of dissipating himself in the service of the State, in broadcasts or lecture tours, in propaganda and pamphlets. As in ancient Rome or China, or modern Russia or U.S.A., the artist will have a sense of responsibility to a world-wide audience, which he must control. But that should be the only temptation for him in what will at last be a serious world, a world in which the new conquerors avoid the mistakes of the old and bring to the opportunities of victory the wisdom and dignity that they learned in defeat.

War journalism and war oratory have produced an unchecked inflation in our overdriven and exhausted vocabulary. Dictatorial powers to clean up our language should be given to a Word Controller.

The first act of the Word Controller (Mr. Shaw would be a good choice) should be to issue licences (like driving licences) to all journalists, authors, publicists, orators, and military spokesmen. Without such a licence it would be a criminal offence to appear in print or on the platform. The licences of all those found using the words *vital*, *vitally*, *virtual*, *virtually*, *actual*, *actually*, *perhaps*, *probably*, would then be immediately cancelled. This surprise action of the Word Controller would at once eliminate most journalists and politicians, and all military spokesmen. These words should be unmolested, and protected, for several years. The words *democracy*, *liberty*, *justice*, *freedom*, *jackboot*, *serious consideration*, *island fortress*, *love*, *creative*, and *new* should be suspended for six months, and the licence endorsed of anyone found using them. Lists (constantly brought up to date) of forbidden clichés with a scale of fines should be posted on every notice-board. The Word Controller, at any rate during the few hours of office before his powers turned his head, would be non-political. His aim would be to reshape the English language to its original purpose as an instrument of communication, and an invention for expressing thought. Thus the expression "The town is virtually surrounded" would become "The town is, or is not, surrounded," "vital necessity" would become "necessity," and a scientific machine for weighing words would demonstrate that while such terms as "coronary thrombosis" are as full of content as when first minted, other verbal coins are worn too thin for the public slot-machine and must be withdrawn from circulation. As he became more autocratic and more like other controllers he would find out that there is a connection between the rubbish written, the nonsense talked, and the thoughts of the people, and he would endeavour to use his censorship of words in such a way as to affect the ideas behind them, or, rather, he would give priority to statements of fact over abstractions, and to facts which were accurate rather than incorrect.

Applying himself to art, the Word Controller will remark that no great literature can be made out of the split-mind which is now prevalent. The unadulterated aggressive instinct creates its art; the detached and meditative attitude is also valid, but blended they destroy each other and produce the hotchpotch of standardized, lukewarm, muddled propaganda through which we are floundering. An artist must be in the war or out of it. He must go to America or to Ireland or to prison if he wants to write, or else fight and read the newspapers: the moment he becomes undecided, well-meaning and guilty, he is Hamleted out of service as a writer; however much he concentrates on the Atlantis of the past, or the Utopia of the future, he will be made to suffer in the present. For we live in an imperfect world: history punishes the ignorant and the mistaken: the wicked are left to punish themselves.

In the times in which we live a writer should not be able to put down more than two or three lines without making it obvious whether he has anything to say. The Word Controller, by banning the verbal camouflage of those who doubt, who twist, who are on the make, or who hope for the best, would clarify propaganda and leave literature safely where it belongs, in the hands of the very sane, or the very mad.

We are all prisoners in solitary confinement: when at last we give up trying to escape through mass emotion or sexual union there remains for us only the wall alphabet in which we tap our hopes and thoughts. Nobody should learn this alphabet who can abuse it, who jerry-builds the English language as if it were the English countryside, who wastes the time of his fellow prisoners by tapping out stale rhetoric, false news, or untranslatable messages, and so brings a perfect achievement of civilization into confusion.

What are the three characteristics of Puritan verse? Poverty of imagination, poverty of diction, poverty of experience—the characteristics, in fact, of Puritan prose and Puritan painting. If we examine an imaginary poet, for example, John Weaver, "whose austere verse, eschewing all tricks and facile solutions, so clearly depicts the dilemma of the intellectual in the period of *entre deux guerres*," we find that, of any age between twenty and forty, he is "the child of professional parents, was educated at a major university and a minor public school, has Marxist sympathies, and is at present trying to reconcile communism with religion, pacifism with war, property with revolution, and homosexuality with marriage." He will have been published in "*New Verse*, *New Writing*, and *New Directions*, and will have produced one volume of poems [I am quoting from the Introduction] called *The Poet's Thumb*." "John Weaver is most actively interested in politics and took part in several processions at the time of the Spanish War. Indeed, his particularly individual imagery discloses an extreme awareness of the contemporary situation.

> Come, Heart, we have been handed our passports,
> Love's visa has expired.
> The consulate of Truth is closed
> And virtue's signature no longer valid,

and many other poems show that he was among the first to await, like MacNeice, 'The Gunbutt on the door.'"

For an interesting fact about Weaver is that, though several years younger than Auden and MacNeice, he is completely dominated by them. He imitates their scientific eroticism, their Brains Trust omniscience, without the creative energy of the one or the scholarship of the other, just as he assimilates the fervour of Spender and the decorum of Day Lewis into his correct, flat, effortless, passionless verse. And it is Weaver, now at an O.C.T.U. or in the Air Force Intelligence, who is responsible for some of the badness of war poetry, who used to write " Comrades we have come to a watershed," and now talks about " Love's tracer bullets," even as his brother Paul, who once painted ascetic winter streets for the East London Group, is responsible, with his fossilized landscapes of tanks and hangars, for some of the badness of War Art. An element of Puritanism is always present in a good artist, but in a minute quantity. The Puritan poet of the 'thirties has been all Puritan, he has been afraid of life and repelled by it, and so has acquired no experience to digest; caught in the pincer-movement of the dialectic, he has picked up the modern vice of arrogant over-simplification, nor has he developed his imagination by reading or travel. As a person he is incomplete and therefore as an artist sterile, the possessor of a desiccated vocabulary which is not his own, but which he has timidly inherited from his poetic uncles. Auden and Spender made use of this vocabulary to chasten the Georgians, and, having served its purpose, it should have long been discarded. Such poets as John Weaver, who exist rootless in the present without standards or comparisons, are doomed to swift extinction, for the war has proved a godsend to bad artists, allowing them to make honourably, and for their country's good, that surrender to normality which in peace-time is only accepted after a long and terrible struggle.

There will always be poetry in England: it is the concentrated essence of the English genius, distilled from our temperate climate and intemperate feelings, and there will always be critics who claim that it is dead. But poetry is going through a bad patch. The sophisticated intellectual poetry of the 'twenties is exhausted. Poetry was taken down a cul-de-sac to get away from the Georgians, and now it has to find its way back. The academic socialism of the 'thirties was not strong enough to revive it, we are waiting for a new romanticism to bring it back to life. This will happen when the tide of events sweeps round the lonely stumps on which our cormorants have been sitting and gives them a fishing-ground—for one of the difficulties of John Weaver has been the isolation of his mood from the uneasy fatuity of between-war England, and another, the hitherto sheltered, unwanted, uneventful character of his life. Now that events have caught up with his prognostic and he is no longer out of step with the rest of the population, his work will be deepened and simplified.

This process is only just beginning. As an industrial nation we lag behind: our factories are not the largest, our generals not the wisest, but as an ancient civilization that is not neurotic, where thought once more is correlated with action, and which fights for its beliefs, we should, in those invisible exports like poetry and fine writing, be in a position to lead the world.

The death of Sickert, unhonoured, almost unnoticed, reminds us that we live in a philistine country. Camden Town, Dieppe, Paris, Bath, Brighton, Venice, the places he loved and painted, recall to us that art once was international, that the greatest English painter could yet stem off from the art of France and Italy, could be as English, and as Continental, in the piazza of St. Mark's, or a South London music-hall; by the Porte Saint-Denis, or by a brass bedstead off the Tottenham Court Road. Looking at his best pictures, such as the French and Venetian landscapes shown at the Redfern in 1940, or the *Granby Street* shown recently at the National Gallery, we are conscious not only of superb technique, but of the sacred moment, of the absorption of the painter in what he sees, which by talent and patience he is able to communicate. It is the communication of this sacred moment which constitutes a work of art. The vision might be insane, like Van Gogh's, or ponderous with sanity as in Degas or Cézanne, but it existed. Our tragedy is to live at a time when it does not. In a continent which is exterminating itself, a country which is socializing itself, a world that is destroying its standard of living, the existence of the great artist, the free personality, of the solitary smouldering creative figure whose thought and imagination challenge eternity, becomes more and more precarious. If we want great art after the war we must restore the freedom of Europe to our artists, and also guarantee them economic security. The defects of War Art arise through the personality of the artist being shrunken by being fitted in to the military structure, and by his being denied the freedom of Europe, and so cut off from the masterpieces of the past. The sacred moment which the artist is too self-pitiful to communicate or too shallow to perceive has vanished.

As the war goes on, intimations of the kind of world that will come into being after the war become clearer. It will be a world in which the part played by the English will be of supreme importance. In fact, one might say that the whole of English history, tradition, and character will be judged in the future by how we rise to the occasion of the post-war years. England will find itself in the position of one of those fairy-tale princes who drift into a tournament, defeat a dragon or a wicked knight, and then are obliged to marry the king's daughter and take on the cares of a confused, impoverished, and reactionary kingdom. That kingdom is Europe, the new dark continent which must perish if it cannot attain peace and unity, and which is yet in a constant eruption of war, economic rivalry, and race-hatred.

England is the weakest of the three great post-war powers: unless it has behind it a strong, united Europe it must be overwhelmed by America, either involuntarily or in a tug-of-war with a Communist Europe and Russia. If England fails to unite Western Europe it fails as a world power, if it succeeds and can hold a balance between American Capitalism and Soviet Communism, defending Western Europe from the reactionary imperialism of one and the oppressive bureaucracy of the other, it will prove itself the greatest and wisest middleman in History. To achieve this, England must resurrect that political wisdom for which it was once famous and produce a scheme for Europe which will incorporate the socialist idealism of Russia with the humanist individualism of America and which will lead towards the gradual atrophy of European race-hatreds and nationalist pretensions. Every European war is a war lost by Europe; each war lost by Europe is a war lost by England. When the struggle for our lives is over, the struggle for our standards of living will have only begun, and our standard includes the liberty to go where we like, stay where we like, do what we like and pay how we like.

To achieve and deserve this leadership will require courage and wisdom, with an appreciation of the complexity of European affairs and a sense of trusteeship for the European spirit which we are still far from possessing. But Europe is more than a political concept, it is still the chief breeding-ground of ideas, the laboratory, the studio, and the reference library of the world's art, science, and imagination. If England is to help Europe, it must assume the cultural as well as the moral and political protection of Europe, it must restore liberty of expression, economic security, and mental audacity to the world of art and ideas.

This is a most difficult task, because England—the only country in Europe where a man may still paint or write very much what he likes, and find a market for it—is nevertheless a philistine country. Worse still, the philistinism is an essential factor in the national genius, and forms part of the stolid, practical, tolerant, pleasure-loving, responsibility-taking English character. There is no other civilization in the world so old, so mellow, so wise, and so polite which can yet so happily dispense with respect for learning, love of art, or intellectual curiosity. The French are saturated in these things; the Americans worship culture even though they are inclined to do so for the wrong reasons; the English, to whom will fall the task of restoring paper and ink and paints and canvases to occupied Europe, dissipate their aesthetic instinct in ball-games, card-games, dart-boards, and foot-ball pools. Even the culture of England in war-time is a most haphazard affair.

A visit to the French Exhibition at the National Gallery (the best picture show since the war started) brings the problem closer. Why is not English painting better? Why do we raise Sargent instead of Renoir, Munnings instead of Degas, Pre-Raphaelites instead of Impressionists? The climate of the Ile de France is hardly different from that of Southern England: many of the scenes chosen by the Impressionists are not in themselves beautiful; their gardens are inferior to English gardens; their tall, red-roofed villas almost as ugly as ours; their magical light is not peculiar to the Seine valley. What have they got that we lack?

Can the question be answered sociologically? The art of the Impressionists and their followers is the supreme flowering of bourgeois society. Many of the Impressionist painters were well-to-do people; they were not only secure in their patrons, they were secure in their investments; all through their lives several of them never had to worry about money. This is not all-important, but it is a great addition to a sense of vocation. They were also secure in their aesthetic philosophy. They believed in devoting a long life to the worship of beauty and the observance of Nature. Politics, society, family were all represented, but they were not the important things. There was a certain Chinese humanism about them; they loved their friends and painted them admirably in their favourite surroundings, they enjoyed, in moderation, the good and simple things of life, they were not ashamed of man's place in Nature, nor of urban civilization with its alcoves and café-tables, nor of old age with its arm-chairs and book-shelves. If the highest expression of their art is such a landscape as the Renoir of Argenteuil, a vision of watery paradise, or the Seurat of a wood or the Pissarro of La Roche-Guiyon, there are two smaller pictures which perhaps betray more of their secret. One is a tiny Manet of a dark bistro-interior, which reveals all the poetry of city-life; the other is Vuillard's portrait of Tristan Bernard in his garden. The garden is hideous—grass with a flinty rose-bed, against the brick of a Normandy villa—and the bearded poet is rocking back in it on a cane chair. The effect is of a civilization as sure of itself as a poem of Li-Po or Po-chüi. One sees immediately that the English could not paint like that because Kipling or Meredith or Henry James would not rock about so irreverently—because the English imperialist bourgeoisie, though just as stable as the French, had that extra moral and mercenary conscience, had too much money, too much sense of duty, and so could never give off such a light and heavenly distillation as Impressionism. Whistler and Sickert succeeded because they were not English, and at the price of a Harlequin defence-mechanism which never left them.

When we restore the arts then to Europe, we can do one of two things: we can attempt to restore to bourgeois civilization sufficient order and stability to enable the cream of art to come to the top, or we can develop a civilization which will permit a new art to arise. If we adopt the second course instead of trying to put back the nineteenth-century Humpty-Dumpty on the wall, then we must radically change our attitude to art here: we must give art a place in our conception of the meaning of life and the artist a place in our conception of the meaning of the State which before they have never known. Never again must our artists be warped by opposition, stunted by neglect, or etiolated by official conformity.

The danger is that the State will take over everything; the

State everywhere has discovered its inexhaustible source of wealth—the working hours of the individuals who compose it. In some countries the discovery is a few years old, here it is only two—and woe betide us if we had not made it—but more woe still if we cannot unmake it, if we cannot break the tyranny of State, here and everywhere else, after the war, or never again will we have an hour to call our own. Being a small State-owned country we will have to work twice as hard to compete with the large State-owned countries, like some wretched Cock-house at school whose members never dare break their training. For the State-owned nation will have nothing in common with the dream of international Socialism, since it will always be in total competition with the others, and therefore have to ration and overwork its members while taxing both their work and their earnings. Its weapons will be propaganda, bureaucracy, and a secret police with every man his own informer. For every child born there will be one to spy on it—for life. Our dossiers will open with the first words we say! And this will continue till a revolution is made and world Stakhanovism succumbs to the cry of "Liberty, Inequality, and Inefficiency."

The effects of State control are already apparent in art. We are becoming a nation of culture-diffusionists. Culture-diffusion is not art. We are not making a true art. The appreciation of art is spreading everywhere, education has taken wings, we are at last getting a well-informed inquisitive public. But War-Artists are not art, the Brains Trust is not art, journalism is not art, the B.B.C. is not art, all the Penguins, all the C.E.M.A. shows, all the A.B.C.A. lectures, all the discussion groups and M.O.I. films and pamphlets will avail nothing if we deny independence, leisure, and privacy to the artist himself. We are turning all our writers into commentators, until one day there will be nothing left for them to comment on. "A great work by an Englishman," wrote Hopkins, "is like a great battle won by England. It is an unfading bay-tree." How true that is to-day, and how tragic if *les lauriers sont coupés*.

This year we celebrate the centenary of Henry James, a man who, if he had never written a novel, would be considered the first of short-story writers, and if he had never written a short story, the noblest of letter-writers, and if he had never written anything would by his talk alone be known as a great man. To-day he is more than that, for he has become the symbol of a certain way of life, a way that is threatened not only by the totalitarian enemy but by the philistine friend, and yet a way which in an unpropitious age has helped masterpieces to be created and artists to live; the path of what James called "the lonely old artist man," who is so easily destroyed and so quite irreplaceable.

Thirteen years ago Edmund Wilson, in his *Axel's Castle*, attacked this outlook. He criticized all the great individualists—Joyce, Proust, Valery, Yeats, and Mallarmé—on the ground that they had carried the investigation of the ego to a point at which it had become unbearable, and he asserted that the great literature of the future could only arise from a corporate and socialist view of art as the expression not of the individual but of the mass. This literature has not yet arisen, and ten years later, in *The Wound and the Bow*, Edmund Wilson seems to have returned to the conception of the artist as an isolated wounded figure, as different from the social realist as is a huge lightning-stricken oak from a Government conifer plantation.

It is difficult to prove that any age has been propitious for the artist; Socrates was condemned to death, so were Seneca and Petronius, Dante was exiled, the age of Louis XIV was one of both civil and religious persecution; the nineteenth century, as the lawsuits against Flaubert, Baudelaire, Hugo, etc., show, was not much better; and in the twentieth century there are whole tracts of Europe where to be a writer is to invite a firing-squad. "Silence, exile, and cunning" are the artist's lot, and, exquisite though his happiness will be when his public, educated at last, mobs him like a film-star, we may be wiser to assume that, for our lifetime, "silence, exile, and cunning" it will remain. For this reason it is necessary to keep the memory of these giants like Henry James and Flaubert, or Baudelaire and Mallarmé, always before us, even if we never read them, for they are the saints of modern bourgeois art, whose virtues—sensibility, intellectual courage, renunciation, and consecrated devotion—emanate even from the mere storing of their books in our rooms. They are sacred relics which we need not too often disturb.

The tragedy of our civilization is that a specialized education has segregated an advanced artistic minority from the main body as with a tourniquet. In the interests of the masses (and therefore by his logic, of art), a Communist may be willing altogether to wash out this "advanced" literature and, from a level open to all, to make a fresh start which, with an educated proletariat, might lead in fifty or a hundred years to a new and happy art made by artists as integrated in the State as were the builders of medieval cathedrals in the Church. But anyone who does not accept the overriding authority of the proletariat must feel that, since art has advanced so far, even if down the wrong turning, it is too late to turn back. In relation to his public the artist of to-day is like the spelaeologist of the Peak or of the Causses of Southern France; he walks at first with his companions, till one day he falls through a hole in the brambles, and from that moment he is following the dark rapids of an underground river which may sometimes flow so near to the surface that the laughing picnic parties are heard above, only to re-immerse itself in the solitude of the limestone and carry him along its winding tunnel, until it gushes out through the misty creeper-hung cave which he has always believed to exist, and sets him back in the sun.

1940-43.